Abiding
in
Christ

Abiding
in
Christ

The Essence of Christianity

A
DAILY
DEVOTIONAL

by

REIMAR A. C. SCHULTZE

CTO Books
PO Box 825
Kokomo, Indiana 46903

Published by:
CTO Books
An outreach ministry of Call to Obedience
PO Box 825
Kokomo, Indiana 46903
www.schultze.org

To purchase additional copies, contact:
BookMasters, Inc. toll free: 1-800-247-6553

Publisher's Cataloging-in-Publication Data
(Provided by Quality Books, Inc.)

Schultze, Reimar A. C.
  Abiding in Christ : the essence of Christianity : a daily devotional / by Reimar A. C. Schultze. -- 1st ed.

  p. cm.
  Includes bibliographical references and index.
  LCCN 2002112359
  ISBN 0-9724411-0-7

  1. Jesus Christ--Prayer-books and devotions--English.
  2. Christian life. 3. Devotional calendars. I. Title.

BT306.5.S38 2002   242'.2
                                                    QBI02-701947

Printed in the United States of America.

Contents

About the Author vi

Forward vii

Introduction ix

Abiding in Christ:
The Essence of Christianity:
A Daily Devotional 3

Bibliography 369

Scripture Index 370

Order Page 374

About the Author

Reimar Schultze was born in Nazi Germany in 1936. Because of their Jewish heritage, the family suffered much hardship from anti-Semitic laws and attitudes as the Holocaust unfolded. They miraculously escaped the heavy bombings in Hamburg, Germany that killed most of their neighbors. After fleeing Nazi persecution into eastern Germany, Reimar's father died and a fifth child was born. These events qualified the family to escape their city on the last refugee train before the Red Army invaded. Additional miracles delivered the Schultzes from torpedo boats and mines during their evacuation to Denmark, where they were interned for two years with 36,000 other refugees.

Pastor Schultze first heard the call of God in his heart at the age thirteen. Several years later he was saved under the ministry of English evangelist Major Ian Thomas and came to the U.S. at age nineteen. After he graduated from college, he worked as an administrator for the U.S. Public Health Service. When he answered the call to the ministry, he received a M. Div. from Asbury Theological Seminary and has now pastored for 36 years. He and his wife, Marcia, have four children and six grandchildren. Pastor Schultze has served his current congregation for 25 years.

The Call to Obedience

In 1974, Pastor Schultze began the habit of praying several hours daily. That same year, with a vision to teach, train, and build disciples, he founded his Call to Obedience ministry. His monthly sermon letters, which are currently mailed to two dozen nations, became the inspiration for this devotional book. The radio branch of the Call to Obedience ministry began in 1977 and has expanded to include three worldwide short-wave stations. These sermons are designed to both challenge and encourage the average Christian in his daily walk of obedience to Christ. Other helps and an expanded version of Pastor Schultze's testimony are also available on his web site at www.schultze.org

Foreword

The divine-human encounter of God with man and man with God demands our total attention and heart-response. Mortal man was created for the purpose of daily heart-fellowship with God—not mind-fellowship. Evil entered man's heart while he listened to Satan and allowed the path of evil to become dominant. The Bible makes it very clear that our greatest need is to live by heart-obedience to God in simple faith each day. Modern, professing Christianity has drifted dangerously to a head-response to God. True Christianity, that of abiding in Christ daily, must proceed from our hearts.

This author uses his head but writes from his heart, and he lives from his heart Self-denial and obedience to the Holy Spirit and the Word. Knowing Reimar Schultze for many years, I have seen an unusual mind at work, yet I am most impressed by his heart. His monthly devotionals have challenged our minds, but more importantly, have convicted our hearts. Throughout the years, I have carefully kept and used these messages to encourage others in my own ministry.

Most devotionals stop short of getting to the "crux of the Cross" in daily abiding in Christ by surrendering our Self-wills to Christ. The Self-will, the carnal man that rules and reigns in most professing Christians, is frightening. This devotional confronts this issue.

My library has many daily devotional books. Some are deeply profound while others encourage child-like simplicity and are more easily adapted to daily living. I believe this devotional spans both. Oswald Chambers' recorded words have been great food to my soul. This author takes me a step farther. I have seen the fruit of the message written upon these pages, and more fruit is promised by Jesus in John 15:2:

"...and every branch that beareth fruit, he purgeth it, that it may bring forth more fruit."

I have seen where the author works in his study, but my

heart is stirred most by where he waits upon God and intercedes with God in prayer: in the loft of his barn. Go with him in your heart to the barn, live in your heart while you read, and your fellowship with the Holy Spirit will grow daily.

Dr. J. Carl Rouintree, D. Min.

Introduction

In John 15, Jesus says, *"If ye abide in me..."* (vv.4-5). Notice that He does not say, "If I abide in you," but *"If you abide in me"* (emphasis added). Before our conversion to Christ, we can say that Jesus chose us, for He said, *"Ye have not chosen me, but I have chosen you..."* (John 15:16). The whole process of salvation began with God and not with man, as John also says in his epistle, *"Herein is love, not that we loved God, but that he loved us, and sent his Son to be the propitiation for our sins"* (1 John 4:10).

But after we are born of God, the choice for our intimate relationship with Christ is with us and not with Him. The fact of and the working out of our salvation is in our continually choosing Him: His will, His ways, His holiness and His fellowship. Once we stop choosing Him, once we stop seeking *"first the kingdom of God and his righteousness"* (Matt. 6:33); once we stop abiding in Him, we cut ourselves off from God to become fruitless branches only worthy to be cast into the fire (John 15:6).

We must see the imperative of abiding in Christ. It is for this purpose that we are born of God. We must come to the end of the misconception that once Christ has chosen us to be His own that He will continue to choose us, regardless of our behavior, our moral soundness, and self-gratifying plans.

Both the Old and New Testaments are saturated with God's continued call upon His people to respond to Him in order to stay in fellowship with Him. Everything after God's choosing us depends very much on whether we keep choosing Him. It is with this that the whole history of the Hebrews begins. God chose Abraham out of Ur of the Chaldees, but how Abraham fared after that depended upon how he responded to the One who called him at every turn of events. Here begins God's "if...then" theology. We see it repeated throughout the Scriptures: Ex. 19:5-6; Lev. 26: 18, 23-24; Deut. 7:12; Matt. 6:14-15; John 14:15; 15:7; Rom. 8:13; 1 Thess. 3:8.

When Jesus said, *"If you abide in me,"* He merely continues to stress our responsibility, hence, His love call to abundant and everlasting life is continuous. It is absolutely necessary that our response to it also be continuous, that we "abide in Christ."

So, you ask, how do we abide in Him? The missing link that connects us to abiding in Christ, that allows His living waters to flow through us, is Self-denial. Jesus said to His disciples, *"Whosoever will come after me, let him deny himself, and take up his cross, and follow me"* (Mark 8:34). Jesus died on the cross to save us, but we need to die on our cross to keep what He has given us. Only then can we grow *"unto the measure of the stature of the fulness of Christ"* (Eph. 4:13).

This crucifixion of the old Adamic nature is a choice that we must keep making, as Paul says, *"I die daily"* (1 Cor. 15:31). A day is made up of twenty-four hours, and hours are made up of minutes, and minutes of seconds. We must choose moment-by-moment submission to Christ. But the moment we allow Self-will to have its way, we cease to abide in Christ, fruit-bearing discontinues, our spiritual branches – the fruit of the Spirit – dry up and wither, and the poison of the fruit of the flesh begins to enter our life.

True Christian living is only found as we are abiding in Christ. It is this life that produces purity, fellowship, fruitfulness, and joy unspeakable and full of glory. This precious life of abiding will be free from criticism, fault-finding, anger, jealousy, envy, the lust of the eye, the lust of the flesh, and the pride of life.

At the heart of this devotional is an earnest cry of this needy servant to every Christian that, now, after Christ has chosen you, you will choose Christ as a place of everlasting residence. As you read through the pages of this book, I trust you will find yourself breaking through the overcast of disappointments, discouragements, and spiritual paralysis into the light of God's promises He has destined for you to experience.

Reimar A. C. Schultze

Abiding
in
Christ

Abiding in Christ

*There is therefore now no condemnation
to them which are in Christ Jesus, who walk
not after the flesh, but after the Spirit.*

—Romans 8:1

Here, in the most sweeping way, the apostle Paul declares the essence of Christianity: *in Christ*. No phrase is more characteristic of Pauline writings than *in Christ*. In fact, there are 74 references to *in Christ* in Paul's epistles. Why are the words *in Christ* so important? Because there is no grace outside of Christ. The truth is, Christ is grace, and grace is Christ. To abide in Him as a branch abideth in the vine is to abide in grace. To abide in Him is to *"walk in the light, as he is in the light...and the blood of Jesus Christ his Son cleanseth us from all sin"* (1 John 1:7).

To abide in Christ is to abide in His love. To abide in Him means that we are void of selfish ambition, faultfinding, unbelief, and jealousy. To abide in Him is to actually have Him live His life in us and through us. That is, it is to deny ourselves and let our Lord live His life in our bodies as He lived in His own body 2000 years ago. Yielding to Jesus in self-denial is the missing link that connects conversion to the life of abiding in Christ.

Oh, what dynamic words are these two words: *in Christ*. To believe in Christ and the gospel without *abiding* in Christ provides no life in Christ; it provides neither grace nor salvation. But, if we actually abide in Him, we shall walk even as He walked, as the Scriptures say, *"...because as he is, so are we in this world"* (1 John 4:17).

Yes, it is only as we are in Christ that there is no condemnation, for our salvation is in abiding. We arrive at the place of abiding by denying Self and walking *"not after the flesh, but after the Spirit."*

3

January 2

Praise in the Pit

--==mmₙₙmm==--

*This thou knowest, that all they
which are in Asia be turned away from me.*
—2 Timothy 1:15

Paul was well aware of the life of suffering. *"...five times
received I forty stripes...Thrice was I beaten with rods, once
was I stoned, thrice I suffered shipwreck...in perils of
waters, in perils of robbers,...In weariness and painfulness,
...in hunger and thirst..."* (2 Cor. 11:24–27). Yet, all these physical afflictions were nothing to Paul compared to the "all in
Asia have forsaken me."

Yes, Paul's pulpit seemed to have been in a pit, yet never
pitiful. While in this pit, Paul wrote his "prison epistles"
which we know as "praise epistles," proving to us that Christianity works victoriously even in the most miserable of
circumstances. Friend, are you letting your prison epistles
become praise epistles?

Paul's theology of praise in the pit helped him to lay the
foundation for the arena of faith. Truly, this pit religion
meant that Paul's faith was first tested before it was
published as a faith that sings when it could have wept.
The church of Asia is no more, but the product of Paul's
faith lives on, not pitifully but triumphantly! Yes, Paul's
writings help all of us in our pits of life.

Are you in a pit? If so, rejoice! Has trouble upon trouble
come into your life? Do as Paul did: rejoice! Remember that
man's most desperate hour is God's greatest opportunity to
show forth His power and glory in earthen vessels (2 Cor.
4:7).

As much as our flesh dreads suffering and death, let us
remember that Jesus came to suffer and to die. If we suffer
and die as He did, our fruit shall be as sweet as His. People
may turn away from us, trials may abound unendingly, but
none of these things will prevent the abiding fruit that comes
out of a surrendered life.

No Time Out

Then took they up stones to cast at him:
but Jesus hid himself, and went out of the temple...
And as Jesus passed by, he saw a man
which was blind from his birth.

—John 8:59–9:1

If there was ever a reason for Jesus to take time out to sulk, to feel sorry for himself, to bind up his wounds, to get depressed or discouraged, and to become absorbed in self-pity, this was one of those times. Here at the Feast of Tabernacles, He had received one of the harshest tongue-lashings from the Pharisees ever, He was accused of having a devil, and now they got ready to kill Him. But Jesus, walking out of the temple, instead of trying to find a place of retreat—a juniper tree—immediately saw a man who was born blind. And He healed him!

My friend, when you are ill-treated, accused, misunderstood, called names, cast out of a church meeting, do you still see the needs of others as Jesus did? Do you still comfort the widows? Do you still give bread to the hungry? Do you still notice the torn coat of your brother? Do you still join in the prayers of the saints for revival? Or do you stop seeing all the needs of humankind but your own?

Yes, let us not think that we are like Jesus when we are rejected and spoken evil of unless we also react like Jesus—taking no time out for self-pity—but going right on with the mission to help the needy and to seek and to save that which is lost. Take no time out.

Plant Your Roots in the Right Place

*Rooted and built up in him, and
stablished in the faith, as ye have been taught,
abounding therein with thanksgiving.*

—Colossians 2:7

There were many forces pulling on the Colossian believers, such as traditions, philosophies, and false teachers. The forces that were pulling on those early Christians are still with us today. Therefore, the answer to these pulls and attractions is that we be rooted in Christ. Paul says, *"For in him dwelleth all the fulness of the Godhead bodily"* (Col. 2:9).

Paul was rooted in Christ! What are you rooted in? Some people are rooted in past religious experiences, so they live in the past rather than feasting on the fresh streams of today's faith. There are some who are rooted in bitterness over something that happened years ago. Some people are rooted in resentments, in religious schedules, works, baptism, confirmation, and religious pride. None of these will help us to receive of the fullness of the Godhead, which will put a spring in our step and a song in our soul each day. Only by being rooted in Jesus Himself will we have sustaining, divine life within us.

And now, my friend, how do we become rooted in Christ? The answer is, we must die to Self. Jesus said, *"Except a corn of wheat fall into the ground and die, it abideth alone: but if it die, it bringeth forth much fruit"* (John 12:24). Yes, only as we give up the old life will our roots go down into Christ, and then our spiritual branches will spring upward. Plant your life in the soil of the Lord Jesus, and your fruit will abound and remain forever.

Come to the Rock

*But they that wait upon the Lord shall renew
their strength; they shall mount up with wings as
eagles; they shall run, and not be weary; and
they shall walk, and not faint.*

—Isaiah 40:31

Before an eagle can mount up each morning, he has to spend a considerable amount of time preening himself on the rock. The process of preening includes, first, the straightening of the feathers. Feathers tend to get tangled up a little; therefore, they must all be properly realigned.

Next, the eagle runs his wing feathers through his beak, and he presses them so as to guarantee a smooth and efficient wing surface for flight. The eagle will not leave the rock until his feathers, around 7000 in all, have been checked and maintained in order to meet the high standard required for flying.

We are called to be eagle saints. We are called to come each morning to Christ our Rock. We are called to get all our attitudes properly aligned and to press our thoughts and motives into conformity with God's perfect will. This takes time and effort and yielding to the prompting of the Holy Spirit. When we have done this, we are then prepared to soar into the high altitudes of God's blessings, and we will be able to face every storm that may come our way.

As the eagle is bound to fail unless he first comes to the rock, so are we also bound to fail unless we come to our Rock. But if we do come to the Rock each day, then we "shall run, and not be weary" and we *"shall walk, and not faint."*

Walking with God Is Possible

These are the generations of Noah:
Noah was a just man and perfect in his
generations, and Noah walked with God.

—Genesis 6:9

What a beautiful picture this is. Are you walking with God? Would you like to walk with Him? Noah walked with God before the Law, before Christ, before the Holy Spirit was poured out, and before the Bible and hymn books were printed. Then should there be any reason why we cannot walk with God?

Now, walking is preceded by the embarrassing experience of stumbling and falling. Walking is an art to be learned, and not a gift to be received. It requires a good deal of practice. Anyone who is not willing to face the humiliating process of falling and failing, while others laugh and the devil says you can't, is never going to walk with God.

Oh, my friend, take heart, because you can learn to walk with God. When Noah was born, he was born with the same depraved humanity as you and I. He had similar mood swings as you and I, and he had to fight his way through the same fog of doubt and the same storms of accusations to reach the goal as you and I do. Yet, Noah walked with God, and he was the only one in his generation who did. Dear one, take up the challenge for which you were born again: to walk with God.

Sin and Righteousness Cannot Live Together

*Whosoever is born of God doth not
commit sin; for his seed remaineth in him:
and he cannot sin, because he is born of God.*

—1 John 3:9

J ohn was an expert when it came to stating things in black and white. While others see life in shades of gray, John separates the dark from the light. In this verse, John is saying that sin is the ultimate measure of man's spiritual state. *"Whosoever is born of God doth not commit sin"* tells us that it is as natural for the man who is in Christ not to sin, as it is for the man outside of Christ to sin.

The "seed" mentioned in this verse refers to Christ and to Christ's deposit of the Holy Spirit in the heart of man. Once His Spirit is present in the believer, sin becomes repugnant to him. God's true children are disgusted with nakedness, lying, disobedience, strife, and slander. Their anxious souls are like that of Lot's who, in the midst of the wickedness of Sodom, was vexed, oppressed, grieved, exhausted, and distressed by sin. Sin is a foreigner and an unwelcome guest to those in Christ.

To John, righteousness could never coexist with sin in the same heart. And when sin tries to make a subtle attempt to enter a holy heart, it is recognized and immediately thrown off, just as a fly about to land in a pot of honey is swatted away.

Paul, in agreement with John, says with great confidence that we who are born of God are free from sin, and that sin shall no longer have dominion over us (Rom. 6:9–11).

Fact Versus Feeling

*And the Lord God called unto Adam,
and said unto him, Where art thou?*

—Genesis 3:9

Here you have the first question of biblical history: *"Where art thou?"* Notice that this is not a question of feeling, but a question of fact. God did not want to know how Adam felt, but where he was. There is no place in biblical literature where God ever asked anyone how he felt. Yet this is one of the most dominant questions in American society.

We in America are so hypersensitive to our feelings. We have been highly influenced by Germanic psychoanalysis to look inward, thereby greatly impairing us in our look upward toward God. If we want to make strong progress in our Christian development, we must abandon this inward look, this frequent self-examination, this excessive probing of our state of emotions.

It is certain, facts matter much more than feelings. You may not feel that God loves you, but the fact is that He demonstrated His love to you at Calvary. *"But God commendeth his love toward us, in that, while we were yet sinners, Christ died for us"* (Rom. 5:8). You may not feel as if your prayers are reaching heaven, but the fact is that God hears the cries of the destitute. *"Call unto me, and I will answer thee"* (Jer. 33:3). You may not feel victorious, but the fact is, if you obey Him, you are victorious. *"And being made perfect, he became the author of eternal salvation unto all them that obey him"* (Heb. 5:9).

So, the question to you this day is not how do you feel, but where are you with God?

Faith Needs Dressing Up

*And beside this, giving all diligence, add to your
faith virtue; and to virtue knowledge; And to knowledge
temperance; and to temperance patience; and to patience
godliness; and to godliness brotherly kindness;
and to brotherly kindness charity.*

—2 Peter 1:5–7

This faith Peter is referring to is something like naked faith, a faith yet undressed, a faith in its simplest, primordial form. Such faith is like a house without furniture, carpet, and fixtures. It is livable but not comfortable. Such faith is like an automobile without a radio, rear view mirrors, heating, or air conditioning.

When we first come to God, we have such faith. Abraham had such primitive faith, and it got him to Canaan. Samson had it, and it helped him to do great miracles.

But this initial faith is an undressed faith. It lacks in the areas of virtue, knowledge, godliness, and self-control. New and young faith may suffice for many tasks, and it may be livable, but it is yet far from what God can make of it or intends for it. This undressed, raw faith lacks the beauty and grace of Christlikeness. Hence, this faith explains Abraham's behavior in Egypt, Samson's crudeness, James and John's revengeful spirit in wanting to burn up Samaria, and Paul and Barnabas' violent dissension.

Let us not underestimate simple faith, but let us also not remain in such faith. Let us dress up our faith and add to it all the divine virtues so that it will be perfected, making us like "little Jesuses" at home, at work, and at church.

What Will You Send Away?

*And when he had sent the multitudes away, he
went up into a mountain apart to pray: and when
the evening was come, he was there alone.*

—Matthew 14:23

Oh, what a preacher He was, to send the multitudes away
so that He could pray! How important are the multitudes?
Yet, how much more important is it to pray? What can a
man give to a multitude if he does not come apart to pray?
What can you give to your marriage, to your children, to
your job, to your church, without your time alone with God?

If you have ceased in your times alone with the Master,
begin again. Wait upon the Lord each day. As you become
quiet, He will speak to you. He will take inventory of your
soul: your attitudes, your motives, your reactions, and your
thoughts. He will search the innermost chambers of your
heart. He will ask you to surrender your spots, wrinkles,
blemishes, and all that is unholy, unloving, and unChristlike,
in order to make you clean. He will transform you little by
little, for saints are not made overnight. As you continue to
behold His face and His glory, and confess and abandon your
shortcomings, you will be changed into the image of the Lord,
"from glory to glory, even as by the Spirit of the Lord" (2 Cor.
3:18).

Yes, Jesus sent the multitudes away so He could pray.
Whatever is in your life that prevents you from praying,
send it away. And when it is time for you to speak, your
words will be more than just sounding brass and a tinkling
cymbal.

Life and Death Are Friends

I am crucified with Christ: nevertheless I live;
yet not I, but Christ liveth in me: and the life which
I now live in the flesh I live by the faith of the Son
of God, who loved me, and gave himself for me.

—Galatians 2:20

What does it mean to be crucified with Christ? What is this paradox that one can be crucified and live at the same time? What is this great truth that one can only live with Christ when one is dead?

Oh, my friend, this is a marvelous mystery, first explained by Jesus to the Greeks when He said to them, *"Except a corn of wheat fall into the ground and die, it abideth alone: but if it die, it bringeth forth much fruit"* (John 12:24). In the victorious Christian walk, life and death always coexist. The moment we cease to die to Self, spiritual life in Christ also ceases. In Christ, life always comes out of death, and life is always sustained by the death of Self.

So, only as we crucify our Self-life, and the affections thereof, can Christ live in us. The moment we leave self-denial, our abiding in Jesus and His abiding in us become history. We can only follow our Savior by bearing our cross. *"And he said to them all, If any man will come after me, let him deny himself, and take up his cross daily, and follow me"* (Luke 9:23).

Self-will Is the Cause of Sin

*And he said to them all, If any man will
come after me, let him deny himself, and take
up his cross daily, and follow me.*

—Luke 9:23

It is obvious that without self-denial one cannot follow Jesus. What air is to breathing, water to a fish, and land to a farmer, self-denial is to victorious living. To reject self-denial is to choose to be spiritually barren, for Self will never take one step after Jesus.

Self-will is the mother of all misery and sin. It is sin personified in every unsanctified person. Sin is not the origin of evil, but Self-will is. Eve did not sin because she had a sinful nature but because she chose what her Self-life wanted. In fact, Eve was sinless. She was perfect. It was not sin that made Eve sin, nor was it the devil. The devil brought temptation, but the devil did not make Eve sin. The refusal on Eve's part to deny Self was the cause of her sin. So, can you see that Self-will is a cause and that sin is an effect?

It is also Self-will that brings Christians into lukewarmness, that breaks up marriages, and fills our prisons. It is this Self-will that prevents us from following Jesus. Yes, it is this Self-will that must be denied and crucified daily so that we may be the true followers of our Lord. And as Self-will took man out of the Garden of Eden, so Self-denial will bring him back into it. There is nothing in the Self-life to sustain life, therefore, abiding in Jesus as the branch abides in the vine is our only hope (John 15).

In Christ

*Therefore if any man be in Christ,
he is a new creature: old things are passed
away; behold, all things are become new.*

—2 Corinthians 5:17

Why are there so many precious believers who act, think, and live so much like old creatures? They have been born again, yet, their conversation and interests turn so much more easily to sports, politics, and personal problems than to their Lord. Where is this *"all things have become new"* with them? The answer is found in the two most vital words of Pauline theology, *in Christ*. Paul does not say, if any man be born again that *"he is a new creature,"* but he says, *"if any man be in Christ,"* that is, if he is abiding in Christ, *"he is a new creature."*

Yes, one absolutely cannot abide in Christ but by being born again. Rebirth is the beginning point of being in Christ. But the beginning will only be sustained by our taking up our cross daily and following Him in humility. It is this which keeps us in Christ. It is this that sustains the *"new creature"* life. Hence, Paul admonishes us all, *"As ye have therefore received Christ Jesus the Lord, so walk ye in him"* (Col. 2:6).

One might well be born of God in one hour, and then make one's own selfish choices in the next hour. So, therefore, the whole point of this Pauline theology can be condensed into two beautiful words: *in Christ*. Let us come to Him, walk in Him, and remain in Him and with Him forever.

Is God Enough for You?

That I will not take from a thread even to a shoelatchet,
and that I will not take any thing that is thine, lest
thou shouldest say, I have made Abram rich.
—Genesis 14:23

In the "battle of the kings," Lot and most of the citizens of Sodom and their goods fell into the hands of the enemy. But Abraham and his 318 servants valiantly returned all of these people, with all of their goods, to their homes. Subsequently, the king of Sodom tried to reward Abraham for his kindness (Gen. 14:21). But Abraham turned down all rewards.

"After these things the word of the Lord came unto Abram in a vision, saying, Fear not, Abram: I am thy shield, and thy exceeding great reward" (Gen. 15:1). Because Abraham turned down the rewards of men, God became his reward! Dear one, if you forsake all, God will also become your reward, now and forever.

Oh, what self-indulgent Christians we are. We want and need so much in rewards, in things, and in attention in order to be happy. May the Spirit of the Lord convict us all of our earthly attitudes and demands. May we turn thumbs down to man's pitiful gifts to serve the Lord God for Himself only.

God is good. Is He good enough for us to want nothing else but Him, knowing that in Him all things are ours, and we are His? God wants to be our exceeding great reward. Let Him be so for you!

The Mighty Few

*Then saith he unto his disciples, The harvest truly
is plenteous, but the labourers are few.*

—Matthew 9:37

Why would Jesus have said that the laborers are few when there were hundreds of priests and Pharisees all around Him? The answer is simple. Few were willing to pay the price to enter into Christ's harvest as laborers. Jesus said, *"Because strait is the gate, and narrow is the way, which leadeth unto life, and few there be that find it"* (Matt. 7:14).

In Noah's time, only eight souls were worthy to survive the flood. In Ezekiel's day, in spite of dozens of prophets, priests, and Levites, God had to say, *"And I sought for a man among them, that should make up the hedge, and stand in the gap before me for the land, that I should not destroy it: but I found none"* (Ezek. 22:30). Out of 603,000 men who left Egypt, only two entered into the Promised Land. And Luke 14 tells us that of all those who were bidden to the Great Supper, none tasted of it.

Yes, many are called, but few have ever qualified to be chosen. And yet, God has worked mightily through His few. Consider all that He did through Noah, Abraham, Joseph, Moses, Deborah, Samuel, Elijah, John the Baptist, Peter, and Paul.

Oh, how sobering is the word "few," and yet, how vital it is for us to be counted in that number. Get onto the strait and narrow path today, enter into the field of harvest, and see what mighty works God will bring to pass in you and through you.

A Shortage Unfulfilled

*There was a man sent from God,
whose name was John.*

—John 1:6

That great man of prayer, E. M. Bounds, remarked, "What the church needs today is not more and better methods, nor more efficient machinery, but men sent from God."[1] *"There was a man sent from God, whose name was John."* Nothing is more refreshing today amid the clang of sounding brass and tinkling cymbals than to know that there is a man among us who is sent from God.

Men sent from God do not reflect their private views or institutional opinion, nor do they yield to the pressures and expectations of other men. They do not seek promotion, honor, or gain in the church. Men sent from God reflect God and promote His glory. Men sent from God have the greatest delight in communing with their Maker. Men sent from God do not compromise to save themselves, nor do they use religious methods to boost their egos. Men sent from God, through years of solitude, servanthood, and humility, have tuned their ears to clearly discern the voice of God. They live by that voice every moment of their private and public lives, regardless of circumstance.

Oh, how the church needs men sent from God. She needs them as much as automobiles need gas, ships need compasses, farmers need land, and ducks need water. Let us pray that somewhere, in some homes, God will raise up a new generation of men sent from God, men who will entirely belong to Him, who will always do His will.

Complete Your Surrender

Remember them which have rule over you,
who have spoken unto you the word
of God: whose faith follow...

—Hebrews 13:7

Our spiritual instincts tell all of us that Christianity without surrender is impossible. So, we surrender to God; of course, at least theologically. But if we have so many "surrendered" Christians, why do we have so much trouble in our churches, in our homes, and on our jobs? Why is the average evangelical pastor nudged out of his church and on to another one every two to three years?

One reason for this is our lack of submission to man, the forgotten element in our surrender to God. God has not only designed a pecking order for chickens, predators, and cattle, but also for man. In most stations of life, we are either called to lead or to follow. The whole history of the children of Israel makes a good case study of man's tragic dilemma if he does not follow men appointed of God. Paul says, *"Wherefore I beseech you, be ye followers of me"* (1 Cor. 4:16).

No government can function without the submission of its citizens to its laws. No business has ever prospered without its employees doing what the boss says. No school can function without its students following the guidelines of the principal. No army has ever won a battle, unless she obeyed her generals.

Yes, my friend, complete your surrender by the realization that God and His appointed leaders are closely intertwined. Jesus said to his apostles, *"He that receiveth whomsoever I send receiveth me; and he that receiveth me receiveth him that sent me"* (John 13:20).

Stoning Rights Terminated

*Now Moses in the law commanded us, that such
should be stoned: but what sayest thou? This they said,
tempting him, that they might have to accuse him.*

—John 8:5–6

In the story of the adulterous woman, the Pharisees' real
agenda was not the stoning of the woman but the stoning of
the Son of God. We read in John 5:18, *"Therefore the Jews
sought the more to kill him."* The adulterous woman was
only a tool in the hands of the murderers. Jesus was their
prize. Now, why did Jesus not consent to the stoning of the
woman in order to satisfy the Law of Moses? Here is my
thought on this matter:

If the woman was to be stoned for adultery, so the Pharisees should have been stoned for intent to murder; so should
all men in the temple have been stoned who had looked at a
woman with a lustful eye, which Jesus also called adultery;
so should the rest who had had evil thoughts, resentments,
jealousies, and any disobedience. The incarnate Christ,
through the Holy Spirit, is God's fullest revelation to man
of the holiness of God, and in the presence of that holiness,
no sin can stand and live. Compared to this pure holiness,
all sinners are worthy of death. Jesus said, *"He that is without sin among you, let him first cast a stone at her"* (John
8:7). Only Jesus was without sin. The stoning rights of men
are over, even of the best of men. *"For all have sinned, and
come short of the glory of God"* (Rom. 3:23).

Through Christ, the triune God has become more holy to
us. Through Him, sin has become more sinful in us, and grace
has become more abounding toward us. All this is displayed
in the story of the adulterous woman. Here, all become sinners; here, all are placed at the feet of Jesus for their need
of forgiveness; and here, all are told to go and sin no more!
Yes, man's stoning rights are over. Judgment is altogether
in the hands of God, and may you and I leave it there.

Earthly Faith Versus Heavenly Faith

*And the waters covered their enemies: there was
not one of them left. Then believed they his words;
they sang his praise. They soon forgat his works;
they waited not for his counsel.*

—Psalm 106:11–13

"Then belived they his words." The question is: When did
they believe His words? They believed His words only
after they saw. This is a shallow faith. This is a worldly
faith, an unblessed faith, and therefore it is a faith that lacks
perseverance in the face of difficulty.

The words *"Then believed they"* in verse 12 were soon
followed by *"They soon forgat his works."* in verse 13. All
the way from Goshen to the Red Sea, Israel did not believe.
Her faith was based on the physical, and their physical
senses saw an angry Egyptian army behind them and a large
body of water in front of them. There was not one physical
thing that they could attach their faith to, so they did not
believe until the waters opened up, until they had physical
evidence to believe. Again, such faith is not faith at all, for
*"faith is the substance of things hoped for, the evidence of
things not seen"* (Heb. 11:1).

Moses' faith, however, did not come out of the physical.
He also saw the Egyptian army and the waters, but his faith
was locked onto the invisible God and onto His promise of
protection in the midst of despair and hopelessness. Therefore, Moses could say, *"Fear ye not, stand still, and see the
salvation of the Lord, which he will shew to you to day"* (Ex.
14:13). The people's faith was earthly, and it took them to
an untimely death. Moses' faith was heavenly, and it
endured unto the end.

We Need an Endurance Theology

───◦∭◦∭◦───

But he that shall endure unto the end,
the same shall be saved.

—Matthew 24:13

Continuing on the subject of the perseverance of the saints, it is self-evident from this proclamation of our Lord that if there ever was a time when we needed an endurance theology, it is in these last days.

We already have a deliverance theology, deliverance ministries, deliverance literature, and a deliverance mentality. Almost everyone wants to be delivered instantly from sickness, suffering, difficult relationships, persecutions, and tribulations. Today's deliverance theology is dangerously faulty, because it leaves out God's marvelous plan of tempering and maturing his people. For this reason, Paul admonished Timothy to *"endure hardness, as a good soldier of Jesus Christ"* (2 Tim. 2:3). In other words, he was hinting to Timothy to beware of a deliverance theology.

My friend, is there a challenging relationship in your life with your pastor, spouse, or someone in church or at work? Do not abandon it. We do not become stronger by continually backing out of the fiery furnaces of life. It is there where our spots, wrinkles, blemishes, and such things are cleansed out of us. Suffering in this world is not our enemy, but rather a noble friend and teacher. Is it, therefore, any wonder that one of the first revelations of God concerning Paul, the architect of Christian theology, was, *"For I will shew him how great things he must suffer for my name's sake"* (Acts 9:16). Yes, the first doctrine of Christ came out of the furnace of affliction.

"Beloved, think it not strange concerning the fiery trial which is to try you, as though some strange thing happened unto you: But rejoice, inasmuch as ye are partakers of Christ's sufferings; that, when his glory shall be revealed, ye may be glad also with exceeding joy" (1 Pet. 4:12–13).

Single-mindedness Brings Light

*I press toward the mark for the prize of the
high calling of God in Christ Jesus.*

—Philippians 3:14

$\mathbf{W}$e see in this Scripture a man (Paul) concentrating and focusing on one object and going after it with all his might. Paul's words parallel the words of Jesus, *"The light of the body is the eye: therefore when thine eye is single, thy whole body also is full of light"* (Luke 11:34). This explains why Jesus was a bright and shining light, because He always did the will of His Father. The intensity both of the beauty and power of light that you emanate is in relationship to your focus upon the mark, Christ Jesus.

Unfortunately, such bright divine lights as the early saints have become rare in the church, and many a young Christian has to look at the top athletes of the world for their illustrations and inspirations for singleness of purpose.

May the Lord God Almighty convict and convince us that the most focused persons are to be in the house of God, that the only goal worth pressing toward with single-minded energy is that of finding and doing the will of God. May His kingdom come again amongst His people, driving out cheap and lukewarm religion which is unable to say with Paul, *"but this one thing I do"* (Phil. 3:13).

Servants Are Rejected
—Slaves Are Received

*But made himself of no reputation, and took
upon him the form of a servant, and was
made in the likeness of men.*

—Philippians 2:7

Jesus took on the form of a servant, and the Greek meaning for servant is *doulos* or "slave." The word *doulos* occurs at least fifty times in the Greek New Testament, yet it is erroneously translated in most passages as "servant." So, the first thing I want you to do is replace the word "servant" in the New Testament with the word "slave."

Secondly, consider the practical, obvious difference between a servant and a slave. A servant maintains his own rights. A slave has no rights. A servant punches the clock at 8 AM and again at 5 PM, and then he goes home and does his own thing. Because many Christians think they are servants, they punch in at 10 AM for church each Sunday, they punch out at noon, and then watch television or do whatever they please for the afternoon. Then, they punch back in at the evening service and then back out, to indulge themselves in personal pleasures which bring leanness to their souls.

Because many believers consider themselves servants rather than slaves, they consider any call beyond their scheduled attention to religious duties or worship an infringement upon their rights. Servants have rights and can hold onto their rights, but slaves have been bought with a price, and they are not their own.

So, my friend, are you a servant or a slave of Jesus?

No Disappointments in Christ

*For the scripture says, "WHOEVER BELIEVES
IN HIM WILL NOT BE DISAPPOINTED."*

—Romans 10:11 NASB

In Christ Jesus, there is no disappointment. In the world, there is tribulation, heartache, hurt, insufficiency, and failure. But, as we live out our lives in Christ Jesus, the negatives of the world will be overcome by Christ's great pluses. The key is *in Christ*. The call is to abide in Him as a branch abides in the vine, and so we shall bring forth much fruit.

Take your needs, your heartaches, your burdens, and your disappointments, and bring them to Christ. *"Casting all your care upon him; for he careth for you"* (1 Pet. 5:7). Jesus said, *"Come unto me, all ye that labour and are heavy laden, and I will give you rest"* (Matt. 11:28). *"Be careful for nothing; but in every thing by prayer and supplication with thanksgiving let your requests be made known unto God. And the peace of God, which passeth all understanding, shall keep your hearts and minds through Christ Jesus"* (Phil. 4:6–7). There it is again: *"...through Christ Jesus."*

Let us believe in Him with all our hearts, and let us give Him all our disappointments. Then, by His life and power, we shall move from the negatives to the positives. And we shall know Christ Jesus as the great "divine plus" in every circumstance, relationship, and mood of life.

God Is Not Endangered

—⊸Ⅲ〰Ⅲ⊷—

*And when they came to Nachon's
threshingfloor, Uzzah put forth his hand
to the ark of God, and took hold of it; for the
oxen shook it. And the anger of the Lord
was kindled against Uzzah; and God
smote him there for his error; and
there he died by the ark of God.*

—2 Samuel 6:6–7

There are many things that are better left alone. Uzzah's intentions were good, but here he was not judged for his intentions but for his actions. His actions were those of disobedience. For, no doubt, he knew the specific instructions on how to handle the ark.

Yet, this matter of disobedience goes deeper than the act. Uzzah failed in his intimacy with God. It appears that his vision of God was as small as the ark, in that he did not want God to be turned over or to fall out of the box.

Our impulsive reactions often reveal more about us than first meets the eye. How do we react to our spouse, children, or pastor when the unexpected and unsettling thing suddenly happens? Our reactions tell us and others what is truly in our heart and where we are in our vision.

God was not in the ark, because heaven is His throne and the earth is His footstool. Even when there seems to be a shaking and a stumbling in his plans, programs, ministries, and servants, we would be far wiser not to fret. It is best not to put our hands on any matter too quickly. God will somehow know how to take care of Himself, His work, and His servants.

Take Ye Away the Stone

*Jesus therefore again groaning in
himself cometh to the grave. It was a cave,
and a stone lay upon it. Jesus said,
Take ye away the stone."*

—John 11:38–39

When Jesus arrived at the grave of Lazarus to do the greatest physical miracle of His ministry, He did not call for a prayer meeting. He called for the removal of the stone that blocked the entrance to the cave.

There is a tendency with many of us to believe that prayer is the solution to everything. Oh, how quick we are to say we have not prayed enough. But there are times when it is not more prayer that is needed but simply the removal of a stone.

In this story, it was the stone of unbelief and not the lack of prayer that held up the miracle. The moment Jesus heard of Lazarus' sickness several days prior to His arrival at the cave, He had prayed for Lazarus and was confident that Lazarus would live on, as He kept reaffirming to His followers (John 11:11, 23). At the grave He said, *"Father, I thank thee that thou hast heard me"* (v. 41). No, it was not more prayer that was needed, but the removal of that which prevented prayer from releasing its power.

"Take ye away the stone." Check your heart for stones. If it is not the stone of unbelief, it may be the stone of earthly ambitions, of pride or jealousy, of bitterness or resentment, of withholding your tithe and offerings, of prayerlessness, of faultfinding, or it may be the stones of self-pity or rebellion that hinder your prayers from being answered.

How many times have we prayed on and on for weeks, months, and years, even in great earnestness and with fasting, yet, if we had just removed the stones from our heart, we would have had the answer long ago?

"Take ye away the stone," and do it today!

Imaginations Versus Staying Power

Casting down imaginations, and every high thing that
exalteth itself against the knowledge of God, and bringing
into captivity every thought to the obedience of Christ.

—2 Corinthians 10:5

Abram was able to enter into Canaan but not able to stay there in his early life. Like Abram, many of us have trouble with "staying faith." You see, "starting faith" and "staying faith" are not the same. What is it that caused the staying faith of Abram to fall apart? Rational human expectations— or, as Paul puts it, imaginations—were at fault. Abram was still a newcomer to the household of faith. He obviously expected that God, being all-wise, would send him to a good land with friendly people. The rational mind would have chosen the fertile plains of the Ukraine in the north where there was good land and perhaps a people more akin to Abram's faith.

As we read the story of Abram following God's lead to Canaan (Gen. 12), we find him frustrated by imaginations. God sent his servant, Abram, to the rocks to live among a people totally alien to all that Abram believed. To top it off, God sent a famine to Canaan to welcome him. Abram's faith, therefore, became mixed and weakened by his imaginations of what he thought God would or should do when He told him about going to Canaan. His faith, now weakened by reason, took him down to Egypt. And, in Egypt, Abram created such turmoil and confusion in Pharaoh's house that it led to his disgraceful expulsion from that land.

Well, my friend, how clearly now rings the truth of Paul's words, *"Casting down imaginations."* Let us cast out and down our imaginations of what we think should be, and let us accept what God has for us so that our faith will have "staying power"!

Dislodged, but Not Conquered

And there was a famine in the land: and
Abram went down into Egypt to sojourn there;
for the famine was grievous in the land.

—Genesis 12:10

The tragic thing about this verse is it tells us that Abram went "down." Indeed, did he ever go down, both physically and spiritually. He stopped building altars once he left Canaan. He stopped hearing from God. He told a "half-lie" about Sarah, which was really a full lie. He endangered his wife. He angered Pharaoh and treated him unfairly. He brought serious diseases on Pharaoh's household, and he picked up an Egyptian maid who brought him seeds of trouble. Yes, Abram went down.

The last verse in the chapter says, *"And Pharaoh commanded his men concerning him: and they sent him away, and his wife, and all that he had"* (Gen. 12:20). That is a kind way of saying that Pharaoh expelled Abram from Egypt. Egypt was nothing but trouble, and Abram allowed the famine and the ungodly people of that land to drive him out.

But, thank God, our text also says Abram went into Egypt to sojourn there. To sojourn means to abide temporarily. Abram knew that Egypt was not his home. Abram had no intention of living there, for his vision for Canaan did not perish. So, after much failure, he went back to Canaan, and he never left again.

Yes, Abram was dislodged for the moment, but, in time, he became a conqueror. If you, too, have been dislodged by a lack of faith, return to your spiritual home, to where God's will for you is.

Storms Will Be Brewing

*And straightway Jesus constrained his disciples to get
into a ship, and to go before him unto the other
side, while he sent the multitudes away.*

—Matthew 14:22

Jesus ordered His disciples to go before Him to the other
side of the lake. Soon, the disciples found themselves in a
mighty storm. The ship was tossed, and they began to see a
ghost! Yet, they were there by revelation. Once God reveals
something to you, there is no guarantee that the journey
will be easy, that the car will not break down, that the marriage will not hit bumps, or that the church will be exactly
what you have been looking for. On another occasion, the
disciples crossed the sea (Matt. 8:24), and by the time they
had gone a little way, the boat was full of water. Revelations are no guarantee that we shall not have to contend
with storms, dark places, and water in the boat.

The Lord was gracious enough to reveal the house he
wanted me to have. I had already looked at five houses, but
when we came to the sixth one, the Lord told me, "This is
your house." Here was a colossal farmhouse built in the early
1900s, with a chicken coop, a rabbit building, and a large
barn standing over thirty feet tall. When I took the stairs
into the basement, I found six inches of water staring up at
me from the floor, saying, "Welcome home, city boy!"

When God reveals His will to you, you will be tested,
tried, and refined. But remember, He will be in the boat
with you, even when it is full of water.

Revelation or Reason?

*And Simon Peter answered and said, Thou art the Christ,
the Son of the living God. And Jesus answered and
said unto him, Blessed art thou, Simon Barjona:
for flesh and blood hath not revealed it unto
thee, but my Father which is in heaven.*
—Matthew 16:16–17

Peter had the revelation that Jesus was the Christ. The two primary sources of knowledge are revelation and reason. Revelation comes from God, and it tells us what we otherwise would not know, but reason comes by our senses. A clear revelation of Christ is one of our greatest personal and corporate needs.

Because Peter had a revelation of who Christ was, he never strayed far from Jesus. Jesus, therefore, became Peter's all-consuming love, his passion, and his life. Is it possible that the lack of fervor and personal sacrifice in many of today's believers is a result of their never having had a revelation of Christ? Is it not likely that too many worshipers know Jesus only by reason, by word of mouth, by hearsay, by Bible study, or by history, as a man can only know Aristotle, Beethoven, or Columbus?

What we know in our heads will seldom touch and move our hearts, because we can easily abandon that knowledge in the time of testing and trials. Head knowledge never makes us disciples but only fickle, religious performers. Revelations, however, make us men and women who will hold on to Jesus with fervency, love, and passion, both in life and in death. Do you have the revelation that Jesus is the Christ, the Son of the Living God?

Glory and Embarrassment in the Same Week

———⟨⟨⟨⟨⟨⟨⟩⟩⟩⟩⟩⟩———

But he turned, and said unto Peter,
Get thee behind me, Satan: thou
art an offense unto me.

—Matthew 16:23

Yesterday, we learned that Peter had just declared his revelation of Christ. Immediately following that, Jesus gave Peter the keys of the kingdom of heaven. What greater thing could have happened to a young fisherman who had just begun to follow Jesus? How many older, mature saints have spent thirty or fifty years in following our Lord—such people as scholars, theologians, preachers of renown—but have never been equally honored as Peter was in a moment of time?

Jesus said to Peter, *"And I* will *give unto thee the keys of the kingdom of heaven"* (Matt 16:19). But, my friends, herein lies the weakness of youth, for all too often it thinks it already has that which is still only a promise. Peter immediately began to act with authority as if he was already the chief apostle, for when Jesus spoke about his coming death, Peter rebuked Him by saying, *"Be it far from thee, Lord: this shall not be unto thee"* (v. 22). Then Jesus rebuked Peter as if Peter was Satan himself, saying, *"thou savourest not the things that be of God"* (v. 23). Oh, how quickly we can fall from moments of ecstasy, vainglory, and self-importance to feel like the scum of the earth!

Here we have a chief apostle in the making, and in his first attempt at following his calling, he is told that he is totally disinterested in the things of God. If there was ever a time for this young fellow to quit, it would have been then. But thank God, Peter didn't quit. Remember, he had a revelation of who Christ was. And with such a revelation, you, too, will not quit whenever a rebuke comes from God or man.

Peter Did Not Quit

*And after six days Jesus taketh Peter, James,
and John his brother, and bringeth them
up into an high mountain apart.*

—Matthew 17:1

A week had not even passed since the unfortunate incident of Peter having been soundly rebuked by his Lord as being unspiritual. Many people, if not all of us, find ourselves occasionally in similar situations. Having failed in some way, we feel that we might as well quit. Many have quit the Master, having been called much less than "the devil himself" by their pastors.

For some, the twig they stumbled over never to darken a church again has been nothing more than being left out of a meeting others were invited to, or not having been called by the pastor for a long time. If we fall over things like that, how are we going to be followers of Jesus and handle His rebukes?

But, *"after six days Jesus taketh Peter..."* Glory to God! Hallelujah! After six days, Peter was not in his boat sulking. He was not spreading the news that Jesus was a hard taskmaster. No! After six days, Peter was still there. He had simply hung on to the revelation that Christ had given him. He swallowed the rebuke, put himself back together, and hung on to the robe of Jesus, knowing that the waves of the sea that take us down will also bring us back up.

So, after these six days Jesus *"taketh Peter...and bringeth them up into an high mountain apart."* The man whom Jesus had called Satan a week earlier was now chosen with two others of all the people in the world to see Jesus' glory with Elijah and Moses. Yes, this tells us that we must never give up on Jesus, and He will never give up on us. It tells us that there is an "up" for all His people once they are down.

Armed or Unarmed?

For the word of God is quick, and powerful,
and sharper than any twoedged sword...

—Hebrews 4:12

The devil tries to get us out of the Word of God, because he knows that it is a two-edged sword. Without the Word of God, we are unarmed. So, you say, "But, Pastor Schultze, I do live by the Word of God." Let us have a checkup.

Do you rejoice evermore? That is written in the Word, isn't it (1 Thess. 5:16)? Do you, as a husband, strive with all your heart to love your wife as Christ loved the church? That is the Word of God, isn't it (Eph. 5:25)? Do you, as a wife, submit to your husband as unto the Lord, without contention and resentment? That, also, is the Word of God (Eph. 5:22). Do you forsake the assembling of yourselves together, or are you selective about which church services you are going to attend and which ones you are going to stay away from (Heb. 10:25)? Have you, from your heart, forgiven others their trespasses as Christ has forgiven you (Matt. 6:14–15)? Do you speak idle or foolish words (1 Tim. 5:13)? Are you a jester (Eph. 5:4)? Do you keep yourself unspotted by the world, or do the television programs you watch tell otherwise (James 1:27)? Is the Word of God *"living and active"* within you and working through you to change others?

Jesus lived by the Word, and He let the devil know so when He was tempted (Luke 4:4). The Word was His weapon, protection, covering, comfort, and deliverance.

Greater Works than These

━━◅◦◦◦▻━━

*He that believeth on me, the works that I do shall he
do also; and greater works than these shall
he do; because I go unto my Father.*

—John 14:12

Evidently, as we see from this passage, the works that Jesus
did cannot be the greater works we shall do. The works of
Jesus, such as healing, casting out demons, and miracles,
defy natural law, but they are not the "greater works." In
this verse, Jesus points to *"greater works than these."*

Perhaps the greatest clue as to what Jesus had in mind
in reference to greater works is to be found in His high-
priestly prayer (John 17). He prayed for us to be sanctified
by abiding in the Word, through the precious Holy Spirit,
and through the blood of the Lamb, that we may become
one even as the Father and the Son are one, so that the
world may believe.

So, whenever you look at acts of healing, exorcisms, and
miracles of various sorts, you are looking at the lesser works
of the kingdom, even as great as they are in themselves.
For these works are mostly of a temporal rather than eternal nature. They also are more external than internal.

Jesus said, *"greater works than these,"* and these greater
works come as we yield to the Holy Spirit. It is these works
that will transform sinners into saints and that will bring
saints to the end of strife, division, jealousies, and judgments. These works will usher us all into a oneness like
that of Pentecost, bringing multitudes to their knees,
confessing that Jesus Christ is Lord. Yes, this happened
before at Jerusalem, and whenever we pay the price it will
happen again anywhere in the world.

Beware!

*...so Absalom stole the
hearts of the men of Israel.*

—2 Samuel 15:6

Many an associate pastor has stolen the hearts of the people by taking them away from the "old man of God" or the senior pastor. The spirit of Absalom is still with us. We love beauty, we love excitement, we love youthful vigor, and we love action, drama, and eloquence. For many a minister who is called to a congregation, there is an Absalom on the staff or in the pew, a spoiler, one who is not ashamed to usurp authority over the leader.

An Absalom is one who is deceitful, conniving, and cunning, a thief stealing the people of God from their superior under the guise that "God is leading." An Absalom is someone who, like Aaron, takes advantage of the murmuring and discontent of the people with their God-appointed Moses. May all the Absaloms know that their "father" Absalom died with a spear through his heart while hanging on a tree.

If we don't like the senior preacher, let us pray for him until we like him. And if we are too lazy to pray, let us leave the church instead of taking a part in an insurrection. Remember, *"the powers that be are ordained of God," "and they that resist shall receive to themselves damnation"* (Rom. 13:1, 2). Absalom stole the hearts of the men of Israel. Can you assure your senior pastor that your heart is with him?

The Fall of Solomon

*And the Lord was angry with
Solomon, because his heart was turned from the
Lord God of Israel, which had appeared unto him
twice, And had commanded him concerning this
thing, that he should not go after other gods: but
he kept not that which the Lord commanded.*

—1 Kings 11:9–10

Solomon is in our minds predominantly for his great wisdom and the literature of the Proverbs, Ecclesiastes, and the Song of Solomon. He went down in history because God gave him an understanding heart, so that there was none like him before him, neither would there arise any one after him like unto him (1 Kings 3:12). Solomon started his kingship humbly, for he said at the beginning, *"I am but a little child: I know not how to go out or come in"* (v. 7).

Solomon built the first temple. Solomon prayed a prayer of dedication for that temple that brought down the fire of heaven and put every priest and Levite on his face. Oh, how God used Solomon. But as you look at the end of his life with his having a thousand wives, we say, "Oh, how have the mighty fallen." And the Lord became angry with Solomon.

How is it that men so mightily used of God sometimes come to the end of their lives in total disfavor with God? The answer here with Solomon is that in all his love for God, he never ceased to sacrifice and burn incense in the high places (1 Kings 3:3). Solomon never made a clean cut with paganism. And that which simmered in his heart for years finally took over and destroyed him.

Let us examine our hearts for any duplicity of devotion so that we, having run well, will not fail at the end.

Be Slow to Judge

*For he shall have judgment without
mercy, that hath shewed no mercy; and
mercy rejoiceth against judgment.*

—James 2:13

James says that judgment without mercy will be shown to anyone who has not been merciful. This tells us that if we have judged another person, then on Judgment Day, God will judge us the same way. If we want to have any of the mercy of God when we stand before the judgment seat of Christ, we had better show a lot of mercy toward the people we meet in this life.

If we have not prayed as we should every day since our conversion, we will need God's mercy on Judgment Day. If we have not loved everybody the same since our conversion, we will need God's mercy on Judgment Day. If we have been skipping and missing in our giving, we will need God's mercy on Judgment Day. If we have spoken idle words, complained, and have had impure thoughts, we will need God's mercy on Judgment Day,

If we have not obeyed God in everything, if we have bought things we should not have bought, if we have watched television programs we should not have watched, and if we have missed church services, dear ones, we will need God's mercy on Judgment Day. If we have gone where God did not want us to go, we will need God's mercy on Judgment Day. Yes, we all have failed, we all have sinned, and we all need God's mercy. So, let us also be merciful to our brothers and sisters in their transgressions and weaknesses. *"For with what judgment ye judge, ye shall be judged: and with what measure ye mete, it shall be measured to you again"* (Matt. 7:2).

Being Careful One with Another

*Welcome the weak believer, and do
not criticize his views. One person has faith
that allows him to eat everything, but a weaker
one confines himself to vegetables. The one who
eats should not feel contempt for him who abstains,
nor should the one who abstains censure him who
eats; for God has accepted him. Who are you to
censure another's servant?...One person gives
preference to one day above another day,
while another person steems every day.
Each person should be fully convinced in his own mind.*

—Romans 14:1–5 BERKELEY

Here were Christians who judged other Christians by what they ate and by what days they worshipped. Dear ones, *"mercy triumphs over judgment"* (James 2:13 BERKELEY). The one who eats, Paul said, should not feel contempt for him who abstains, nor should the one who abstains censure him who eats, for God has accepted both. Since God receives the man who is a vegetarian as much as the one who is not, what business do we have in judging one or the other?

We are experts at judging people, because the judgmental spirit is deeply rooted in our carnal nature. We judge our brothers and sisters at church. We judge our minister on his sermons, on his car, on his home life, on his personal habits, on what he does on his day off, on how he spends his money, and on how he makes his calls to parishioners. Many sit in judgment of most everyone nearly all the time.

No, dear ones, we are not called upon to sit in judgment. Instead, we are called upon to love one another, for love is the fulfilling of the law.

Be Busy with Prayer

And it came to pass in those days,
that he went out into a mountain to pray,
and continued all night in prayer to God.

—Luke 6:12

Prayer is the greatest force in the universe available to man, because God has chosen it as the means by which he is moved to act. Prayer can span the widest oceans, cross the highest mountains, and reach into every prison, hospital, and presidential palace. Prayer can stop armies and change the course of history.

Prayer is that force which causes the devil to tremble, because prayer links up with the omnipotence of God. That is why the devil ferociously fights prayer. He will first do all he can to prevent us from getting to prayer. He will try to stop us on the intellectual, the emotional, and the spiritual level. And then, once we have pressed through the first battle and entered into prayer, the devil will try to stop us by ridicule, by accusations, by giving us blanks in our thoughts, by making us sleepy, and by bringing up our old sins. But after we have pressed further, and we are well into prayer, the devil will tremble and flee as we plead the blood of Jesus and as we begin to praise Him for His goodness and mercy.

Prayer is that force which gets things done that otherwise would never get done. Give yourself to prayer. Take the telephone off the hook if you need to. If it is necessary, put a sign on the door, saying, "Busy talking to God. Come back later." Jesus could not succeed without prayer, and neither can we.

Miracles Call for Repentance

━━⊰⊱━━

Then began he to upbraid the cities
wherein most of his mighty works were
done, because they repented not.

—Matthew 11:20

It says here that Jesus began to upbraid the cities. Jesus denounced the cities because they did not repent after He did miracle after miracle in their midst. Nowhere did Jesus do so many works of God as in the Decapolis, the circle of ten cities surrounding the Sea of Galilee.

So, our text continues by saying in verse 21, *"Woe unto thee, Chorazin! woe unto thee, Bethsaida! for if the mighty works, which were done in you, had been done in Tyre and Sidon, they would have repented long ago in sackcloth and ashes."* Think of it. If the mighty works that Jesus performed in these Jewish cities had been done in the Gentile cities, they would have repented—not just with lip service but with sackcloth and ashes.

This teaches us that the greatest amount of stubbornness, pride, and hardness of heart today may be amongst God's covenant people, the Christians. Yes, these failings may be found in churches where God is doing many mighty works, where He is giving great revelations, and where He sends the finest of His men. However, just because Jesus does a lot of mighty works in a certain church is no sure proof that that church is better. In fact, it may be the opposite, that this church is in great need of repentance. Such was the case with Capernaum which Jesus denounced as a city being worse than Sodom, and condemned her to hell.

My friend, let us be aware that the signs and proofs of God amongst us are more than just miracles. They are warnings to us to repent in sackcloth and ashes.

No Retirement!

*In the sweat of thy face shalt thou eat bread, till thou
return unto the ground; for out of it wast thou taken: for
dust thou art, and unto dust shalt thou return.*

—Genesis 3:19

In this passage, we have the beginning of the Judeo-Christian work ethic. The first principle of the work ethic is that a Christian is to earn his bread by the sweat of his brow. In God's economy, there is no plan for idleness. The apostle Paul says, *"For we hear that there are some which walk among you disorderly, working not at all, but are busybodies...we command and exhort...that with quietness they work, and eat their own bread"* (2 Thess. 3:11–12). The welfare state is not the creation of the Bible. We must share our bread with those who cannot work—the rest should work with diligence.

The second principle of the Judeo-Christian work ethic is that there is to be no retirement. We must work until we return to the dust because idleness is dishonorable, selfish, and unblessed. Many a man says at age sixty, "I have worked hard, I have saved retirement money, and I deserve to quit to see the world." Such men ought to know that these "I's" display enough selfishness to take them out of God's perfect plan for their lives. Too many people with means, once retired, become absolutely useless to the church, because they often come and go as they please. So, neither the man of God nor God Himself can count on them for anything.

The Bible says no to retirement. A slow down and change, yes, as our strength ebbs away, but idleness and selfish indulgence have no place in the kingdom of God. Your secular work may come to an end soon, but your service to the Lord will only cease at the grave. So, delay your retirement a few more years, and then retire for eternity at God's expense. God has a work to do for each of His children until they return to the dust.

From Pit to Palace

*Therefore all things whatsoever ye would that
men should do to you, do ye even so to them: for
this is the law and the prophets.*

—Matthew 7:12

Here in this passage, we find that the third principle in the Christian work ethic is to "Do unto others as you would have them do unto you." By taking this principle to work, we incorporate the Sermon on the Mount into the workplace. How often has an employer asked an employee to do something, and the employee responded by saying, "That is not my job. I was not hired for that, and I am not getting paid for it." The golden rule causes us to cheerfully do whatever our superiors require of us. "Do unto others as you would have them to do unto you" brings the law and prophets with us into our offices, factories, and hospitals. This principle helps us to be the light of the world and the salt of the earth at every place of employment.

There is no Christian witness at any workplace without this work ethic. There is no blessing or anointing unless we do as Jesus said. Bringing Jesus with us to our work gives us fellowship with Him right there in the factory and the office. And, as we apply this ethic at work, so it is also meant to be applied to our conduct toward our neighbors and brothers and sisters in Christ. No doubt, it is this work ethic that took Moses from the mud of the Nile, and Joseph from the pit, into Pharaoh's palace. There is no way of telling where it will lead you!

Strikes and Sabbaths

...be content with your wages.

—Luke 3:14

Now, the fourth principle of the Christian work ethic is to *"be content with your wages."* In this passage, John the Baptist was speaking to the Roman soldiers because they apparently had been striking or, at least, murmuring about their pay. John's answer? Repent! Repent of what? was the question. The answer was to repent of the murmuring, striking, and complaining spirit.

The apostle Paul said a similar thing in Hebrews 13:5, *"be content with such things as ye have."* First Timothy 6:6, *"But godliness with contentment is great gain,"* tells us that we are gaining more in the long run by not striking or complaining about our wages.

The fifth element of the Christian work ethic is the Sabbath. Consider these verses: *"Six days thou shalt do thy work, and on the seventh day thou shalt rest"* (Ex. 23:12); *"Remember the sabbath day, to keep it holy"* (Ex. 20:8); and *"Keep the sabbath day to sanctify it"* (Deut. 5:12).

It is almost impossible to build a strong Christian home when the mother and the father work on Sundays. I know we need firemen, policemen, and hospital personnel on Sundays as much as on any other day. However, there is no need at all for a Christian to sacrifice his Sunday to connect a yellow wire to a red wire on an assembly line. That is uncalled for. If you do that as a Christian, you may very well still be in Egypt, stamping mud to make bricks on the Sabbath.

God wanted His people out of Egypt because He wanted His people together to worship Him. The God of the Hebrews is also the God of the Christians. Therefore, six days of work and one day for worship is the rule. It is best for the soul, mind, and the body, simply because God said so.

HUMILITY: the Key to Revival

God resisteth the proud,
but giveth grace unto the humble.

—James 4:6

This verse tells us what God assists and what God resists. It tells us what God works through and what He does not. This verse reveals to us to whom God gives a tail wind and to whom He gives a head wind.

Since God is against the proud, you will never find the Holy Spirit in any person who has pride in his heart. Likewise, you will never find the Holy Spirit within a church or congregation that has pride in her accomplishments, growth, doctrine, denomination, mission, or educational programs. If there is any congregational pride, the Holy Spirit cannot work in that body of believers. They may call the finest evangelist and the best musicians to hold revival meetings, and everything may be planned to the highest standard of excellence, yet pride will prevent revival. Pride *always* prevents true revival. Pride in the midst of all this excellence will be as a fly in a glass of milk, making it unfit to drink.

Oh, how we need a baptism of humility. How we need to clothe ourselves with the apron of humility just as Jesus did when He washed the disciples' feet. Men take pride in religious accomplishments, in their bloodlines, in their heritage, in physical strength, and in good deeds. We must not have pride in anything, because pride goeth before destruction, and *"no flesh should glory in his presence"* (1 Cor. 1:29). Remain humble, and you will find the Lord a present help in every time of need.

February 13

HUMILITY: a Garment of Excellence

...and be clothed with humility.

—1 Peter 5:5

Peter said that we must be clothed with humility, and that means we must be meek. We must give God all the glory. We must realize that whatever good we have is a gift of God.

Those clothed in humility have the favor of God, the power of God, and the blessings of God. They have strength to do what God wants them to do. They are the ones whom God is working through to accomplish His eternal purposes.

The hands of pride cannot hold on to the gifts of God. The hands of pride are weak, and this is why destruction follows wherever there is pride. The proud cannot hold on to their successes. They cannot hold on to the revelations of God. They cannot hold on to prayer and endure. They fail in the Gethsemanes of life.

Joseph was a man of great humility. Because of his humility, he was able to hold on to the Lord, the dreams of the Lord, and the revelations of the Lord. In the end, this humility brought Joseph great favor with Pharaoh and with his brothers who had once despised him.

The power of God is with the humble. The blessings of God are with the humble. The wisdom of God is with the humble. The kindness of God is with the humble. The compassion of God is with the humble. The revelations of God are found in the hearts of the humble, and the hands of the humble are indeed the hands of God. Clothe yourself with humility, for it is indeed the garment of excellence!

HUMILITY: an Ornament of Grace

By humility and the fear of the Lord
are riches, and honour, and life.

—Proverbs 22:4

Humility is the way to all that God has prepared for us before the foundation of the world. Humility will never fail. Humility is not a loser. Humility can be kicked around, knocked about, abused, slandered, shot at, falsely accused, spat upon, pressed, pierced through, crucified, and buried. All that, but humility will never die. It is indestructible. Each time, it will rise up to resume its journey where it has left off.

Humility took Joseph from the pit to the palace. It took Moses from being an arrogant court official to being the meekest man on the face of the earth. It took Jesus from the throne of His glory into the deepest depth of servanthood. It took Paul from the self-righteous ranks of the Pharisees to becoming the chief architect of Christian theology.

Humility fights no battles, yet it wins all wars. Humility does not defend itself, yet it is never defeated. Humility seeks nothing for itself, yet it has everything. Humility rests at the foot of the cross, yet it touches all of the universe. Humility in the hearts of men is what causes angels to wonder and God to smile. Humility draws grace, forbearance, and forgiveness and converts them into Christlikeness. Yes, humility is the garment of excellence but also an ornament of grace.

Feathered Food

*The people asked, and he brought quails, and
satisfied them with the bread of heaven.*

—Psalm 105:40

In this passage, we learn that there is both a perfect will
and there is a permissive will of God. To state it in the
context of this verse, God's permissive will is quail, and
God's perfect will is manna.

Quail is what Self wants. Manna is what God wants. Quail
was blown in from a bird migration route, but manna was
created anew each day by God Almighty. Quail had the seeds
of corruption and death in it. Manna had the seeds of life
and health in it.

There was nothing in the manna harmful to man. It
contained no bacteria, no viruses, nothing infectious—there
was nothing imperfect within it. Hallelujah! It was all good,
all pure, all perfect—until it was abused. When it was
abused, *"it bred worms, and stank"* (Ex. 16:20). And that
teaches us another lesson: when God's perfect will is abused,
beware of the consequences!

Unfortunately, many religious people want quail, the
permissive will of God, rather than manna, the perfect will
of God. Many times, someone will want a certain house, a
certain car, or a certain vacation. It is something they
always wanted or dreamed of. The desire for that can be so
great that the soul of that person will not rest until God is
weary of his pleading and reluctantly gives what is asked
for. But, oh, if we ask for that which is not His perfect will,
it will have feathers, beaks, claws, and intestines in it. It
will never satisfy.

Let us never ask for quail, for it contains the seeds of
disappointment and death. Rather, let us only ask for manna
and find that *all* of it is good!

The Tolerance of Sin

And because iniquity shall abound,
the love of many shall wax cold.
—Matthew 24:12

The tolerance of sin in the church is equal to participation therein. That is, if we tolerate sin, and we do not warn the wicked, we are just as guilty as if we committed those sins ourselves. Ezekiel tell us, *"if thou dost not speak to warn the wicked from his way...his blood will I require at thine hand"* (Ezek. 33:8). Is this admonition only to prophets of old, or is it to all of us in the priesthood of believers?

I believe no nation in the world has as many churches, religious broadcasts, books, and Bible studies as America. Yet in nakedness, adultery, drunkenness, and crime, we exceed many. We have a Christianity without the lordship of Jesus, without the government of the Holy Spirit, and without holiness in many of our churches.

At first, the professing church decided to tolerate sin so that grace would abound. But, of late, she has made peace with sin altogether. The new gospel of love has become a cloak to hide our iniquities rather than a power to save us from them. We should have discovered by now that this new gospel is not grace-abounding, but sin-abounding.

We have nakedness on our television and movie screens because we tolerate immodesty in our churches. We complain about government workers wasting time, but we say little about our need to redeem the time because the days are evil. We complain about schools not teaching our children the three "R's," but we do little to graduate our children from Sunday school with the three "S's": saved, sanctified, and serving.

God wishes to cleanse our nation, and He is waiting for repentant hearts. May we all become despisers of evil and watchmen on the wall.

I Shall Not Want

The Lord is my shepherd;
I shall not want.

—Psalm 23:1

In English, "I shall not want" means that I shall not come short of what I need. With Jesus as our Shepherd, we have everything we need. Everything! If we do not believe that, then we make God a liar. Wherever you are, child of God, whether it be in great sickness, financial trial, persecution, accusations, misunderstanding, or deprivation of opportunities, you have all you need in Him.

Our main problem is truly accepting and truly, inwardly comprehending this great truth with joy when we are in the storms of life. All too often, we cannot accept this, because we are not well enough acquainted with our God. Perhaps, we have spent too much of our time living in the shallows of Christianity. So, when He commands us to cast out our nets into the deep at night, totally exhausted, we find our faith is gone. Yes, unbelief too frequently tells us that it will do no good, that we have tried it before and that our strength is not sufficient for the task.

Oh, our God is altogether lovely, a Friend who sticks closer than a brother, a Friend who holds the whole world in His hands. Yes, *"The Lord is my shepherd"* is not for the superficial to comprehend, neither for the prayerless nor the unsurrendered to fathom. Rather, it is the lifeline to those who have learned to trust the Lord their God with all their heart, and to those who have ceased to lean on their own understanding. Yes, dear one, the Lord knows your need; He is with you, and He will never fail you.

Three Types of Men

*For ye are yet carnal: for whereas there is
among you envying, and strife, and divisions,
are ye not carnal, and walk as men?*
—1 Corinthians 3:3

*But the natural man receiveth not the
things of the spirit of God...But he that is
spiritual judgeth all things.*
—1 Corinthians 2:14–15

Here is the whole description of man: there is a natural man, a carnal man, and a spiritual man. To get this distinction clearly, we must not allow ourselves to get bogged down with the Greek, rather we must look at those terms as Paul uses them theologically.

The *natural* man does not perceive the things of the Spirit because he is an unconverted man. He has never come to Jesus. The natural man, according to Paul, is alienated from God, *"dead in trespasses and sins...Wherein in time past ye walked according to the course of this world"* (Eph. 2:1–2). The natural man is in darkness, and spiritual things are foolishness to him.

The *carnal* man, as Paul uses the term, is a person who has been converted by the blood of Jesus and the work of the Holy Spirit, but who refuses to deny Self. Such was the case with the Corinthian Christians.

The *spiritual* man is one who has been born of God, and he lives a life of obedience, ever crucifying the flesh and the affections thereof. So, one of Paul's main reasons for writing his letters to the churches is to bring carnal Christians into a life of full obedience and surrender to Jesus Christ.

There is a natural man, there is a carnal man, and there is a spiritual man. Which of these types describes you?

Yet Carnal?

*For ye are yet carnal: for whereas there
is among you envying, and strife, and divisions,
are ye not carnal, and walk as men?*

—1 Corinthians 3:3

Are you yet carnal? How long are you going to be yet carnal? What are the characteristics of carnality? Does the gospel have a cure for carnality? If so, what is it?

Carnality has its roots in the disobedience of Adam and Eve. When this first couple ate of the Tree of Knowledge in that precious, holy garden of God, something awful of the nature of the Serpent entered into them and consequently polluted their spiritual bloodstreams.

Adam and Eve were expelled from the garden because carnality cannot live in the garden of God. In fact, carnality is enmity against God (Rom. 8:7). Carnality cannot please God. Carnality fights, bites, and butts. It is jealous, envious, selfish, foolish, divisive, lustful, covetous, and resentful.

When we are born again, we are forgiven of all the sins we ever committed. Our sins are removed as far as the east is from the west (Ps. 103:12). But even though we are converted, we still have the carnal nature, even as the Corinthians were still carnal, as noted in our verse for today.

Oh, dear friend, the cure for past sin is the cross of Christ. The cure for the nature of sin, the carnal nature within us, is in *our* taking up our cross, denying our Self-life, and following Jesus. As we deny this carnal nature, crucifying it moment by moment, and follow Jesus, the Lord will sanctify us. And no longer will it be said of us, *"ye are yet carnal."*

Prevent Balks

And Jesus said unto him, No man,
having put his hand to the plough, and looking
back, is fit for the kingdom of God.

—Luke 9:62

There are two absolute essentials for the plowman. First, he is to stay with the plow. Second, he is to never look back while plowing. Once you lay your hand on the plow of the kingdom, you must be done with looking back. You no longer can look back at your past sins, failures, habits, old quarrels, weaknesses, and relationships. You cannot expect to plow straight if you are looking back. Looking back is an invitation to disaster. Kingdom plows cannot operate with a backward look.

When a plowman looks back, his eyes leave the work ahead of him, and he leaves a balk, or a ridge, not turned. Every time he looks back, he leaves another balk. The balks become islands of weeds that reinfect the whole field. We cannot attain holiness and purity with balks in our hearts. They come from looking back.

There is an insatiable desire within us to be current on the quality of our performance. There is a constant groping for assurance causing us to ask, "How am I doing?"

We always want to know if our rows are straight behind us. The temptation to look back and check is so tremendous. Yet, we must resist these temptations, for energy spent on the past equals energy lost for the future. The only way to prevent islands of weeds is to look straight ahead, ever looking to *"Jesus the author and finisher of our faith"* (Heb. 12:2).

I AM

*And Moses said unto God, Behold, when I come
unto the children of Israel,...what I shall I say unto them?
And God said unto Moses, I AM THAT I AM: and he said,
Thus shalt thou say unto the children of Israel,
I AM hath sent me unto you.*

—Exodus 3:13–14

In sending Moses to Egypt to deliver His people, God wanted Moses to know that the secret of victory was in the conquest of the present and not in the plans of the future. God did not want Moses to think of Him as the One who was or who shall be, but as the One who is!

God is always all He can be. When we are not what we can be or ought to be, He is all He can be. God is never anything less than 100 percent at any moment.

"And God said unto Moses...Thus shalt thou say unto the children of Israel, I AM hath sent me unto you." "The God of the moment has sent you." As the God of the moment puts everything He has into every moment, so He wants all of His children to put everything into each moment. For it is in the present moment where life is.

We never fail in the past, nor in the future. For the past is gone, and the future is not yet here. All that is left for us to fail in is the now. And if we seek first the kingdom of God in each moment, our lives will be 100 percent successful.

So, singer, do not consider important only the moments while you sing; and surgeon, do not consider important only the moments of your surgery. All moments between are equally important and sacred, and must be redeemed for God. Let the great I AM, the God of all moments, fill every moment of your every day.

If your life consists of regrets over the past and worries over the future, you have no present. Be an I AM Christian.

Are We Willing to Be Meddled With?

We will not have this man to reign over us.

—Luke 19:14

At the root of this expression from Luke is a deep-seated rejection of any external authority that threatens our Self-life. Self wants to rule and not to be ruled, unless that external rule is the creation of its own will for the sake of its own benefit.

We have willed the rule of our government from the police officer up to the senator to grant us protection and assistance in the pursuit of our own desires. But we do not will any authority that will meddle in the personal affairs of our lives and meet our wills head-on.

It is those authorities who interfere with our plans and who challenge our will which cause us to say, "We do not want this man to rule over us." This is exactly what the parable intends to teach us; namely, that God will meddle in our personal affairs, changing our plans from day to day. Are we willing to have Him meddle?

Because we do not like a God who interferes with our honeymoon and funeral plans, or with our purchases of oxen and land, we have created our own god of convenience, claiming all along that we still worship the God of Abraham.

If we don't like the ruler who threatens our plans, hopes, schedules, and dreams, the only way out is to find a flaw in him which, in our minds, will disqualify him to reign over us. The Pharisees knew that. They either had to submit to Jesus' rule or to find fault with Him as a way out.

May God deliver each of us from that spirit which caused the Pharisees to excuse themselves and eventually to plot the murder of the One sent to save them and to rule over them.

Resting Is Trusting

There remaineth therefore a rest to the people of God.
For he that is entered into his rest, he also hath ceased from
his own works, as God did from his.
—Hebrews 4:9–10

What is this rest that God has for us? This rest is the life of trust. This rest is ceasing to do our own plans, to make our own arrangements, and to go forward in our own strength. In the life of God, whatever is of the flesh is dead from the beginning. This rest is not sweating, nor worrying, nor fretting, nor being anxious over life's situations. This rest is trusting in the promises and in the Word of God, the revelations of God, the benevolence of God, the knowledge of God *"that all things work together for good to them that love God, to them who are the called according to his purpose"* (Rom. 8:28). Resting is trusting, and trusting is resting.

When Abram came to Canaan and found famine, he did not rest. Abram, in his unrest, went south. Israel was supposed to enter the Promised Land at Kadesh-barnea, but they were not trusting nor resting in the promises of the omnipotent God. Therefore, they could not enter in because of their unbelief. When Lazarus died, Mary and Martha were in unrest because they did not know that the Resurrection was in the midst of them to meet their need.

Yes, there is a rest for the people of God: a glorious rest, a joyful, trusting, and God-pleasing rest. In this rest, there is neither disappointment nor embarrassment for *"whoso-ever believeth on him shall not be ashamed"* (Rom. 9:33).

Many Shall Be Offended

Great peace have they which love
thy law: and nothing shall offend them.
—Psalm 119:165

The obedient, surrendered Christian is a stranger to hurt feelings. Hurt feelings are the result of an exaggerated self-image. Hurt feelings are the result of pride and arrogance. All those who are offended, who are subject to hurt feelings, have never been broken of that kingly, carnal nature.

David came to the point where he was beyond hurt feelings, where he knew he was only a worm. Jesus never had hurt feelings. He humbled Himself to be a servant of all. The Syrophenician woman displayed no hurt feelings when she was called a dog by our Savior. The apostle Paul was beyond offense, for he knew he was the chief of sinners.

So, hurt feelings are a signal that Self has not been crucified. When Self is hurt, it retaliates by unkind words, accusations, resentment, and anger. Our feelings are hurt in relationship to the amount of pride we possess. How many people do you suppose have lost out because of hurt feelings? How many people have left prayer meetings, choirs, Sunday school classes, churches, and old friendships because they have been "hurt"?

Dear one, take your hurts to Jesus and ask Him to break you and to slay that carnal nature out of you, and you will come to the end of those hurt feelings. Jesus predicted that in the last days *"shall many be offended"* (Matt. 24:10). You need not be one of them!

A Kingdom beyond Measure

*Blessed are the poor in spirit:
for their's is the kingdom of heaven.*

—Matthew 5:3

To be poor in spirit is to possess, not part, but *all* of the kingdom of heaven. Never in the history of man has as much been given away for so little.

Paul gave a fleeting description of the kingdom when he said it was righteousness, peace, and joy in the Holy Spirit. But Jesus' description is much broader. In parables, he compares the kingdom to a pearl, a treasure, a sower, a net, ten virgins, leaven, a mustard seed, and a man traveling into a far country. Oh, what is this kingdom of heaven, and what riches are in it? How can it be described? It is so great that one can find a piece of it in everything God has created, and yet, were we to put all of these pieces together, we would still have only a little segment of the whole.

We enter the kingdom through humility and brokenness. We stay in it through childlike trust. And we find all things we need by keeping it a priority, for Jesus said, *"seek ye first the kingdom of God, and his righteousness; and all these things shall be added unto you"* (Matt. 6:33).

Oh, how great is the kingdom. It is both incomprehensible and comprehensible. It is a divine mystery and, yet, a present reality to all the lowly in heart.

Our Walk Is More Important than Our Talk

For if ye live after the flesh, ye shall die: but if ye through the Spirit do mortify the deeds of the body, ye shall live. For as many as are led by the Spirit of God, they are the sons of God.

—Romans 8:13–14

The Bible, in this eighth chapter of Romans, puts all of mankind into two categories: those who walk in the flesh, and those who walk in the Spirit. The final criterion for our salvation here is not condensed into a religious experience, but rather, it is found in our walking in the Spirit. It is possible to be born again without ever taking a single step to follow Jesus.

According to the apostle Paul, it is essential to our newfound faith that we walk with God by the leadership of the Holy Spirit. In all of his thirteen epistles, we see Paul emphasizing this walking in the Spirit of the living God. Unless we follow Jesus daily, we will walk in the flesh, and we are "yet carnal," as Paul says of the Corinthian Christians.

So then, there are spiritual Christians, and there are carnal Christians. Jesus likened the carnal Christians to the foolish virgins and the spiritual Christians to the wise virgins. All the virgins were washed by the blood of the Lamb, which the word "virgin" implies. They were all pure to start with, but on their way to the wedding feast, only five maintained their purity and walked with God.

Dear ones, carnality is shut out of the marriage feast because carnality is enmity against God and it cannot please God. So, let us put to death the deeds of the body of sin that we may live lives led by the Spirit.

The Mind of Christ

*For as many as are led by the Spirit
of God, they are the sons of God.*

—Romans 8:14

To be led by the Spirit is a wonderful thing. It is the evidence that we are the sons of God. Every true child of God is waiting for the guidance of the precious Holy Spirit. But to be led by the Spirit has a wonderful prerequisite, and that is to have the mind of Christ. The context of today's verse is, *"For to be carnally minded is death; but to be spiritually minded is life and peace"* (Rom. 8:6).

So, being led by the Spirit comes out of Christlikeness. It comes out of having the mind and the Spirit of Jesus who *"thought it not robbery to be equal with God: But made himself of no reputation, and took upon him the form of a servant"* (Phil. 2:6–7). To have the mind of Christ is to be forgiving, long-suffering, merciful, loving, courageous, selfless, self-denying, helpful, and sacrificial. It is not only looking after one's own things, but also after the things of others (v. 4). If we have the mind of Christ, our life in Him will be a life led by the Spirit.

Oh, how many imagine they are led of the Spirit who, as yet, are strangers to the mind of Christ, who are yet carnal, contentious, resentful, proud, and self-assertive? My friend, let us not think that we can be led by God until we have become obedient unto death, until Christ saturates our lives with Himself. Only then can we be sure that His leading is true and not just the figment of our imagination.

Enough Faith to Get Out, but Not Enough to Get In

━◆━

So we see that they could not enter in because of unbelief.

—Hebrews 3:19

Israel was never far from the borders of Canaan, but she never entered in. The Israel that left Egypt died in the wilderness. She was delivered from Egypt, but she died in unbelief before she reached the land of milk and honey. She had enough faith to get out, but not enough faith to get in. And because she did not immediately go in pursuit of the Promised Land, she died in the wilderness in the presence of the cloud and the fire, with the manna of heaven in her stomach.

Some of the professing church is in the wilderness of Zin. She boasts that she has gotten out of the old life, but she is too blind to see that unless she enters into the new life, she will also die in unbelief, with manna in her stomach. Yes, untold millions of believers have left the shores of Egypt, have sung the songs of deliverance, and, yes, they even continue to sing them to this day. They have tasted of the heavenly gift, they have drunk of the water from the rock, and yet they are not able to enter into the sanctified victorious life of Canaan because of unbelief.

We must be aware that we, as a born-again people like unto Israel of old, can die without grace on the wrong side of Jordan, in the very presence of the fire, the cloud, the divine manna, and the water from the rock. Let us determine today not only to leave Egypt, but also to enter into Canaan. For it is for this purpose that we were born of God.

Like unto Us

Jesus wept.

—John 11:35

The gods of the world are made of wood, stone, silver, and gold. They have eyes that see not and ears that hear not. They also have a mouth, but they do not speak. They have no heart, and they have no feelings.

Our Deity has ears to hear, eyes to see, a mouth to speak, and a heart that feels. Our God is not someone that is cold and absolute, but He is like unto us, for we are made like unto Him—even in His own image.

Observe from the following examples that our God is capable of experiencing the whole range of emotions of humankind: God sorrowed that He made man when He saw the wickedness in the days of Noah. The *anger* of the Lord was kindled when Moses made excuses for not going to Egypt. Jesus *wept* over Jerusalem, and He had *compassion* for the multitude, for they were like sheep having no shepherd. Jesus was *incensed* when He saw the money changers in the temple, and He was *exceedingly sorrowful* when He prayed in Gethsemane.

Yes, Jesus has feelings just like us. Yes, *"we have not an high priest which cannot be touched with the feeling of our infirmities; but was in all points tempted like as we are, yet without sin. Let us therefore come boldly unto the throne of grace, that we may obtain mercy, and find grace to help in time of need"* (Heb. 4:15–16). *"Jesus wept."* His tears tell us that He is real.

Fear and Wisdom Are Inseparable

The fear of the Lord is the beginning of wisdom.

—Psalm 111:10

There are many fears: the fear of losing one's job, the fear of a marriage breakup, the fear of children going astray, the fear of war, the fear of famine, the fear of bankruptcy, the fear of an economic depression or recession, and so on. We need none of these fears. There is only one fear that we need, and that is the fear of the Lord. If we have that fear, all other fears are vanquished, because the fear of the Lord gives us the wisdom to tackle the most difficult circumstances of life.

The fear of the Lord will take us through every storm, and through every dark valley and wilderness. By it, we come to the divine wisdom which is *"better than rubies; and all the things that may be desired are not to be compared to it"* (Prov. 8:11). Yes, *"The fear of the Lord is the beginning of wisdom: and the knowledge of the holy is understanding"* (Prov. 9:10).

Oh, how much we need the fear of the Lord. This is why the Bible first introduces us to the fear of God before we learn of the love of God. Unless we first have the fear of God, we will never come to the divine wisdom that prevents us from abusing God's love and mercy. The fear of God puts us onto the strait and narrow path where His right hand and holy arm will never fail us.

Fear God, for your wisdom and protection will depend upon it. *"Teach me thy way, O Lord; I will walk in thy truth: unite my heart to fear thy name"* (Ps. 86:11).

Venomous Leaders

*O generation of vipers, how can ye, being evil,
speak good things? for out of the abundance
of the heart the mouth speaketh.*

—Matthew 12:34

Here is a group to whom Jesus spoke directly and not in parables: the Pharisees, the scribes, and the scholars. Jesus did not want these men to leave His meetings saying one to another, "Now what did He mean?"

When Jesus saw the multitudes He was moved with compassion, because they fainted and were like sheep that had no shepherd. And why were they without shepherds? The reason was that the men who were supposed to be shepherds were busy finding fault with Jesus. They were jealous of Him. They followed Jesus to judge Him, condemn Him, and put Him to death. They were as vipers hanging on branches, ready to drop on their prey and destroy it.

So, they dropped in on a woman in the act of adultery. How did they plan that? How much satisfaction did they get out of that? What did they see that perhaps they should not have seen? Oh, what vipers they were, not knowing that Jesus did not come to destroy the world, but to save it. With the shepherds having this mindset, no wonder people fainted! For where there is no compassion, people faint and scatter.

So, you can see now why Jesus did not talk to these leaders in parables. He wanted them to know His ultimate displeasure, and so He addressed them as a generation of vipers, whited sepulchers, and hypocrites. May we beware of such leaders whose only interest is in themselves, who are falling far short of the vision and compassion of our Lord Jesus.

Where Have We Been?

⸺◦⫘⟨⟩⫘◦⸺

*Who shall ascend into the hill of the Lord?...He
that hath clean hands, and a pure heart.*

—Psalm 24:3–4

When we begin to come before the Lord, our first concern
must be cleanness of hands and purity of heart. What did
our hands do yesterday? Where did they guide our automobile? What books did they handle or television programs
did they turn on? Do we have clean hands?

We must ask the Holy Spirit to help us review the works
of our hands. We must ask Him to help us review our hearts
by asking Him to help us examine our reactions, our
thoughts, our desires, our impulses, and our meditations.
Most of us need to make slight corrections in our attitudes,
motives, and reactions each day.

"Who shall ascend...?" We must have clean hands and a
pure heart before we can ascend the hill of worship, praise,
adoration, and intercession. We must take obedience with
us into the hour of prayer, for we will only come to *know* as
much about God as the degree to which we are willing to
obey Him. But as we pray, we must also listen. As we pray
and listen, God will show us the places of rebellion, apathy,
doubt, disobedience, and criticism we need cleansing from.

However, in the soul-searching process, let us know that
the scrutiny and the conviction of the Holy Spirit are not to
condemn us but to make us whole through confession, for
*"if we walk in the light...the blood of Jesus Christ his Son
cleanseth us from all sin...If we confess our sins, he is faithful and just to forgive us our sins, and to cleanse us from all
unrighteousness"* (1 John 1:7, 9). Praise God! By virtue of
His provisions, we can *"ascend into the hill of the Lord"* and
worship Him in the beauty of holiness.

HOPE: Shattered and Unshattered

*And hope maketh not ashamed; because
the love of God is shed abroad in our hearts by
the Holy Ghost which is given unto us.*

—Romans 5:5

This hope that Paul talks about is hope as an assurance of our salvation. Paul says that as long as Holy Ghost love dwells in our hearts, this hope will never make us ashamed; it will never lead to shipwreck; it will never disappoint or delude us.

There are many hopes and dreams which may come to naught for many of us: our hope for a godly son or daughter, our hope for good health, our hope for an easy marriage relationship, or our hope for success in business or ministry. Oh, how many hopes have already been shattered in our lives, and how many are yet waiting to put us to shame, disappointment, or delusion? Is there anyone who has not experienced some hope unfulfilled?

Noah's hope for some response to his preaching was shattered. Moses' hope to take Israel into Caanan at Kadesh was lost in the sands of the desert. Elijah's hope that he would take fifty men over Jordan with him ended in disappointment. Jesus' hope for Capernaum vanished when, having experienced more miracles than any city, she would not repent. Paul's hope to unify all believers into one body to which God could bring the latter rain, went with him to the grave.

Oh, but praise the Lord, the love of God shed abroad in our hearts will never let us lose the hope of our eternal salvation. With that in mind, despite all of life's disappointments, we can go on, assured that we will see His face.

The Kingdom of God or the Kingdom of Heaven?

*And said, Verily I say unto you, Except ye
be converted, and become as little children, ye
shall not enter into the kingdom of heaven.*

—Matt. 18:3

*Verily I say unto you, Whosoever shall
not receive the kingdom of God as a little
child, he shall not enter therein.*

—Mark 10:15

I am quoting these two verses from the synoptic gospels to settle the question of whether the kingdom of God and the kingdom of heaven are two different kingdoms, or whether they represent the same kingdom at different stages, such as the kingdom of God representing God's kingdom on earth and the kingdom of heaven representing God's kingdom in the afterlife.

If we believe in the full inspiration of the Bible, if we believe that *"no prophecy...is of any private interpretation,"* if we believe that God moved men to write the Bible *"as they were moved by the Holy Ghost"* (2 Pet. 1:20, 21), then we know that the kingdom of God and the kingdom of heaven are two expressions of one and the same thing. Were it not so, Matthew, on explaining the principle of entering the kingdom, would not have used the "kingdom of heaven" while Mark was allowed to use the "kingdom of God" to express the same truth. The Holy Spirit is not the author of confusion. The Holy Spirit allowed both renderings, the kingdom of God and kingdom of heaven, for they speak of the same truth.

Therefore, from now on, let the confusion end. As there are many names for Jesus, there are many names for His kingdom, the kingdom of heaven and the kingdom of God being just two of them.

The Will of God

*Not every one that saith unto me, Lord, Lord,
shall enter into the kingdom of heaven; but he that
doeth the will of my Father which is in heaven.*

—Matthew 7:21

*And why call ye me, Lord, Lord, and do not
the things which I say? Whosoever cometh to me,
and heareth my sayings, and doeth them, I will shew
you to whom he is like: He is like a man which built an
house, and digged deep, and laid the foundation on
a rock: and when the flood arose, the stream beat
vehemently upon that house, and could not
shake it: for it was founded upon a rock.*

—Luke 6:46–48

These verses tell us that the kingdom of heaven is only entered through obedience. We may be born again, we may sing, pray, worship, and profess; yet, if we are not doing the will of God, we may have lived in vain.

Not doing God's will is doing the will of our Self-life and is collaborating with Christ's archenemy, the devil himself. Selfishness is the extension of the kingdom of evil into the heart of man. Hence, the apostle John rightly states that he who sins is of the devil.

Wherever Self has its way, there is iniquity and rebellion against God. Whenever a husband or wife insists on the way of Self, the spirit of wickedness is turned loose on the marriage. Whenever a congregation demands programs other than what the Holy Spirit leads, the spirit of the Prince of Darkness is released into that church.

Doing God's will divides the disciples of Jesus, the possessors from the professors, the wheat from the tares, and the sheep from the goats. Christianity without obedience is like a cloud without rain. We must seek His will at all times and at any cost. Yes, let us obey!

"She Hath Done What She Could"

⟿⟿⟿⟿⟿⟿⟿

*She hath done what she could: she is come
aforehand to anoint my body to the burying.*

—Mark 14:8

There are very few persons who will face Judgment Day with such comforting words as Mary of Bethany received, *"She has done what she could."*

There are three recorded instances where Mary met the Master. She is first found sitting at Jesus feet while her sister Martha was busy serving. Jesus said of her, *"Mary hath chosen that good part, which shall not be taken away from her"* (Luke 10:42). Next, Mary is found meeting Jesus when He came to raise her brother Lazarus from the dead. As she came to Him, *"she fell down at his feet,"* touching Him deeply (John 11:32–33). Finally, we see Mary anointing the Lord Jesus for His burial, emptying ointment from an alabaster box worth one year's salary (Mark 14:3-9). And, indeed, it is quite possible that this box of blessing was her inheritance.

If she would have anointed Jesus with just a few drops of that ointment, one would think that it would have been enough. She could have kept the rest to travel the world, to buy beautiful clothing or new furniture. But, no, whenever Mary was with Jesus, she gave all she could. So her inheritance became His inheritance, and His inheritance became her inheritance. Three times Jesus and Mary were brought together in a wonderful feast of sacred devotion and entire consecration. They both had the same spirit in that they both gave all they could, and that they both did all they could.

Loved one, you may not have an alabaster box. You may not be called to shed your blood to save someone else. But you can give what you have. If you do all you can, you will be on a similar level as Jesus and this woman were, and your story, too, will be worth telling all over the world.

Staying in Divine History

---

*As touching our brother Apollos, I greatly desired
him to come unto you with the brethren: but his will was
not at all to come at this time; but he will come
when he shall have convenient time.*

—1 Corinthians 16:12

Even though Apollos apparently received his first church
from Paul, he did not seem to aspire to the "apostles first"
doctrine. The "apostles first" doctrine was so clearly evident right after Pentecost when the church continued in it
(Acts 2:42), and when her believers laid everything down at
the apostles' feet (Acts 4:37).

Paul, by the Holy Spirit, reiterated the "apostles first"
doctrine in 1 Corinthians 12:28, *"And God hath set some in
the church, first apostles."* But most of the churches Paul
established and pastored did not receive such doctrine very
well. And what we see here in our text today is the tip of an
iceberg of the reluctance of many of the first pastors to
respond to Paul as the first Christians responded to Peter.
Here we have a glimpse of the tragic breakup of apostolic
authority in the church and the movement toward indepen-
dence and the more convenient, democratic type of church
government.

How different would Apollos' ministry have been had he
been willing to be sent by Paul when Paul made request for
him to go to Corinth? When Apollos chose his will over
Paul's, I think he stepped out of divine history, never to be
heard of again, just as the fifty prophets with Elijah and
Elisha disappeared from the scene once they refused to follow their masters (2 Kings 2–6).

Be as wise as Aquila and Priscilla. Know who is sent from
God, hang on to such persons as long as God bids you to,
and you shall remain in divine history.

Redeem the Moments

Behold, now is the accepted time;
behold, now is the day of salvation.

—2 Corinthians 6:2

Although the main intent of this verse is to tell us that we are now in the dispensation of grace, there are, however, others things that we can learn from it. For instance, there is never anything more important than the moment. Yesterday's battles are history. We can do nothing to change that. The future has not yet arrived, but the now is the accepted time—it is here.

Unfortunately, too few live in the now. Many are lost in the memories of the past, and others are caught up in the dreams of the future, so we fail in the challenges at hand. We need to learn something about the sacredness of each moment in order to redeem the moment, so that our past will start looking better and our future more promising. We also need to learn that no one moment is any more sacred than another.

For example, early Sunday morning, the preacher of a large church thinks about that sacred, great moment when he shall stand before his congregation. But in his final moments of preparation, his wife says, "Husband, our son cannot find his medicine. Do you know where it is?" and he sharply rebukes his wife for interrupting his important preparation for that great moment in the pulpit. He is not aware that at the moment of his rebuke, he lost his anointing for the pulpit. He did not consider that the moments on the way to church were just as sacred as the moments to be redeemed in church. When we crush, bump, bruise, and disappoint others on our way to our "great moments," we destroy the blessing and anointing of those moments.

All of time is sacred to God, and each moment must be captured for the glory of His name.

Me? Follow a Man?

And they two went on.

—2 Kings 2:6

In God's eyes, Elijah was good enough to be followed, but there were fifty prophets who did not agree with God on that. To God, Moses was good enough to be followed, but most of the nation of Israel found him unworthy. To God, Jeremiah was called to be a prophet unto the nations, but the people in his own village held him in disdain. To God, Jesus was good enough to be followed, but the multitudes forsook Him, and the Pharisees engineered His crucifixion. To God, Paul was good enough to be followed, but when he came to the end of his life, he was cold, hungry, penniless, distrusted, and all those in Asia had forsaken him. Only Timothy was like-minded with him.

"And they two went on." Elisha said to his master, *"As the Lord liveth, and as thy soul liveth, I will not leave thee"* (2 Kings 2:4). Since the double portion of the Spirit came out of his following a man of God, perhaps we had better take a second look at the arrogance expressed by so many, "I will never follow a man. I only follow Jesus." Yes, history tells us that it can be very dangerous to follow men. But the Bible tells us here that it can be just as dangerous not to follow men.

There are quite a few passages in the Scriptures where following God's men is equated with following God Himself (John 13:20; 1 Cor. 11:1; Matt. 10:14–15, 40). Has the church stopped following men sent from God, or has the church ceased to produce men worth following? When God brings a true man of God to us, may we be faithful to follow him even as Elisha followed Elijah.

Honor the Living or Dead

⊸◦⊸◦⊸

*And when the sons of the prophets which were to
view at Jericho saw him...they came to meet him, and
bowed themselves to the ground before him.*

—2 Kings 2:15

After Elijah's colorful transition to heaven, the fifty prophets now committed themselves to a new master, Elisha. They *"bowed themselves to the ground before him,"* but their dedication to Elisha was just as hollow as it had been to Elijah. They respected both, but they obeyed neither the one nor the other.

The prophets requested to send out a search party for the lost Elijah, but Elisha said no. Still, they continued to urge him until he gave in (2 Kings 2:17). For three days, these fifty sons of the prophets sought for the remains of their dead, old master. They were not ready or willing to pay the homage due to him when he was yet alive, but now they were willing to build him a monument when he was dead.

Yes, Elijah had one follower while he was alive; he had fifty when he was dead. After three days, these fifty gave up their search for Elijah's body. But, then what did they do? They made the same mistake over again. They did not follow Elisha either, who had the double portion of the Spirit!

Now, notice the two groups of people in all of church history on this matter: (1) those who honor the prophets while they are alive, and (2) those who will honor them only after they are dead.

Alone, Elisha walked to Jericho to cleanse the spring. Perhaps the fifty viewed him from afar as they did his predecessor. But these fifty soon passed into oblivion, while the true follower, Elisha, rose higher and higher in God's precious anointing. From washing Elijah's hands, he now had become more than his equal. Yes, perhaps there is, after all, great virtue in following a man who follows God.

Democracy or Theocracy?

───◦⑅∿⑅◦───

*And laid them down at the apostles' feet: and distribution
was made unto every man according as he had need.*

—Acts 4:35

What we see here is theocratic government in operation.
Churches are either theocratic or democratic. In the former,
the government is from above by revelation. In the latter,
the government is from below by vote or election.

Speaking metaphorically, in a theocracy, the pyramid is
started from the top; that is, God begins with one man
(apostle, prophet, pastor, etc.). Then God calls others to
follow that man. In a democracy, government is started from
below with many. The many will elect themselves a leader
whom they make accountable to them. If the leader serves
them well, he is kept; if not, he is replaced by another.

In recent years, more and more churches have recognized
that a theocratic government is worthy of reconsideration.
In fact, as successful as democracy has been in protecting
us from anarchy on the one side and dictatorship on the
other, it has no precedence in biblical history.

"Remember them which have the rule over you" (Heb. 13:7),
and *"Be ye followers of me, even as I also am of Christ"* (1
Corinthians 11:1) are other admonitions toward theocratic
government.

All of the Bible tells us that whenever people followed
God-ordained leaders, the flames of revival burned across
the land even as they did in Acts 4. Democracy, government
from below, has never and will never bring revival. So, perhaps, the following questions are worth pondering: Are we
reluctant to return to theocratic government because of a
lack of Christlike, God-ordained leaders? Or are our hearts
too hard to submit ourselves to such men? Remember,
theocracy is God's only acceptable government, and that will
never change.

"Lord, Make Us Pure"

———⚬⚏⚬———

And when he is come, he will reprove the world of sin,
and of righteousness, and of judgment.

—John 16:8

The modern church has many fine programs, but she falls short in purity. She has programs for the widows, the divorced, the youth, the toddlers, the married, the lost, the poor, the sick, the prisoners, the hungry, and the neighborhood. Unfortunately, often, those won to Christ are won into programs to be attended and doctrines of denominational distinction to be believed in. This cycle has repeated itself from generation to generation.

Oh, we need a program for purity and power, that conviction may fall and holiness of heart may triumph in every believer. We need a program which provides deliverance from criticism, faultfinding, covetousness, prayerlessness, jealousy, the spirit of competition, pride, jesting, adultery, fornication, divorce, and foolish talk. As long as these elements abide in our churches; and no matter how wonderful our other programs are, how beautiful our music, or how attractive our buildings; Holy Ghost conviction cannot flow through us with power to convict the world of sin, righteousness, and judgment.

In general, conviction will only flow through any body of believers in proportion to its corporate surrender to God. May we redouble our efforts to be holy and pure. Let us *"lay aside every weight, and the sin which doth so easily beset us,"* and let us pray with greater fervency and sincerity, *"Create in me a clean heart, O God; and renew a right spirit within me"* (Heb. 12:1; Ps. 51:10).

Avoid God's Anger

―⊸◦⊸◦⊸―

And they all with one consent began to make excuse...
Then the master of the house being angry said...
—Luke 14:18, 21
And the anger of the Lord was kindled against Moses.
—Exodus 4:14

The Lord is not only angry at the wicked every day, but He also gets angry at us for making excuses. Jesus, in telling the Parable of the Great Supper (Luke 14:16–24), let us know how He feels when we do not obey immediately. Excuses such as *"I have bought a piece of ground,...I have bought five yoke of oxen,...I have married a wife"* (vv. 18–20), raise dark clouds between us and Him. In fact, such excuses can shut us out of the Great Supper forever, as this great parable tells us, *"For I say unto you, That none of those men which were bidden shall taste of my supper"* (Luke 14:24).

Likewise, Moses invoked the anger of the Lord for making excuses for not going to Pharaoh. His first excuse was that the children of Israel would not believe. His second was that he was slow of speech. His third was that someone else would do better than he. But despite all these excuses, Moses' story ends better than the characters in the Parable of the Great Supper. For Moses, thereafter, never made another excuse for the rest of his life. Oh, yes, he had his questions from time to time, but he had no more excuses. From that point forward, his life was a "yea and amen" to everything God ever said.

May it also be so for us, lest the anger of the Lord keep us from the Supper of all suppers.

The Kingdom of God

*Thy kingdom come. Thy will be done
in earth, as it is in heaven.*

—Matthew 6:10

Jesus gave His disciples only one specific prayer—commonly called The Lord's Prayer—and the first petition of that prayer is: *"Thy kingdom come."* Also, in another part of the Sermon on the Mount, He admonishes us to seek first the kingdom of God. Through these passages, we learn what should be every man's and woman's priority. Jesus wants the Baptists, the Lutherans, the Roman Catholics, the Presbyterians, and each one of us to make *"Thy kingdom come"* a priority. Isn't that wonderful?

It is only in the kingdom where God's will reigns supreme. Even though we may pray, witness for Jesus, teach the Bible, and sing in the choir, there will be no fellowship in the Holy Spirit unless His kingdom has come to dwell within us.

Oh, how wonderful it is that Jesus tells us that among all the visible, perishable kingdoms of the earth, there is an invisible, eternal kingdom. In this kingdom, we can have peace in the midst of war, joy in the midst of tribulation, and righteousness in the midst of a crooked and perverse nation.

No wonder Jesus went everywhere preaching the gospel of the kingdom. No wonder He told one kingdom parable after another. No wonder He came as a king, saying, *"My kingdom is not of this world"* (John 18:36). No wonder His sermon to the multitude on the mountain began with, *"Blessed are the poor in spirit: for their's is the kingdom of heaven"* (Matt. 5:3). No wonder the devil wanted to give Jesus all the perishable kingdoms of this world in exchange for His everlasting kingdom. Christianity without the kingdom is impossible. Christianity is the kingdom of God.

March 16

The Kingdom and the Church

*From that time Jesus began to preach,
and to say, Repent: for the kingdom
of heaven is at hand.*

—Matthew 4:17

It is remarkable to observe that Jesus has never been known to have preached a single sermon about the church. Rather, He went to every village preaching the gospel of the kingdom. This is not to say that the church is not important. But the doctrine of the church is purely an apostolic doctrine, and it was not introduced until the kingdom of God had come to dwell in the hearts of men.

There are distinct differences between the kingdom and the church. The kingdom is within and is personal. The church is corporate and is without, visible to the world. The kingdom is pure while the church may have spots, wrinkles, and blemishes. The kingdom is one, but the church may have divisions. The kingdom is unchanging and unshakable. The church is ever changing and often shaken by events and disappointments. The kingdom is governed by the King of kings, but the church generally is governed by men, by its commissions, boards, and committees. In the kingdom, everything is constant, but in the church, there is frequent turmoil and upheaval. When the church is at her best, then the church is as the kingdom.

Jesus preached the kingdom. He had no other message. And repentance followed by rebirth puts us at the very doorstep of that kingdom. Therefore, Jesus said, *"Except a man be born again, he cannot see the kingdom of God"* (John 3:3). May our prayers be that the church be more like unto the kingdom of God.

Abiding and Prayer

*If ye abide in me, and my words abide
in you, ye shall ask what ye will,
and it shall be done unto you.*

—John 15:7

In this text, we see the relationship between abiding and prayer. Most prayers outside of abiding in Christ are futile, except for prayers of mercy in certain situations. Abiding means simply, obeying. And obedience means self-denial, for Jesus said, *"If any man will come after me, let him deny himself, and take up his cross daily, and follow me"* (Luke 9:23).

So, the very lifeblood of abiding is self-denial and obedience. For us to have spiritual life, for us to abide in Christ, we must say no to Self. To abide, we cannot do what we want, arrange, or plan. Wherever Self is asserted, abiding ceases.

But if we abide in Christ, His desires become our desires, His plans become our plans, and His Spirit will be in us. His prayers will become our prayers, and *"...whatsoever ye shall ask in prayer, believing, ye shall receive"* (Matt. 21:22).

When we abide in Christ, we become one with Christ and one with one another, and the kingdom of God will be in operation in our hearts in its richness, glory, love, and provision, and in its *"righteousness, and peace, and joy"* (Rom. 14:17).

Abiding and Much Fruit

*I am the vine, ye are the branches. He that
abideth in me, and I in him, the same bringeth forth
much fruit: for without me ye can do nothing.*

—John 15:5

Each one who abides in Christ brings forth much fruit. The
Amplified Bible reads, *"abundant fruit."* Abiding in Christ
puts every Christian on the same level with fruitfulness. It
is the level of "muchness."

No one who abides in Christ brings forth *little* fruit, or
even *some* fruit, but *much* fruit. That is true of the young,
the old, the learned, the unlearned, the mature, and the
immature. The sum may be thirtyfold, sixtyfold, and an hun-
dredfold, but for all of them it is *much.* This *"much fruit"* is
not the work of man, nor of the wisdom or cunning of man,
but it is by the Holy Spirit flowing through surrendered
lives.

For the nature of this fruit, we go to the connection
between Jesus and Paul. We find that connection in
Galatians 5, where Paul says, *"But the fruit of the Spirit is
love, joy, peace, longsuffering, gentleness, goodness, faith,
Meekness, temperance: against such there is no law"* (vv. 22–
23).

Yes, praise the Lord for the *"much fruit"* which is the
result of a healthy relationship between the vine and the
branches, free of growth-retarding disease and debilitating
infections.

Therefore, my friend, if you do not bear much fruit, you
are likely to be outside of Christ. If that is the case, then
enter back into the marvelous life of abundance in Christ
Jesus today.

No Death Means No Fruit

*Except a corn of wheat fall into the
ground and die, it abideth alone: but if it
die, it bringeth forth much fruit.*

—John 12:24

Without dying, there is no fruit. Regardless of what you do as a Christian or how hard you try as a minister of the gospel, you have no fruit without dying. You may spend hundreds of hours in prayer, and you may be a devoted Bible scholar, yet, without dying, there is no fruit. This is both a biological and spiritual law. You may do Christian works, visit the sick and the lost, teach Sunday school, yet, without dying, it will be all in vain. It is only in dying that we live and that the Holy Spirit can enter into our work. And it is only in dying that our work becomes His work.

The way to fruit is so simple, so wonderfully simple, that everyone can get there. All that is required is a continuous, voluntary death to Self. This was the call of Jesus when He told His disciples, *"If any man will come after me, let him deny himself, and take up his cross daily, and follow me"* (Luke 9:23).

"Except a corn of wheat fall into the ground and die..." There is a finality about this death. It is this finality that leads to fruitfulness. Anything less than total death is not death. Anything less than total self-denial comes short of bringing in the harvest.

The fruit is not in the sickness unto death, nor in the groaning or the suffering, but in the death of Self itself. The dead never moan or groan; they are plain dead and wonderfully alive in Jesus. Oh, how fitting the words of Paul at this point, *"I am crucified with Christ: nevertheless I live; yet not I, but Christ liveth in me"* (Gal. 2:20).

Take up your cross and do only what Jesus bids you do, and much fruit will be the natural outcome.

Lost at Home

⸻◍⸻

*Because that, when they knew God, they glorified him not
as God, neither were thankful; but became vain in their
imaginations, and their foolish heart was darkened.*

—Romans 1:21

Here, we learn that the first step toward backsliding is not a deliberate act, nor is it a willful sin, but rather the neglect of the duty of giving thanks. When a man ceases to thank God, to praise and glorify Him, he is on the way to the pigpen.

The prodigal son left his father long before he left his father's house. His older brother had never left his father's house but had, in fact, left his father, too. Here were two sons who had left their father while still at home, one further expressing his rebellion by physically leaving his father's house, and the other by a bad attitude. Neither son was in oneness with his father (Luke 15:11–32).

There are many people who are working hard in church like the elder son worked hard for his father, yet they are as far from the Father as the prodigal son was when he spent his substance in riotous living. We leave the Father when we cease to praise and glorify His precious name.

So, the devil wants all of us out of praise. He does not mind if a Christian prays an hour, or reads ten chapters of the Bible each day, or if he preaches, teaches, or counsels out of the Word of God. The Pharisees did all that. As long as the devil has a Christian who is praiseless and thankless, he has a Christian whose imagination is vain, whose thoughts are warped, and whose heart is dark.

So, there are those who leave the Father by leaving the church, and there are those who leave the Father while yet remaining in the church. In both cases, the culprit is a praiseless life. Keep your praises so that you will never become a prodigal in a far-off land or at home.

Can You Say It?

━━◁◀◖◗▷▶━━

Father, I have sinned against heaven, and before thee.
—Luke 15:18

These three words, *"I have sinned,"* are three of the most powerful words in the world. Nothing of eternal value for mankind has ever begun without those three words. Every man who has ever walked with God has had to say these words, *"I have sinned."*

Every man of God who has backslidden and who wants to come to God again must first say these words, *"I have sinned." "*Not my brother, not my sister, but it's me, oh Lord! Standing in the need of prayer."[2]

More good has been done by these words, *"I have sinned,"* than all the money given to the poor, than all social welfare, than all the inventions of man to improve life on earth, and more than all the religious programs of the church.

Sin separates us from God, and the first step toward God is always the confession of that which separates us: our sins. If I harbor even one sin in my life, my spiritual growth is halted. In every case, I, like the young prodigal, can only resume my journey back to the Father's house by that simple confession, *"I have sinned."*

No matter how much I do, whether I double my church giving, church attendance, Bible reading, or prayer time, nothing can restore me to spiritual growth until I confess my sin and forsake it. Nothing but our sincere confession will bring an expedient response from the Father to meet us, to forgive us, and to restore us to full fellowship.

Is it any wonder, therefore, that Jesus said, *"I say unto you, that likewise joy shall be in heaven over one sinner that repenteth, more than over ninety and nine just persons, which need no repentance"* (Luke 15:7).

Be Not Deceived

Know ye not that the unrighteous shall not inherit the kingdom of God? Be not deceived: neither fornicators, nor idolaters, nor adulterers, nor effeminate, nor abusers of themselves with mankind, Nor thieves, nor covetous, nor drunkards, nor revilers, nor extortioners, shall inherit the kingdom of God. And such were some of you: but ye are washed, but ye are sanctified, but ye are justified in the name of the Lord Jesus, and by the Spirit of our God.

—1 Corinthians 6:9–11

Paul had to tell the Corinthians not to be deceived. Why? Because there were people in that church, as there are today, who think that once they are born again, they can continue in these sins mentioned and still inherit the kingdom of God. Paul says they cannot.

Jesus' gracious forgiveness is never a ticket for sin, but always a call to "go and sin no more." It is a ticket unto righteousness and holy living.

The grace of God is to be received gratefully but not to be abused through spiritual or physical debauchery. Yet, this is what the prodigal did. He abused grace, and it led him to the pigpen. Prior to his return, the son, who once lived under the grace of his father, was called "lost" and "dead."

So it is with all those who have come to the knowledge of the Lord and Savior Jesus Christ and are entangled again in the evils of this world. For many of them, *"it had been better for them not to have known the way of righteousness, than, after they have known it, to turn from the holy commandment delivered unto them"* (2 Pet. 2:21).

But, thank God, the prodigal came home; the son that was lost was found; the son who was dead was alive again. So, aren't you glad that Paul says of the kingdom possessors, *"such were some of you,"* and not "such are some of you"?

The Point of Reference

―⁓―

*Therefore shall a man leave his father
and his mother, and shall cleave unto
his wife: and they shall be one flesh.*

—Genesis 2:24

The woman came out of the man. She was built out of his rib. So, this is what love is all about. The woman keeps longing for his body, from whence she was taken, and his body keeps longing for the rib that he lost, which is the woman. Only as the two come together will there be a fullness, a "one-fleshness."

This one flesh cannot be experienced outside the union of a man with a woman. It is the will of God and a gift of God to every man and woman, excepting those who are called to be eunuchs for Christ's sake. How, then, can this oneness, this one flesh, be enjoyed to the ultimate?

The answer is in Ephesians 5. Ephesians 5 is the divorce eliminator of the Bible. It is the "happy-marriage enhancer." Here, you find two rules and only two—one for each partner to keep. The rule for him is to love the wife, *"even as Christ also loved the church, and gave himself for it"* (v. 25). For her, it is to submit to her husband *"as unto the Lord"* (v. 22). It is as simple as that—one rule for each—not ten or twenty of them.

Each rule has Christ as a point of reference. To him, it is to love *as* Christ loved, and to her, to submit *as* unto Christ. Oh, my friend, since Christ is the point of reference in all we do, how can we help but be happy and in harmony one with another if we follow Him?

So, husbands love, and wives submit, and the romance will go on and on as Christ Jesus smiles upon you.

The Way to Love

———◄═══╗♫╔══►———

So ought men to love their wives as their own bodies.
He that loveth his wife loveth himself.

—Ephesians 5:28

"So ought men to love their wives as their own bodies."
Consider all that we do for our bodies. We feed our bodies
with food that will foster strength and health. We, likewise,
give fluids to our bodies. We clothe our bodies appropri-
ately for each occasion, for the work to be done and for the
company to be kept. We keep our bodies clean, and we protect them from disease and injury. We take special care for
the most visible parts of our body: the face and the hair. We
give our bodies rest whenever necessary. We relax our bodies when tensions build up.

"So ought men to love their wives as their own bodies." As
we care for our own bodies, so then, we should care for our
wives in thoughtfulness and tenderness. The supreme
example of how men ought to care for their wives comes
from Christ's care for his bride, the church. Christ gave Himself unto her and for her. There is nothing that Christ will
withhold from His bride. Christ will give anything that will
comfort her, strengthen her, purify her, and honor and
protect her.

Husbands, love your wives. It is not only a command and
a necessity but a privilege; for as we love our wives, so we
love ourselves. *"He that loveth his wife loveth himself."*

Indeed, we may pray much, we may be faithful in church,
in witnessing and tithing, but if we as husbands don't love
our wives as Christ loves the church, our Christianity is
nothing but wood, hay, and stubble. For if Christianity does
not begin at home, it does not begin at all!

Husbands Must Love as Jesus

*Husbands, love your wives, even as Christ also
loved the church, and gave himself for it.*

—Ephesians 5:25

Many a ball game ends in a brawl. That is so, simply because the players are not obeying the rules. There will never be a brawl in any ball game as long as every player abides by the rules. So it is in the marriage or in the home.

All marital and home problems go back to the refusal of its members to live by the rules. Brawls, squabbles, and fights in the home are an indication that someone has broken the laws that govern family life. The marriage relationship, if set up according to God's pattern, is, in itself, a plan of salvation. It saves the home.

As Christ was willing to lay down His life for the church, so a man must decide before marriage whether he is willing to live and die for his woman. Truly, that is what it means by loving a woman as Christ loved the church. Before marriage, a young man had better settle whether this is the woman with whom he will never be harsh, cross, or unkind.

As Christ was willing to live and die for the church—an imperfect church, a spotted church, a blemished church, and an obstinate church—so a man must give himself to his wife in love, despite all of her imperfections. He must give himself to her in a forgiving spirit in all those daily trials of beds made or not, shirts ironed or not, and food overcooked or undercooked.

As Christ constantly forgives us husbands, let us do likewise toward our wives for their shortcomings. *"Husbands, love your wives, even as Christ also loved the church."*

Submit and Adapt

*Wives, be subject (be submissive and adapt yourselves) to
your own husbands as [a service] to the Lord.*
—Ephesians 5:22 AMPLIFIED

The woman was created to be man's helper. This is God's
original design, and it has never been amended by God. *"And
the Lord God said, It is not good that the man should be
alone; I will make him an help meet for him"* (Gen. 2:18).

God's designs offer humankind the ultimate in blessings,
divine protection, and favor. They are not subject to cul-
tural changes or human opinions. Since the Creation, God
has done nothing to change the constitution of either man
or woman. What they were created for then, they are created for now. What relationships He blessed then, He blesses
now. So, *"Wives, be subject to your own husbands."*

So why does man want to change God's perfect design
for womanhood? At the Fall, rebellion against God entered
every human heart. Hence, unsanctified wives do not want
to submit to their husbands, and unsanctified mothers
often choose careers over motherhood, allowing their children to be raised by others. How can a mother birth a child,
only later to abandon it, still expect the Lord's blessings?
How can she pass on biblical character qualities of sacrifice, unselfishness, obedience, and submission to her child
if such qualities are not found in her?

Oh, dear wife and mother, please go back under the
umbrella of God's protective care, although living without
your paycheck may seem naturally impossible at this time.
Believe that the same God who provided for the widow
of Zarephath (1 Kings 17) and who fed the children of Israel
for forty years in the desert is also your God. Begin by
surrendering your heart to God's design, then give yourself
to prayer, and it may not be long until you find help coming
to you from heaven. Sister in Christ, adapt to your husband's
calling, and honor motherhood.

Christ and the Scriptures

*It is written, That man shall not live by bread
alone, but by every word of God.*

—Luke 4:4

These are the two things, then, that men ought to live by: physical bread and spiritual bread. If we live by these, we shall live well. If we neglect either one, death shall be ours!

When Jesus spoke these words, He prefaced them by saying, "It is written." In each case, Jesus met the word of the devil with the Word of God, with an, "It is written." Over and over again, our Lord went back to the Scriptures.

Jesus had committed Scriptures to memory in His youth. He had learned the Scriptures, He lived by the Scriptures, He fulfilled the Scriptures, and He conquered by the Scriptures. The Scriptures sustained His spirit, and, by virtue of them, He drove back the devil. The Scriptures were both His bread and His sword.

I am trying to impress upon you the necessity and the blessings of knowing the Scriptures. *"...man shall not live by bread alone, but by every word of God."* That, indeed, was Jesus' life. So, we are not to live by our feelings, by our opinions, or by what others say about us, *"but by every word of God."*

By the time Jesus was twelve, He knew the Scriptures so well that He confounded the doctors, the scribes, the lawyers, and the Pharisees. Jesus inhaled the Word, and He exhaled prayer. He knew how to discern both good and evil. He knew how to converse with the adulterers, the soldiers, the fishermen, the rich, the poor, the dedicated, the careless, and His enemies in the context of the Scriptures. Jesus defeated the devil by using the Scriptures. *"Study to shew thyself approved unto God, a workman that needeth not to be ashamed, rightly dividing the word of truth"* (2 Tim. 2:15).

Satan and the Scriptures

*For it is written, He shall give his angels
charge over thee, to keep thee: And in their hands
they shall bear thee up, lest at any time
thou dash thy foot against a stone.*

—Luke 4:10–11

Satan also knows the Scriptures. Here in this great temptation of Jesus after forty days of prayer and fasting, the devil gives Jesus scriptural grounds to cast Himself from the pinnacle of the temple. So often, therefore, our fight with the devil is Scripture against Scripture.

Oh, all the things that have been done in the name of Scripture by these great words, "It is written." The priests killed the prophets by "It is written." The Pharisees killed Jesus by "It is written." The Jews killed Stephen by "It is written." The Crusaders killed the Muslims by "It is written." Pastors have been voted in and out of pulpits by "It is written." Christians have been divorced and remarried by "It is written." Churches have been split by "It is written." And we have hundreds of denominations by "It is written," and each one claims to best represent Jesus. Many a congregation has been manipulated to do many a thing by a preacher quoting that which is written.

Hence, knowing the Scripture is not enough. Knowing the Scripture is truly only safe when a person has an intimate relationship and constant communion with the God of the Scripture. For the letter, in itself, killeth, but the Spirit giveth life.

So be careful when someone says, "It is written." Behind that statement could either be the abuse of Scripture by the devil himself or the use of Scripture for the glory of God.

The Poison of Criticism

*But if ye bite and devour one another, take
heed that ye be not consumed one of another.*
—Galatians 5:15

Criticism always violates the law of love. It is a condemnatory and faultfinding declaration, a malicious person-orientated judgment, coming from a pernicious, carnal spirit, which always puts others in a bad light and ruins reputations. A critical person elevates himself above the one he criticizes. It is this critical spirit that caused Paul to appeal to the early Christians, saying, *"Let us not therefore judge one another any more,"* and *"Let nothing be done through strife or vainglory; but in lowliness of mind let each esteem other better than themselves"* (Rom. 14:13; Phil. 2:3).

A person who criticizes has a critical spirit, and such a spirit is no respecter of persons. Hence, your best friend, if he has a critical spirit, will eventually criticize you, too. A person with a critical spirit cannot be led by the Holy Spirit; for if we criticize, we sin, by making ourselves judge over the person we criticize. In doing so, we violate the two greatest commandments (Matt. 22:37–40), and we cause our spiritual growth to cease as well.

Criticism has no place in true Christianity. It takes us out of abiding in Christ Jesus and disconnects us from divine life. Rather than criticize, we should be long-suffering and forbearing with others' faults and weaknesses (Eph. 4:2). As we are long-suffering, the Lord will do a deeper work in our souls, bringing forth much growth in forbearing and loving, in suffering and dying.

So, let us cease biting and devouring each other in order to fulfill this law of Christ: *"A new commandment I give unto you, That ye love one another; as I have loved you, that ye also love one another. By this shall all men know that ye are my disciples, if ye have love one to another"* (John 13:34–35).

The Center of Christianity

So they brought the ark of God, and set it in the midst
of the tent that David had pitched for it: and they offered
burnt sacrifices and peace offerings before God.

—1 Chronicles 16:1

God always dwelt in the center. He dwelt in the center of the tabernacle, which was placed at the center of the congregation of Israel. To be at the center is to be at the controls. David knew that. Do we?

For twenty years prior to this occasion, the ark had been in the hands of the Philistines. Israel lost the ark because they refused to give it its central place. Instead of honoring the prophet Samuel, whom God had raised up to save the nation, they took counsel with the corrupt sons of Eli, the natural successors to the priesthood. In rejecting Samuel, they rejected the centrality of God's government.

Finally, after Israel was broken enough, they *"lamented after the Lord"* (1 Sam. 7:2). Revival came with power because Israel wept before the Lord! The result of this revival was threefold:

1. The centrality of God's government was again recognized by the people by their acceptance of God's anointed prophet, Samuel.

2. God dwelt again in the center of the hearts of His people.

3. The cry for revival brought God back to the center of worship.

So shall it be that when God gets back to the center of our hearts, His glory will come and bless. When God gets back into the center of the church, His glory will hit the church.

God dwells at the center, and the center of Christianity is the cross. Our constant self-denial will keep us in the center, and it will keep us at the cross where the glory is.

Doing the Truth

*But he that doeth truth cometh to the
light, that his deeds may be made manifest,
that they are wrought in God.*

—John 3:21

There is a vast difference between believing the truth and doing the truth. Believing the truth without doing it may qualify us for membership in many a church. But in order to be in Christ's body and to have the beautiful life of Christ flowing through us, we must do the truth.

One of the greatest burdens of any true minister of God is in seeing the wide gap between believing and doing that exists in most of his parishioners' lives. Jesus faced a similar dilemma, causing Him to say, *"And why call ye me, Lord, Lord, and do not the things which I say?"* (Luke 6:46). He also said, *"Not every one that saith unto me, Lord, Lord, shall enter into the kingdom of heaven; but he that doeth the will of my Father which is in heaven"* (Matt. 7:21).

It is a tragedy that in all of biblical history, man has had a tendency to actually equate believing with obeying; whereas, in reality, the two may be worlds apart. The cry of God through Samuel, *"to obey is better than sacrifice"* (1 Sam. 15:22), is reiterated by the words of James, *"faith without works is dead"* (James 2:20). *"Yea, a man may say, Thou hast faith, and I have works: shew me thy faith without thy works, and I will shew thee my faith by my works. Thou believest that there is one God; thou doest well: the devils also believe, and tremble"* (vv. 18–19).

So, believing the truth without doing it makes us no better than the devil himself. Yes, *"be ye doers of the word, and not hearers only, deceiving your own selves"* (James 1:22).

The Lord Sitteth

*In the year that King Uzziah died I saw also
the Lord sitting upon a throne, high and lifted up,
and his train filled the temple.*

—Isaiah 6:1

Moses saw the hinder parts of God. Solomon experienced the glory and the power of God at the dedication of the temple. Several others heard the voice of God. But Isaiah's experience was the most wonderful and sublime of all, for Isaiah saw *"the Lord sitting upon a throne."*

He saw the Lord in dignity, power, and majesty, *"sitting..."* He, the Lord, sits while others stand. He sits while angels wait for His commands. He sits while others fall down to worship Him. He sits while multitudes from every nation, kindred, and tribe sing in sweet adoration. Satan walks to and fro, but our Lord God sits upon His throne, the absolute monarch, Lord of lords, King of kings, the Mighty God, the Everlasting Father.

Through Isaiah, we see God sitting upon a throne, never being shaken by any event in history. He did not shake at Adam's fall in the garden, nor at Cain's murder of Abel, nor at David's fall to Bathsheba. God is unshakable. While nations tremble and fear, God remains a picture of perfect tranquillity, ease, dignity, and self-confidence.

May God give us this vision of Himself. For this vision will steady us and cure us of many a fear, worry, and apprehension. It will help bring to us both wholeness and quietude.

"And every creature which is in heaven, and on the earth, and under the earth, and such as are in the sea, and all that are in them, heard I saying, Blessing, and honour, and glory, and power, be unto him that sitteth upon the throne, and unto the Lamb for ever and ever" (Rev. 5:13).

Rest in the Lord

Rest in the Lord,
and wait patiently for him.

—Psalm 37:7

We learned yesterday that God is resting, and that Satan is restless. God is sitting on His throne. Satan is going to and fro and up and down in the earth. God is at peace, but Satan is in turmoil. God is tranquillity, but Satan is nervousness. Satan does not want us to rest, but God does. So, as there is a rest for the people of God, there is no rest for the wicked.

Yes, I know we are not in heaven yet, and there is a work for us to do on earth. There are prayers to be made, souls to be saved, the poor to be fed, and the needy to be encouraged. However, none of these things should ever rob us of our inner rest. If it does, it is an indication that God is no longer working in us and through us, that God has lost His resting place in us.

When we lose our soul rest, our divine rest, regardless of how religiously good or biblical and beautiful our works may be, it is an indication that we have lost our connection with our Lord. Let us be careful not to cave in to the pressures of life, religious or otherwise, and lose our rest with God.

If you have lost your rest, get reconnected with God, and remember the words of David, the Psalmist, *"Rest in the Lord, and wait patiently for him"* (Ps. 37:7).

Holy, Holy, Holy

And one cried unto another, and said, Holy, holy, holy, is the Lord of hosts: the whole earth is full of his glory.
—Isaiah 6:3

Because it is written, Be ye holy; for I am holy.
—1 Peter 1:16

God is both comprehensible and incomprehensible. He is both immanent and transcendent. That is why we stand in awe before Him. In fact, the oldest meaning of the Greek word for holy is *awe!* You behold Him, and you are speechless and full of wonder, afraid that any descriptive term you use may do an injustice to His sovereignty.

We live in an age in which we have lost our vision of the holiness of God. The seraphim remind us that God is holy—thrice holy. In both Isaiah and Revelation, we hear the same cry, *"Holy, holy, holy."*

You may find the holiest man in the world, but God is holier still. This supreme holiness is so pure, so glistening and burning with the effervescent glory of God that no man can take it in and live.

So, there are degrees of holiness. There was the holy place of the temple, and then, there was the Most Holy Place. The latter was holier than the former. There is the holiness of the saved, and then the holiness of the sanctified; but finally, there is the holiness of the triune God. Only God's holiness is absolute. Ours is relative and contingent. Hence, God did not say, "be ye holy as I am holy," but "be ye holy, *for* I am holy."

Therefore, let us seek holiness, for without it, no man shall see the Lord (Heb. 12:14).

Teach Us to Pray

———⟨⟨⟨⟨∫⟩⟩⟩⟩———

...one of his disciples said unto him, Lord, teach us
to pray, as John also taught his disciples.

—Luke 11:1

To pray better, deeper, and more effectively was the desire of the disciples. Please remember, John's disciples were raised in the Hebrew faith. They went through the rigors of the Jewish educational program. They had memorized many prayers from the Psalms, and they knew the law and the prophets. They, no doubt, had had their bar mitzvahs. But when they saw Jesus pray, they felt like they knew nothing about prayer, and so they said, *"Lord, teach us to pray."*

No man knows himself until he knows himself in prayer. Also, no one knows the mind of God better than in the hour of prayer. Prayer is dialogue. Prayer is a message sent, received, and validated. Prayer is waiting on God. It is petition, intercession, adoration, worship, and praise.

In prayer, and through prayer, we learn to know Jesus in our soul and heart of hearts. We learn more intimately of His saving grace and forgiveness, of the hours of His supreme trial at Calvary, and of the beauty and meaning of His life. Through study, we learn about Jesus, but through prayer, we learn to know Jesus.

Prayer produces a hunger and thirst after righteousness. It makes the soul weary of the world, its goods, music, talk, and toys. Prayer sharpens the spirit of man in the things of eternity. On the potter's wheel of prayer, we maintain flexibility and learn adaptability. So, the only way we can walk in the Spirit is through much prayer, for prayer gives us the vision, the burden, and the passion and compassion of God.

"Lord, teach us to pray," was the desire of the disciples. Let that also be our aspiration.

Kissers or Cleavers

And they lifted up their voice, and wept again:
and Orpah kissed her mother in law;
but Ruth clave unto her.

—Ruth 1:14

"*O*rpah kissed her mother-in-law, but Ruth clave unto her."
Ruth found that all she had within her heart was love for
Naomi and Naomi's God. Here is a Gentile, a Moabite
woman, leaving the graveside of her husband, her father
and mother, her family, her friends, and her country to go
with a woman of God. Ruth attached herself to Naomi with
no earthly blessing whatsoever in sight.

Orpah kissed her mother-in-law and is never heard of
again. Judas also kissed Jesus, but was never found in His
presence again. There are also many people who kiss the
bride of Christ, the church. That is to say, they go along
with the church for a while, but, eventually, when the life of
self-denial is preached, they, too, give the parting kiss. They
have decided that the message is too difficult, and they begin to return to where they came from.

When the times of difficulty, struggles, and strains come,
the "Orpahs" of the church give a farewell kiss. However,
the "Ruths" remain, cleaving to the Rock for strength and
for deliverance, and they are grafted into the natural olive
tree. Because of her loyalty and commitment, Ruth was given
a wonderful husband, and she also became an integral part
of the lineage of our Savior, Jesus.

Let us thank the Lord for those who cleave unto the bride,
the church of the living God, with all her weaknesses and
faults. And so, may we have more in our churches who cleave
than who kiss. Kissing costs you nothing, but cleaving costs
you everything!

Kept from the Promised Land

━━◉◖◗◉━━

Do all things without murmurings and disputings.
—Philippians 2:14

Most people murmur. Some murmur about their spouse, and some about their children. Some murmur about their cars, and some about the taxes they pay. Some murmur about their job, some about their salaries. Some murmur about the church, and some about the preachers. Some murmur about the schools and their teachers. Now, if you made it through this list without having been caught on any of these, congratulations!

It was murmuring that prevented Israel from entering the Promised Land. Dear one, murmuring will keep you from your promised land, and it will get you nowhere, spiritually speaking. No one will get to that which God has destined for them with a murmuring spirit—no one! The murmuring spirit is an anti-Christ spirit, and it will disqualify us from being led by the Holy Spirit.

Now, what is murmuring? Murmuring is a mumbled or private expression of discontent. It is finding fault. It is being critical and judgmental. Remember the words of Jesus, *"For with what judgment ye judge, ye shall be judged"* (Matt. 7:2). What would it be like if Jesus was as judgmental toward us as we are toward a doctor, lawyer, preacher, or tax collector?

Are we not glad that Jesus has a loving, forgiving, compassionate, and merciful spirit? Rather than Jesus murmuring about us, He talks about us as jewels and as His friends when we come to Him with a broken and penitent heart.

Oh, may this terrible spirit of murmuring perish so that the Lord Jesus Christ can dwell within us in power to make us salt and light in the world. Let us heed the warning of the apostle Paul, *"Neither murmur ye, as some of them also murmured, and were destroyed of the destroyer"* (1 Cor. 10:10).

Joy from Above

And the disciples were filled with joy,
and with the Holy Ghost.

—Acts 13:52

The first evident, visible sign of the early church was joy; not a joy that came from below but from above. Hence, these believers were not full of joy by virtue of a program or of getting some earthly gift but by virtue of a relationship of obedience in the Holy Spirit.

This joy from above had nothing to do with earthly circumstances. It was a joy that did not run out when homes were lost, when loved ones were imprisoned, when sickness struck, or when food ran out. It was a joy that had only one condition for its continuance, and that was obedience, as Peter states in Acts 5:32: *"and so is also the Holy Ghost, whom God hath given to them that obey him."*

Jesus also made this heavenly joy independent of earthly conditions when He said through Paul, *"For the kingdom of God is...righteousness, and peace, and joy in the Holy Ghost"* (Rom. 14:17).

So, joy, divine joy, is a gift of God to every obedient heart! And since everybody can obey, everybody can have this joy! The sick can have it, the poor, the learned and the unlearned, the old and young. It can be had in times of adversity as well as in times of tranquillity. Yes, joy, divine joy, was the mark of the early church because obedience was her Christian work.

Oh, let us begin to obey, and the spirit of gloom will depart our churches as the night is sent to bed by the rising of the sun.

Two Kinds of Faith

———◦◦◦———

*Jesus saith unto him, Thomas, because thou hast seen
me, thou hast believed: blessed are they that
have not seen, and yet have believed.*

—John 20:29

Here we find a clear distinction between two kinds of faith: the faith that Jesus blesses and the faith that remains unblessed. *"Blessed are they that have not seen, and yet have believed."*

There is no blessing in believing as a result of seeing. The world says, "I'll believe it when I see it." Friend, there is no blessing in that kind of faith. Even dogs and cats will respond to what they see.

Jesus blesses you for what you cannot see but believe to be true, or believe to eventually become true. That is the whole story of Hebrews 11, which begins: *"Now faith is the substance of things hoped for, the evidence of* things not seen*"* (v. 1). That is, you prove your faith by believing without seeing.

Following those words in Hebrews, we have illustration after illustration of this kind of blessed faith. It is only this faith that endures the fires, the hardships, the disappointments, and all the tests of life. This is so beautifully illustrated as chapter 11 speaks of Moses, *"By faith he forsook Egypt, not fearing the wrath of the king: for he endured, as seeing him who is invisible"* (v. 27).

So, my friend, when you cannot see your way through, believe Jesus anyway. Believe His Word, believe His promises, put your trust in Him, and a blessing will surely come your way.

Enter into the Kingdom

*Verily I say unto you, Except ye be converted,
and become as little children, ye shall not
enter into the kingdom of heaven.*

—Matthew 18:3

Can you see that Matthew gives us a little more on entering the kingdom of heaven than John? John tells us that we need to be born again to "see" and "enter" the kingdom (John 3:3, 5), but Matthew tells us that we also need childlikeness to *"enter...the kingdom of heaven."*

All who are born of God have "seen the kingdom," but only those who have humbled themselves unto utter dependence have "entered" into it.

So, the absence of childlikeness and of utter dependence on God will keep us out of the kingdom just as much as the absence of the conversion experience. We must be made over in our hearts. That is conversion. But we must also be made over in our spirits, and that is becoming as a little child.

What are the characteristics of a little child? A little child cannot dress himself, feed himself, protect himself, or clean himself. He is completely dependent upon his father and mother.

As a little child is subject to the will, plans, wishes, and ways of his physical parents, so must the spiritually born learn to become subject to their spiritual Father in everything.

Yes, conversion belongs to the moment, but becoming as a little child is a constant effort to remain lowly, broken, and contrite at the feet of the Master. It is with this attitude that the kingdom becomes ours. The first beatitude confirms this so beautifully by saying, *"Blessed are the poor in spirit: for their's is the kingdom of heaven"* (Matt. 5:3).

Contentment

*Verily I say unto you, Whosoever shall not
receive the kingdom of God as a little
child, he shall not enter therein.*

—Mark 10:15

Yesterday, we discovered utter dependence as one characteristic of childlikeness. Contentment is another. If a little one is not spoiled, he or she is a picture of utter contentment.

Such a small child can play telephone calling for hours with a string connecting two cans. Such a little one will be as happy in one place as in another, whether it be in mother's, father's, or sister's arms; in a playpen, or a crib. In an unspoiled child, there is adaptability and flexibility. In an unspoiled child, there are no protests, no complaints, no murmuring, no concerns about social status and dress codes. There is no attitude of pride or "I deserve better" or "Why can't I do this?" Yes, of such is the kingdom of God.

Now, do we find such a spirit of utter dependence, perfect contentment, flexibility, and trust in all new converts? Our observations will tell us, not so. This is because, subsequent to conversion, the carnal nature, with its discontentment, selfish, critical, and demanding ways, is yet to be subdued and crucified.

So, dear ones, at the rebirth, you have the joy of conversion, which lasts but for a little moment. But upon entering the kingdom, which comes by childlikeness, you experience divine joy on a perpetual basis as you continue to follow Jesus through self-denial. Yes, you have been born again, but will you go on to the kingdom blessings awaiting you? *"Whosoever shall not receive the kingdom of God as a little child shall in no wise enter therein"* (Luke 18:17).

Go for Excellence!

---•—⊂᪲ᒻᒻᒻ᪲ᒻᒻᒻ᪲—•---

*And this I pray, that your love may abound yet more
and more in knowledge and all discernment; so that ye
may approve the things that are excellent...*
—Philippians 1:9–10 ASV

There are many doors that love can open that otherwise
remain shut. One of the great mysteries of the kingdom of
God is that love can open the doors to greater knowledge
and discernment. Who ever thought that to know more about
God, one must love God more and more?

The Pharisees attempted to gain more of the knowledge
of God by study. Indeed, study must not be scoffed at, for
Paul said to Timothy, *"Study to show thyself approved unto
God"* (2 Tim. 2:15). But study without growing in love will
give us a distorted picture of God and His ways. He who
studies and loves the Lord God with all his heart, soul, and
mind, will be by far the best scholar. The more we love something, the more that something will reveal itself to us.

Discernment is also a fruit of loving God more and more.
The more we love Him, the sharper the lines will become
between good and evil, and between what is pleasing or
grievous to the Holy Spirit. In fact, more love to God will
soon get us dissatisfied with merely distinguishing the good
from the bad. As we go deeper into love, we will soon fine
tune our discernment to see the clear line even between
the good and the excellent.

The shallow Christian will say, "Oh, there is nothing
wrong with that. The Bible does not forbid it." But the lover
of God will say, "If it does not pass the test of excellence, if
it does not put a smile upon the Savior's face, I will not do
it." Dear one, only do that which is well-pleasing in God's
sight. Love God more and more, and His inner light will
become ever brighter in both the knowledge of Him and in
discerning even between that which is His acceptable and
His perfect will. The way of love is the way to excellence!

Enduring the Cross

—━◀▥▥▐ ◗▥▥▶━

Looking unto Jesus the author and finisher of our
faith; who for the joy that was set before him endured
the cross, despising the shame, and is set down
at the right hand of the throne of God.

—Hebrews 12:2

"...Who for the joy that was set before him endured." There are many things in life we need to endure, but the most important thing we need to endure, in order to live with Jesus forever, is our cross. But this cross is not pain and suffering inflicted upon us by the circumstances of life or by our own wrong choices, rather, this cross is Jesus' cross. It is our voluntary choice to crucify or deny Self to do the will of God. Jesus said, *"If any man will come after me, let him deny himself, and take up his cross daily, and follow me"* (Luke 9:23).

As Jesus took up His cross voluntarily out of His love toward God and man, so we must, likewise, take up our cross to be His followers. So, the cross is an instrument of death upon which the old man is crucified, causing Paul to say, *"I am crucified with Christ: nevertheless I live; yet not I, but Christ liveth in me"* (Gal. 2:20).

And what is it that gives us strength to endure the cross? It is the joy set before us! It is the joy of obtaining the promise—life everlasting—and the privilege of sitting in Jesus' throne, for He Himself said, *"To him that overcometh will I grant to sit with me in my throne, even as I also overcame, and am set down with my Father in his throne"* (Rev. 3:21).

Yes, as we look unto Jesus and to the hope of His everlasting fellowship, we have ample inspiration to endure the cross set before us, even as He did.

105

Disciples and Believers

⸺◗▰◖❨◗▰◖⸻

So likewise, whosoever he be of you that forsaketh
not all that he hath, he cannot be my disciple.

—Luke 14:33

The Gospels make a very clear distinction between believers and disciples. All disciples are believers, but not all believers are disciples. Take for example this passage: *"Nevertheless among the chief rulers also many believed on him; but because of the Pharisees they did not confess him, lest they should be put out of the synagogue"* (John 12:42). These chief rulers were believers, but they did not want to pay the cost of discipleship. Consider the man who wanted to follow Jesus but insisted on first burying his father: *"Lord, suffer me first to go and bury my father"* (Matt. 8:21). Think of the rich young ruler who believed Jesus but not enough to give up his wealth to follow Him. These men were believers but not disciples.

Not all believers are disciples. A disciple is one who forsakes all to follow Jesus. A disciple never has an excuse because of prior commitments or human expectations. A disciple never says, "Lord, I wish you had told me sooner, for then I could have come."

Yes, dear friend, Jesus knows all about your prior commitments. He knows all about family expectations and family pressures. He knows all about the complexities of disengaging yourself, and in disappointing people if we choose to follow Him now. All these things matter little to Him, because He is Lord of lords, and we must follow Him like Matthew, on a moment's notice. If we do, He will take care of the consequences of our decisions, and He will do it beautifully and wisely.

So, friend, if you are just a believer and not a disciple, choose to become a disciple today, and you will be numbered amongst God's holy elect.

Coming to the End of Our Excuses

*And they all with one consent
began to make excuse.*

—Luke 14:18

This Lukan passage on the Great Supper is loaded with the distinctions between believers and disciples. These verses give us examples of people held back by oxen, land, marriage, father, mother, wife, children, brother, or sister. *"They all with one consent began to make excuse."* If there is anything in our life which takes precedence over our loving, listening to, and following Jesus, then we cannot be His disciple. And, as soon as we refuse to put Him first in our daily life, we have ceased to be His disciples. This is the narrow way, and few people will take it.

That, my friend, is the substance and the essence of New Testament discipleship: to cease from any and all excuses, and to follow Jesus whenever and wherever He leads. At conversion, it is God's will that we make our last excuse for disobedience and our last choice in the flesh. We will then begin to deny Self, hear His voice, and follow. Thrills, romance, and adventure will be in the making.

Yes, very few have consistently crucified Self and abandoned every excuse for disobedience since the day of their conversion. But no matter how much you have failed, you can make a resolution in your heart today that Self must die and that it shall never again be allowed to rule in your life. May you be willing to pay the price that discipleship demands in order to receive its blessings that will never end.

Don't Just Sit There

*Every place that the sole of your foot
shall tread upon, that have I given
unto you, as I said unto Moses.*

—Joshua 1:3

Here, God gave to Joshua the title, the property rights, of the land of Caanan. This land had everything Israel needed. The houses were built and furnished. The gardens flourished. The crops were planted and the wells were dug. Yet, there was a problem: the land was full of enemies armed to the teeth, battle-seasoned, and battle-ready.

This leads us to this principle: what God has promised, we have to fight to get. Standing on the promises is not good enough. We have to put on the whole armor of God, and march and fight to make the promises come true.

Moses had the title to the land in his back pocket. It was given to him and his generation, as you see in the text by these words: *"as I said unto Moses."* However, Moses and his generation never set foot on the land. How many promises and revelations of God go unfulfilled because people just stand, or go in circles, instead of fighting?

Young man, God has a precious wife for you, but you have to fight impatience and sexual temptations to get to her. And once you have her, you will have to fight to keep the romance going. Young woman, God has a wonderful future for your life, but you will have to fight the pressures of the world in order to gain that future. God has revealed a church or a job for many of you, but you must fight in order to get there and to stay there. Yes, what God has promised, we have to fight to receive, and to keep.

Sign a Contract

*Then Job arose...and fell down upon
the ground, and worshipped.*

—Job 1:20

Job never left the ship of hope. He lost his sons, his daughters, his servants, his property, his health, and the favor of his wife. What did he do after he lost all? He *"fell down upon the ground and worshipped."* His romance with God went on just the same! That is the proof, my friend, that he was a perfect and upright man in all his ways.

The true test of whether we are all for God is that when everything around us falls apart, when our friends leave us, our loved ones question us, and yes, even when disease strikes us a hard blow, we fall down before God and worship Him. Job, long ago, had signed his marriage contract with God to be faithful "for better or worse, in sickness and in health, until death do us part."

There I was, a sixteen-year-old lad returning to my home in Germany, just two days after being saved while visiting in England. I had been deprived of food those two days, and I found myself in a storm crossing the English channel. I was weak, standing on deck, clinging to the railing, watching the sea as the spray of the black waves came up at me. I felt forsaken by both God and man.

The devil talked to me out of that black sea and said, "You will never make it. There is no Christian at home to welcome you." I told him, "Satan, I want to be faithful in sickness and in health. Even if by some failure of mine I go to hell, I will still love Jesus and talk of Him in hell until you get tired of me and spit me out of that pit." Then and there, I signed my marriage contract with God. It was official: for better or for worse!

Loved one, have you signed that kind of contract with God? If not, do so, and your latter blessing shall be greater than your first.

Defeated, but Not Destroyed

*Then came Amalek, and fought
with Israel in Rephidim.*

—Exodus 17:8

Who is Amalek? Amalek represents the carnal nature, the adamic nature, the sinful nature, the old man, the Self-life. Amalek was the grandson of Esau. Amalek was the first one to try to prevent Israel, God's chosen people, from entering into Canaan, which represents the abundant, victorious, sanctified life.

We all have Amalek, the Self-life, within us, but, my friend, there is a way to defeat it. When Moses lifted up his hands to God, Israel prevailed, but when Moses let down his hands, Amalek prevailed. The uplifted hands of Moses represent utter dependence upon God and faith in God's prevailing mercy and power. We cannot defeat Amalek in our own strength.

At this time, Israel had no army, no generals, no captains, and no weapons of warfare such as spears, shields, or chariots. But Israel had God! And since you also have God, you can rely on Him in childlike trust. At that point, the battle becomes the Lord's, and victory is assured. Indeed, it is *"Not by might, nor by power, but by my spirit, saith the Lord of hosts"* (Zech. 4:6).

Moses, through faith and prayer, defeated Amalek. Then Moses said, *"the Lord hath sworn that the Lord will have war with Amalek from generation to generation"* (Ex. 17:16). Yes, Amalek was defeated at Rephidim, but he was not destroyed. Therefore, we must keep fighting Amalek within us until the end of our earthly days. And, thank God, when we see Jesus, all our battles will be over, and Amalek will be cast into the lake of fire forever.

Show Me Thy Glory

And he said, I beseech thee,
shew me thy glory.

—Exodus 33:18

What is it that you desire with all your heart? Is it a position in the church? Is it a home of your own? Is it a spiritual gift? Is it money? Is it a companion? Moses is the only Old Testament character of whom it is said explicitly that he sought God's glory.

Ponder the fact that Moses was reared in the glory and splendor of the Egyptian empire. He was taught, trained, and disciplined to appreciate the finer things of life, yet, he sought for a greater glory: God's glory.

God did show Moses part of His glory at Sinai. He let him see his hinder parts. But 1,500 years later, an angel knocked on the door of paradise and called for Moses and Elijah. In a moment's time, these two men found themselves on the Mount of Transfiguration, beholding a greater glory than God's hinder parts: Christ's glory!

They, in a fuller sense than any others, could say with John, *"(and we beheld his glory, the glory as of the only begotten of the Father,) full of grace and truth"* (John 1:14). Yes, there on the mount, it says that Christ *"was transfigured before them: and his face did shine as the sun, and his raiment was white as the light"* (Matt. 17:2).

"...Shew me thy glory" is a great prayer and a noble request. Yes, God may not show you this glory as he did to Moses, but be assured that if you seek Him like Moses, you will be *"changed into the same image from glory to glory, even as by the Spirit of the Lord"* (2 Cor. 3:18).

More Prayer Is Needed

―◦◦◦◦◦―

...but Satan hindered us.

―1 Thessalonians 2:18

It appears that the great apostle to the Gentiles had a revelation to return to Thessalonica. Although the revelation was there, it was never fulfilled. Satan hindered and stopped Paul from returning to this struggling congregation in Thessalonica. To receive a revelation does not mean that we can rest; it merely shows us on which particular road we can expect to meet the devil.

Abraham received a revelation that he was to be the father of many nations, but he found himself with his face to the ground many times before his first child was born. Joseph received a revelation that he was called to be a great leader, but he had to go through the pit and through slavery to get there. Yes, you will meet the devil on the road to the fulfillment of many a revelation. He will do everything he can to deter you, to discourage you, to disarm you, and to harm you. The devil wants you to give up the revelation altogether, and to make you take the road of reason, least resistance, and convenience.

Yet, my friend, be admonished to never give up going by revelation. Fight to stay on this pathway until the end, and if you can't make it on your own, call on your friends to help you pray. Perhaps, it is because of these encounters with the devil that Paul said in one way or another throughout his epistles, *"Brethren, pray for us"* (1 Thess. 5:25; 2 Thess. 3:1). Yes, let us pray; pray hard, pray frequently, and pray perseveringly that the devil may not hinder us.

We Win by One Way or Another

And I would not have you ignorant, brethren,
that oftentimes I purposed to come unto you
(and was hindered hitherto),...

—Romans 1:13 ASV

We see and understand that Paul had difficult times reaching his destinations. He was hindered many times from doing the perfect will of God. Yesterday's Scripture read, *"Satan hindered us."* It did not say, "Satan hindered me." Hence, the business of getting Paul to Thessalonica or to Rome was everybody's business.

I am sure there are many places men of God have not gotten to because people in their churches have allowed themselves to be hindered in praying for them. However, there is no need to be discouraged if ministers, at times, don't reach their destinations, for *"we know that all things work together for good to them that love God, to them who are the called according to his purpose"* (Rom. 8:28).

The cleverness of God is greater than the wiles of the devil. Those who are faithful in the kingdom will never be cut short, because God knows how to turn temporary losses into long-range blessings. Glory!

Surely, the Thessalonians were robbed of God's choice servant's return visit because many did not pray. It is possible, however, that because Satan hindered Paul from going to Thessalonica, we now have First and Second Thessalonians, through which all Christendom has been able to visit Thessalonica throughout the centuries.

So, dear one, don't be disheartened if a revelation has not come true because of the prayerlessness of others. I ndeed, the prayerless ones will be the losers for it. Instead, be encouraged that the praying ones will always win, nonetheless, even if on a different field of battle and in a different way.

Children, Obey Your Parents

*Children, obey your parents in
the Lord: for this is right.*

—Ephesians 6:1

Dear child, what does it mean to obey your parents? It
means that when one of them says, "George, take out the
garbage," you take out the garbage. How do you take out
the garbage? You take it out with a song in your heart. You
do not go to your father and say, "Why do I have to do all
this when my sister or brother doesn't have to do half the
work I do?" That is not the way you obey in the Lord.
Obedience in the Lord does not make comparison with the
performances of others, but it looks only to God's will.

Someday, you will grow up, and the Lord will ask you to
take the garbage out of your heart. I trust that on that day,
you will not ask, "Lord, how much?" or "Lord, as much
garbage as my sisters or my friend?" Again, you must not
look to others as points of comparison to find your level of
obedience. You must look to Jesus for His standard of
obedience for your life.

When you are grown, He will say to you, "Go to prayer
meeting." If there are only five or six attending, and most of
these skip and miss, will you be faithful in all your house,
as Moses was, and go to prayer meeting?

Obey your parents in the Lord. This means not to
question your parents' authority. It means not to ask for
explanations and not to make comparisons. Obeying your
parents is preparation for obeying God. So, learn to trust
and obey, and you will soon learn that there is no greater
joy in Jesus than when you trust and obey.

Nudging!

*And Sarai said unto Abram, Behold now, the Lord hath
restrained me from bearing: I pray thee, go in unto my
maid; it may be that I may obtain children by her.
And Abram hearkened to the voice of Sarai.*

—Genesis 16:2

There is something like a theology of "nudging." A husband came home one night and asked his little wife how she had moved the heavy refrigerator from one end of the kitchen to the other. She smiled and replied, "By nudging."

Eve nudged Adam to eat of the forbidden fruit. Sarai nudged Abram to sleep with her servant, Hagar. Lot, no doubt, nudged Abram to go into Egypt. Jezebel nudged Ahab to take Naboth's vineyard. Abigail nudged King David not to kill Nabal and his men. Mordecai nudged Esther to appear in the king's palace. Some wives nudge their husbands to go on to early prayer meeting, and some nudge them to stay in bed for a little more needed rest. Some husbands nudge their wives toward a deeper walk with God, and others nudge them toward materialism. What all has been accomplished for good or evil by nudging?

Yes, in many cases you may not be the main player in the theater of life, but you often have just as much power as if you were by utilizing the subtle "nudge." Let us use the "nudge" to exhort one another and to encourage one another unto what is noble, pure, and right.

Affliction Is Better than Pleasure

Choosing rather to suffer affliction
with the people of God, than to enjoy the
pleasures of sin for a season.
—Hebrews 11:25

Paul says that Moses chose to suffer affliction. There are two types of afflictions: those we choose, and those we don't choose.

We all suffer afflictions because of the consequences of our own wrong choices, and we also all suffer afflictions because of the consequences of the wrong choices of others. Then, we sometimes suffer afflictions because of ignorance. All of these are afflictions coming to all mankind, and there is no reward promised in their future life for having suffered these afflictions.

But then, there are afflictions that are peculiar to the righteous. When a man chooses to go all for God, he meets up with a set of afflictions of an altogether different nature and source. These are what we may call the "afflictions of the godly," and the sinner knows nothing about them. It is by virtue of these afflictions that our lives are brought into conformity with Christ and that our souls come to an identity and intimacy with Jesus in the great battle against evil.

Moses chose to suffer affliction when he chose to reject the world and to go with the people of God. Jesus chose to suffer affliction when he decided to leave the glories of heaven to take on the form of a man. Paul chose afflictions when he told his Hebrew friends that he was going to lay down his life for Jesus.

Are all afflictions you suffer the consequence of ignorance or wrong choices, or do you suffer some afflictions which are the consequence of your having chosen to be holy? On the last day, you will be able to trade these latter afflictions in for a special measure of glory and bliss.

A Call to Decisiveness

◄━◄◖◗►━►

...choose you this day whom ye will serve.

—Joshua 24:15

Dear ones, let us talk about these words "choose you." Joshua believed that God's people, by His grace, had the capacity to be the makers of their own destiny. Yet, today's behavioristic philosophy makes man the effect rather than the cause of his circumstances.

Through this philosophy, man has ceased to be the mover. Instead, he has become the moved. It is the world that is making today's man, rather than today's man making his own world. Metaphorically speaking, man has lost his oar, his sail, and his rudder. His boat is no longer following the course of his choice, but rather, it is drifting along the ever-changing currents of time. The man of the world is like a sardine in a can. He is caught, gutted out, smoked, packed, and locked in. The man of the world is trapped. He is the victim of genetics, upbringing, and circumstance.

The man of the Bible is not so. He is the mover, not the moved. He is the cause, not the effect. He is the maker, not the made. He is the pusher, not the pushed. He is the molder, not the molded. He is the painter, not the canvas. He makes his choices, fashions his destiny, and changes his world. The words "I can't" are foreign to the true Christian's vocabulary.

We must not say, "I can't walk with God." We must not find our excuses in the fatalistic philosophy of today. God says, "Choose you." The good news is that we have the choice to get free. We can "do all things through Christ which strengthens us." Therefore, let us stop drifting with the circumstances, and let us choose the way the saints of old have chosen and walked. It will do us good forever.

The Fruits of Bitterness

*Let all bitterness, and wrath, and
anger, and clamour, and evil speaking, be
put away from you, with all malice.*

—Ephesians 4:31

Bitterness corrupts the soul. Bitterness destroys life physically, emotionally, and spiritually. Bitterness prevents us from seeking God.

One would like to assume that Christians are not bitter. But the fact is, Paul had to exhort the believers at Ephesus to put away all bitterness. Whom are we bitter against, and what are we bitter about? At first sight, we may say rather indignantly, "I am not bitter against anyone or about anything." Yet, let's take another close look at ourselves.

We may be saved, active in the church, and faithful in Bible reading and prayer, but, most likely, if we are divorced, or widowed, or if we have lost a child or a parent unexpectedly, if we fight cancer or have lost a job or been demoted, we may be harboring some bitterness. We also may be bitter over something that happened in our church. Paul pleads with us: put away all bitterness!

For King Saul, bitterness produced emotional instability, an uncontrollable temper, a foreign spirit, and unreasonable judgment, finally leading to an association with witchcraft and to suicide. Oh, the awful road that bitterness can put us on.

So, let us look diligently to Jesus lest we *"fail of the grace of God; lest any root of bitterness springing up trouble you, and thereby many be defiled"* (Heb. 12:15). Yes, indeed, put away all bitterness, and do it today. Take your bitterness to Jesus, and let it be cleansed out of you by His precious, sacred, never failing blood.

Sanctified Optimism

*When the enemy shall come in like
a flood, the Spirit of the Lord shall lift
up a standard against him.*

—Isaiah 59:19

Isaiah saw the enemy come in like a flood, but he was unperturbed by it because he also saw the Spirit of the Lord rising up to defeat his enemies. He, among all the prophets, was the most optimistic, the most encouraging, and the most messianic in hope. He sang Handel's *Messiah* before its notes were written. There was a happy hum coming from his lips while gross darkness was over the land. He saw God's light in obscurity.

All the while he saw the vision of the Babylonian captivity being played in his mind, he saw every valley exalted, every rough place made plain, and the glory of the Lord lifted high. In the midst of utmost confusion, he saw the people of God graven upon the palms of God's hands.

When Israel's government was dissolved by the enemy, he saw a government, the increase of which would have no end. Hallelujah! He saw that, with the Son of God, in times of great difficulty, oppression, and danger, God's people cannot lose—they can only quit.

Yes, indeed, when it looks so much like we are losing the fight, we are not losing at all. Let us stay in uniform. Let us not become deserters. Let us believe that *"greater is he that is in* [us], *than he that is in the world"* (1 John 4:4). And we know that *"he is able to keep that which I have committed unto him against that day"* (2 Tim. 1:12).

Yes, dear one, it is not over until it is over. Be slow to judge, and have patience with hope. God will have the last word for every one of His saints, and, no matter what, His last word will always be that we shall be more than conquerors in Christ Jesus our Lord!

Too Good to Be False

———✴———

*And she said to the king, It was a true report
that I heard in mine own land of thy acts and of thy
wisdom. Howbeit...thy wisdom and prosperity
exceedeth the fame which I heard.*

—1 Kings 10:6–7

When a man is both rich and wise, you have a story that spreads. People talk about it. When the Queen of Sheba heard the report about Solomon in her own country, she was not just content reading the gossip columns. She said, "If what I hear is true, I had better not miss it." This Queen of Sheba was one of those rare jewels who still possessed that childlike spirit and philosophy so well expressed in, "It sounds too good to be false."

Children are believers and dreamers. They often cling to their fairy tale stories as if they were real, and they don't want these stories to die. Jesus says that of such is the kingdom of God. Oh, what a tragedy that skepticism and doubt eventually overcome many childlike hearts. This attitude of skepticism kills all dreams and soon settles into many a heart as an almost hellish cynicism which says about any good report, "It is too good to be true."

The Queen of Sheba assembled a large caravan and loaded it with spices, gold, and precious stones to give to one whom she believed to be too good to be false. Thank God, her dreams were not disappointed, and God put her story in the Bible to help us all to cast out our cynicism, pessimism, and doubts, in order that we might dream again. No matter how many times you're disappointed, my friend, keep up the faith, and someday, you, too, might find the great treasures missed by all the cynics.

Whom Do You Feed?

*For it was so, when Jezebel cut off the prophets
of the Lord, that Obadiah took an hundred prophets,
and hid them by fifty in a cave, and fed them
with bread and water.*

—1 Kings 18:4

In the eyes of man, Obadiah was known as the governor of the king's house, but Obadiah knew himself only as a *"servant who feared the Lord from his youth"* (vv. 3, 12). He feared God. He feared God enough not to fear Ahab, the most wicked of all kings (1 Kings 16:30). We either fear man or God.

Obadiah's daily objective was only one thing: bread and water for the prophets, even at the risk of losing his life. Dear friend, bread and water in the time of famine is as wonderful as sumptuous dining in the days of prosperity.

Obadiah risked his life not only once, but each day for possibly one thousand days. It was not an easy task for this governor to steal away hundreds of times, bearing food and water for one hundred men without being caught by Jezebel's informers. But Obadiah never tired of his vision, even though he continually sojourned in one of the most pagan, idolatrous, and adulterous courts of all times.

Obadiah was a light that could not be quenched, a soldier who could not be discouraged, and a governor with a servant's heart. He lived by the principle of Jesus' words, *"be...wise as serpents, and harmless as doves"* (Matt. 10:16). He recognized before Jesus said it that *"He that receiveth a prophet in the name of a prophet shall receive a prophet's reward...And whosoever shall give to drink unto one of these little ones a cup of cold water only in the name of a disciple, verily I say unto you, he shall in no wise lose his reward"* (vv. 41–42).

Obadiah fed the prophets. Whom do you feed?

Give God Your Heart

*O that there were such an heart in them, that
they would fear me, and keep all my commandments
always, that it might be well with them, and
with their children for ever!*

—Deuteronomy 5:29

The Bible refers to the "heart" nearly a thousand times, but "intelligence" is mentioned hardly at all. Does this tell us something?

God looks at the heart. Man looks at degrees and diplomas, at possessions, social standing, physical appearance, and accomplishments. God's concern is with the heart. His observation is, *"The heart is deceitful"* (Jer. 17:9). His cry is, *"O that there would be such an heart in them, that they would...keep my commandments always."* Solomon also says, *"Keep thy heart with all diligence; for out of it are the issues of life"* (Prov. 4:23).

Oh, my friend, Christ wants to be the head of the church, and He is looking for a body that has such a heart as His. He wants us to have a submissive heart, a contrite heart, a trusting heart, a pure, loving, and obedient heart.

The cry of God is for the heart. The cry of much of the modern church is for the head, for intelligent men, for learned and brilliant men to come forth to preach the gospel. But Christ can only lead the church through hearts which are like unto His. That is not to say that God despises intelligence, but it is to say that intelligence without a heart after God's own heart is as dangerous as the religion of the Pharisees was to the religion of Christ.

Christianity is ineffectual unless the heart of man is fully engaged in the purposes of the Lord. Jesus calls you today, dear friend, saying to you, "Give me your heart."

Instant Obedience

*And as Jesus passed forth from thence, he
saw a man, named Matthew, sitting at the receipt of
custom: and he saith unto him, Follow me.
And he arose, and followed him.*

—Matthew 9:9

Here is one of the most beautiful illustrations of instant obedience. In fact, instant obedience is the only obedience— delayed obedience is not obedience. The *"suffer me first to go and bury my father"* attitude was not considered obedience by Jesus (Matt. 8:21). There can be no *"suffer me first"* in the life of discipleship. Neither can there be any attitude of murmuring in disciples' hearts for their plans having been suddenly disrupted, putting them at odds with their fellow men.

Yes, indeed, Jesus is not in the advance notice business. He requires us to be ready anytime for anything, as He is ready for us at anytime for anything. He expects us to trust Him, even to the disappointment and dismay of our fellow men, expecting us to firmly believe *"that all things work together for good to them that love God, to them who are the called according to his purpose"* (Rom. 8:28).

So, Matthew rose up and followed Jesus immediately. He could not notify his boss; he could not balance the account; he could not contact his family. But, yes, all things work together for good. Because of his instant obedience, we have the gospel of Matthew through which millions have come to know God.

Do not let temporary inconveniences and disappointments hinder you from getting to God's great, eternal plan. Whenever He calls you, do as Matthew did: rise up and follow—immediately!

Fasting for the Extra Boost

―――

*Then was Jesus led up of the Spirit into the wilderness
to be tempted of the devil. And when he had fasted forty days
and forty nights, he was afterward an hungered.*

—Matthew 4:1–2

When our bodies are deprived of food, our spirit is strengthened in battles *"against principalities, against powers, against the rulers of the darkness of this world..."* (Eph. 6:12). When our battle is against flesh and blood, we should then eat to the full, but when the battle is spirit against spirit, we should fast.

We first learn in this text that Jesus fasted. Secondly, we learn that some things can only be accomplished with fasting. There is more power when fasting is added to prayer. Now, let us look at some biblical examples to see what God did through fasting.

God prepared to destroy a disobedient Israel after she had made the golden calf. He told Moses, *"...let me alone"* (Ex. 32:10). But Moses would not, and he fasted forty days. God hearkened and spared the people (vv. 11–14).

Ezra led forty thousand men, women, and children to Jerusalem. The king of Babylon loaded them down with wealth as they began their journey. What a target for the bandits and robbers in the unbroken wilderness! Israel was unarmed, but they used the time-tested method of fasting and were delivered from the hand of the enemy.

Nehemiah heard how the walls of Jerusalem were broken down and how its gates were burned with fire. He sat down, wept, mourned, *fasted*, and prayed; and, of course, God heard him (Neh. 1:4).

My friend, Jesus fasted, and He prophesied that when the Bridegroom shall be taken away, then would his children fast. If you are not getting through in prayer with a full stomach, try again with an empty one.

"Get Thee Up"

*And Joshua rent his clothes, and fell to the earth upon
his face before the ark of the Lord until the eventide, he and
the elders of Israel, and put dust upon their heads.*

—Joshua 7:6

Here we see a great man of God, who had never known personal failure, making a dust bowl before the ark of God. Further, observe that it was not only Joshua, but his elders as well, who lay in the dust with their garments torn, throwing dust upon their heads.

Obviously, a crisis had caused Joshua to doubt all of God's promises. The calamity at hand had, to him, risen higher than the promises of God. And whenever a crisis situation becomes greater in our minds than God's revelations, we are bound to have our faces on the ground, throwing dust upon our heads.

This is the kind of picture the devil glories in; but, dear ones, it is a picture God despises. We must get the dust of discouragement out of our lives. We are not born to sit in the dust, but rather to sit in heavenly places in Christ Jesus.

When we as Christians experience failure, it is not time for us to get into the dust, but for us to look at the glory of the redemptive, loving power of Christ's forgiveness. For it is obvious, indeed, that when a man's face is toward the dust, he loses visual perspective of his environment.

Joshua remembered the promises, but he forgot the command, *"Only be thou strong and very courageous"* (Josh. 1:7). Joshua abandoned faith for feelings and forgot that the word was onward, onward, and onward. *"And the Lord said unto Joshua, Get thee up"* (7:10). And so He speaks to all of us who are in the dust of despair, *"Get thee up."*

Why Prayers Are Not Answered

*Then Jesus answered and said, O faithless
and perverse generation, how long shall I be with
you? how long shall I suffer you? bring him hither to me.
And Jesus rebuked the devil; and he departed out of him:
and the child was cured from that very hour. Then
came the disciples to Jesus apart, and said,
Why could not we cast him out?*

—Matthew 17:17–19

The *"Why"* of verse nineteen has been followed by millions of "whys" since that time. Why didn't my mother get healed? Why didn't God protect our mission station from the enemy? Why, with all the prayers, must we tarry and tarry?

The problems of unanswered prayers can generally be attributed to three sources: God, Satan, or man. Let us look at three case histories that illustrate these three points.

God is not willing. The apostle Paul had a thorn in the flesh for which he earnestly asked for deliverance. God was not willing to heal Paul, and He said, *"My grace is sufficient for thee"* (2 Cor. 12:9).

Satan is fighting. When Paul was trying to go to Thessalonica, he had to write to his Christian friends there and say, *"Satan hindered us"* (1 Thess. 2:18).

Man is disobedient. Here is our third and perhaps most common cause of unanswered prayer. *"If I regard iniquity in my heart, the Lord will not hear me"* (Ps. 66:18). Consider also this Scripture, *"Ye ask, and receive not, because ye ask amiss, that ye may consume it upon your lusts"* (James 4:3).

These, my friends, are three reasons for prayers not being answered. Tomorrow, we will consider yet another reason.

His Time, Not Our Time

*And as Jesus passed by, he saw a man which
was blind from his birth. And his disciples asked him,
saying, Master, who did sin, this man, or his parents,
that he was born blind? Jesus answered, Neither hath
this man sinned, nor his parents: but that the works
of God should be made manifest in him.*

—John 9:1–3

Many prayers are not answered because it is not yet God's time. We must allow God His time for His miracles to come about. Our own time for miracles, for deliverance, for healing, is always now. It is not so with our Lord. For the all-wise God, there are bad times, there are good times, and there are perfect times to bring things to pass.

No doubt, this man (notice it does not say youth) had been prayed for, for many years, yet, it seemed to be of no avail. What a wonderful thing if he could have been healed as a child. But such was not God's will. So, great care and sacrifice were required of the parents to raise this blind child. How great it would have been for him to have been healed in his youth so that he could earn his own bread rather than rely on the mercies of others. But, no, God's perfect time was now, as he came into adulthood. It was now and not earlier, nor later, that the works of God should be made manifest in him.

Let us keep praying, and let us keep believing. But let us also know that there is a time and season for everything. Our time is always, but not so His time. Only when things happen in God's time will His glory be manifested to us and through us to others.

Wait

My soul, wait thou only upon God;
for my expectation is from him.

—Psalm 62:5

Waiting upon God is a lost art in the modern church. God waited four hundred years for Israel to get ready to come out of Egypt. Moses waited forty years to get his commission. David waited seventeen years from the time of his call to kingship until he took over the throne. The prophets waited years in the desert to get their prophecies from God. Anna waited in prayer until she was eighty-four to see the salvation of the Lord. John the Baptist, born full of the Holy Spirit, waited thirty years to open his mouth. Paul waited in the Arabian desert to receive the revelations of the kingdom of God. Oh, *"My soul, wait thou only upon God...He only is my rock and my salvation: he is my defence; I shall not be moved"* (Ps. 62:5–6).

Why do we question our salvation? It is because we do not wait upon God. Why do we get flooded by doubts? Because we don't wait upon God for a greater revelation of Himself. Why are we fearful and find ourselves defenseless in the time of trouble? It is because we don't wait upon the Lord for instruction and sustenance. For those who wait upon Him, God is their rock, their salvation, their glory, their strength, their defense, and their refuge. But if we don't wait upon Him, we will forget all of that and fret and be anxious about many things.

Yes, my dear Lord, *"Thou art my hiding place; thou shalt preserve me from trouble; thou shalt compass me about with songs of deliverance"* as I wait upon Thee (Ps. 32:7).

Wait upon God

*The wall fell down flat, so that the
people went up into the city.*

—Joshua 6:20

Israel, under Joshua's leadership, took the city of Jericho. They took the city because they had waited upon God. God gave them the instructions on how to fell the walls. God literally gave them the guidance for victory. The army of Israel did not have a board meeting or a meeting of logistics on the "how to's" of taking a city. They did not have a plan. God had the plan—the perfect plan of victory. So, Israel rested and waited upon God, and victory was theirs.

What board of evangelism or advisory council would ever have thought of a people circling a city in total silence for six days and then bringing it down with a trumpet sound and a shout on the seventh? When we wait upon God and rest, He gives us the directions we need. God's plan may not seem practical, and it may even seem ridiculous, but when God speaks, it is best to obey.

Church history indicates that the more the church ceased from her own works, the more she was able to go by revelation. The more she trusted and rested, the more effective she was in changing the world. Church work in our own strength and by our own wisdom will only do more damage than good. Truly, only God knows how to make the Jerichos fall.

So, if you want your Jericho walls to fall flat, wait upon God, and rest. Wait for His divine instructions. Walking with God, therefore, is not just a matter of going and doing, but it is also a matter of resting and waiting. Therefore, wait thou upon the Lord.

Waiting Is Breathing

*Truly my soul waiteth upon God:
from him cometh my salvation.*

—Psalm 62:1

In this day of rush and run, we need to be reminded of the importance of waiting upon God in prayer, in the Word, and in our walk with Him. Rev. Loran Helm says in his book *A Voice in the Wilderness*:

Waiting upon God is paramount and indispensable. It is as urgent to true Christianity as breathing is to the body. Our waiting upon God must be continuous and unbroken, as the breathing that maintains life. If we do not breathe, we die. If we do not wait on God, we come to spiritual night and barrenness, to spiritual poverty and death.

Unless we wait on God sufficiently, we will not so much as be aware that we simply cannot participate in the kingdom of God until He leads us and directs us.

While you are waiting, God is rooting you downward in His love and His likeness...As you go down in humility, God lifts you in revelation. While your roots are sinking down in lowliness, the spiritual branches are mounting upward. God brings us upward to give us a glimpse of His marvelous Kingdom.[3]

Nothing is more important than the will of God and His kingdom. Yet, it is only as we wait upon Him that we are able to receive His will. Through waiting, we are prepared to enter into the work God has predestined for us. Yes, *"Wait on the Lord: be of good courage, and he shall strengthen thine heart: wait, I say, on the Lord"* (Ps. 27:14).

The Secret of Waiting

Wait on the Lord: be of good courage,
and he shall strengthen thine heart:
wait, I say, on the Lord.

—Psalm 27:14

Not so in haste, my heart!
Have faith in God and wait;
Although He linger long,
He never comes too late.

He never cometh late;
He knoweth what is best;
Vex not thyself in vain;
Until He cometh, rest.

Until He cometh, rest,
Nor grudge the hours that roll;
The feet that wait for God
Are soonest at the goal.

Are soonest at the goal
That is not gained by speed;
Then hold thee still, my heart,
For I shall wait His lead.[4]

The Best Honor Society

———

*Honor thy father and mother; (which is the first
commandment with promise; That it may be well with
thee, and thou mayest live long on the earth.*

—Ephesians 6:2–3

Don't we like what Paul says in Ephesians 6? If we will
honor our father and mother, it will be well with us.

One of the surest ways to success for any young man or
woman is to honor their parents. Young people, the Bible
tells us that honoring our parents will do more good than
joining any honor society in the world. The honor society to
belong to is the one God blesses. It is the one where parents are honored.

To honor our parents is to not judge them. If we have a
judgmental spirit toward a mother or father, we will likely
have such a spirit toward our pastor, teacher, or boss, and
perhaps even some misgivings about God Himself.

The Scripture says, *"Honor thy father and mother."* We
need to do this whether our parents are in their thirties,
forties, eighties, or nineties. We must show respect for our
parents until they leave the earth.

To honor our father and mother means to help, to
encourage, to lift, and to listen to them. For God will not
put any wind behind our sails unless we do so, and unless
we do so consistently.

If you have been disobedient, rebellious, faultfinding, and
resentful toward your parents, then you have not been honoring them. If this has been your attitude toward your
parents, you are headed into a stiff head wind, and you will
be deprived of the blessings God has stored up for you.

So, dear one, to honor our father and our mother is the
first commandment with promise—the promise that God
will give you a spiritual tail wind all the days of your life.

Training unto Discipleship

Train up a child in the way he should go:
and when he is old, he will not depart from it.

—Proverbs 22:6

To train is more than to instruct. Instruction is academic and intellectual, whereas training is actually the formation of habits. Instruction is imparting knowledge, training is developing behavior patterns and character. For example, training a child to make his bed daily is only a success when the child makes the bed without having to be told. Training is getting the child to do things on his own.

Many parents in this busy world sense a great need to spend more time with their children. But just to spend more time for the sake of spending time is not going to save our children. You can spend a lot of time with your dog, but unless you train him, he will not be a better dog.

Training makes better children, which is not just playing with them, or taking them places. No, training prepares your child for discipleship with Jesus.

But, there are limits to training. By training, you can lead a child up to the gates of the kingdom, but training will never usher him in. It takes the Father in heaven to draw a person into the kingdom of God. Jesus said, *"No man can come to me, except the Father...draw him"* (John 6:44). Therefore, many parents unnecessarily condemn themselves by the Scripture, Proverbs 22:6, because, after they have trained their children, their children are still in sin.

This misconception comes from not realizing the limits of training. Paul, the apostle, was trained to be a disciple and a disciplined scholar, but God had to make him a saint. Hence training is our work, but transformation is His work. But then, glory to God, after your trained child has received the Lord, oh, what a wonderful disciple he will make.

The Word and the Spirit

*Thy word is a lamp unto my feet,
and a light unto my path.*

—Psalm 119:105

Most people are trying to receive directions of the Holy Spirit before they have consistently obeyed the written Word. I dare say that our revelations from God are suspect if we don't live by the light of the Word. If a man does not live by the Word of God, how can he be trusted to live by the Spirit of God? Before any of us come under the authority of the Holy Spirit, we must come under the authority of the written Word. Jesus Himself subjected Himself to every word that proceeded out of the mouth of God. He came to fulfill the Law and the prophets, and His ministry was marked by "It is written."

There are thousands of persons who claim to be directed by the Holy Spirit, but their marriages are in disarray; they have strained relationships with their pastors; and their spiritual lives reflect inconsistencies, bad habits, and negative attitudes.

Acts 5:32 tells us that the Holy Ghost is given to those who obey Him. Obeying includes not forsaking the assembling of ourselves together, rejoicing evermore, esteeming others better than ourselves, obeying those who have the rule over us, loving the brethren, seeking first the kingdom of God, being a cheerful giver, and more, much more. I will let you finish the list, if you like.

It is that simple. The person who does not put himself under the authority of the written Word will not be led by the Holy Spirit, regardless of what he says.

Flesh Versus Spirit

...and perfect, will of God.

—Romans 12:2

Every true child of God is led by the Holy Spirit, because every true child of God obeys the Word. For *"He that saith, I know him, and keepeth not his commandments, is a liar"* (1 John 2:4). If we obey, we have the Holy Spirit, we will walk in the Spirit, and we will know that perfect and acceptable will of God.

To walk in the Spirit, we must continually crucify the flesh and the affections thereof. The flesh, or carnality as Paul calls the flesh in Romans 8:7, will never take one step after Jesus. In fact, carnality is enmity against God and is not subject to the law of God. Yet, the deception is, carnality may pray, may go to church, may fast, may tithe, may preach, may exhort, and may even go to the mission field. The Pharisees did all of this, yet, it is they who plotted the death of Jesus.

On the outside, carnality can make itself look religiously beautiful, like a white sepulcher. Yet, within, it can be full of dead men's bones. Within, it can be full of resentments, strife, hate, pride, idolatry, and adultery, which are, according to Jesus, as bad as murder.

Oh, *"The heart is deceitful above all things, and desperately wicked: who can know it?"* (Jer. 17:9). Can you see, then, why carnality must be crucified before we can obey, before we will obey, and before the Holy Spirit can and will lead us?

"My gracious Lord, You know my heart. Please open it up to me, so that I may rightly and thoroughly confess my sins and forsake them. Deliver me from deception, grant me strength to crucify the flesh, and lead me by Thy precious Spirit. Amen."

Born in Prayer

———

...behold, he prayeth.

—Acts 9:11

"Behold, he prayeth." That was not only a statement of fact concerning Paul's present activity at the street called Straight, but it was the description of his entire walk with God.

In the introduction to each of Paul's epistles, he alludes, without fail, to prayer for the saints of God. *"Behold, he prayeth,"* are only three words, and yet they constitute almost the entire life of the apostle Paul. Let us recall some of Paul's declarations concerning prayer: *"For God is my witness...that without ceasing I make mention of you always in my prayers"* (Rom. 1:9); *"For this cause we also...do not cease to pray for you"* (Col. 1:9); *"Night and day praying exceedingly that we might see your face, and might perfect that which is lacking in your faith"* (1 Thess. 3:10).

If a plaque could be hung on the walls of time depicting the life of Paul, it would best be inscribed with the words, *"behold, he prayeth."* Metaphorically speaking, this apostle, from the beginning of his ministry at the street called Straight, to the end, spent his Christian life on his knees.

Preacher, is prayer the mark of your life? Sunday school teacher, is this what your students know you by? Seminary professor, are your lectures more the product of your time alone with God than of your study after man? Businessman, are your decisions born in the closet of prayer? Housewife, are you praying your children into the kingdom of God? *"Behold, he prayeth."* Let this be the epitaph of your life.

You, Too, Can Hear

———∽᷒᷒᷒———

And the Lord said unto him, Arise, and
go into the street which is called Straight, and
enquire in the house of Judas for one called
Saul, of Tarsus: for, behold, he prayeth.

—Acts 9:11

*"**A**nd the Lord said unto him..."* God spoke to Ananias, a disciple of Jesus at Damascus, as he spoke to Moses, Elijah, Jeremiah, and Daniel. God spoke. Ananias, to the best of our knowledge, was not a prophet, an apostle, or even a pastor. Ananias was an ordinary disciple, perhaps just like you and me.

So, let us ask these questions: Since Ananias could hear the voice of God, is there any reason why we should not hear His voice as well? Since Ananias could live by Jesus' voice, why can't we? Were these words of Jesus meant for the first century Christians only, or for all Christians to come: *"...for they* [His sheep] *know his voice"* (John 10:4)?

Truly, there are many pastors who say emphatically that we now have the written Word and that God no longer speaks to us through the Holy Spirit. But, if you ask that pastor why he married his wife, he will say, "The Lord told me." You ask him why he came to this church, and he will say, "The Lord told me." You ask him why he wants to build a larger sanctuary, and he will say, "The Lord told me." If we believe that God ceased speaking to man by His Spirit at the close of the apostolic age, then let us never say again, "The Lord told me," because we contradict ourselves.

Instead, let us realize that in the very written Word we revere so much, Jesus spoke concerning all of us, *"And other sheep I have, which are not of this fold: them also I must bring, and they shall hear my voice"* (John 10:16). May we all hear His voice today and follow Him.

Hearing God's Voice

For this people's heart is waxed gross,
and their ears are dull of hearing.

—Matthew 13:15

Well, my friend, may I prove to you that you have heard the voice of Jesus at least once? Does not Jesus say in Revelation 3:20, *"Behold, I stand at the door, and knock: if any man hear my voice, and open the door, I will come in to him, and will sup with him, and he with me"?*

Every person born of God has heard the voice of Jesus, but not necessarily His audible voice. Nonetheless, Jesus speaks to the heart in that still small voice which Moses heard in days of old, saying to us, "I am calling you. Let me come into your heart."

Yes, all of His sheep hear His voice at least once in the very beginning of their journey with God. But, then, consider the last part of verse 20, *"and will sup with him* [have fellowship with Him], *and he with me."*

How do we have fellowship? What is the essence of fellowship? Is it conversation, hearing, and speaking?

After conversion, if we immediately begin to deny Self and obey the Lord, fellowship with Him will begin to follow, and we will then continue to hear His voice. But, if we cease to obey, our hearts will wax gross, and our ears will become dull of hearing.

The Heart to Ear Connection

━━◌◟◍◟◍◌━━

But blessed are your eyes, for they see:
and your ears, for they hear.

—Matthew 13:16

What caused the disciples to see and to hear, and why did the multitudes neither see nor hear? The answer is that the multitudes had many things in their hearts that prevented them from seeing and hearing.

In verse 15, Jesus said that people's hearts were waxed gross—that is, dull—and therefore, they could not hear. Hence, in the spiritual world, hearing impairment is a result of a spiritual heart disease because there is a heart to ear connection. Jesus said that their *"heart is waxed gross, and their ears are dull of hearing"* (Matt. 13:15). There were many things in the hearts of the people that prevented them from hearing: criticism, complaints, and murmuring, to mention a few.

Do you remember how everyone murmured when Jesus went to eat with the tax collector, Zacchaeus? Luke 19:7 says, *"...they all murmured."* If we have the slightest bit of criticism or a faultfinding, judgmental spirit toward any one person, we violate the law of love, our heart is waxed gross, and our ears become dull of hearing. If we are not consistently denying Self and forsaking all, we also will be prevented from hearing the voice of Jesus.

In the Parable of the Great Supper, Jesus said, *"And they all with one consent began to make excuse"* (Luke 14:18). None of them came because they had not denied Self and inwardly forsaken all in order to clearly perceive the significance of Jesus' call. And this, in turn, led to excuses.

So, my friend, let us ask Jesus to crucify and to cleanse all iniquities out of our hearts, so that we might begin to hear, even as the apostles heard.

God Has Favorites

-⊸⊸⊸∰⟦⟧⟦⟧∰⊶⊶⊶-

Now Israel loved Joseph more than all his
children, because he was the son of his old age:
and he made him a coat of many colours.

—Genesis 37:3

Indeed, it is true that God is no respecter of persons, as we see in Acts 10:34 and James 2:9. But this doctrine must not be stretched beyond its intent. These verses mean only that God does not treat anyone unfairly, nor does He favor people because of wealth, education, popularity, or bloodline.

But, God does have His favorites. And His favorites are generally those who favor Him. God favored Joseph because Joseph favored God. Joseph favored God more than any of his brothers. Israel (Jacob) knew it, and so did God, and thus, the coat of many colors. Consequently, the envy of Joseph's brothers certainly proved that they were far from God, even so far as to contemplate the murder of their brother.

Yes, God treats everyone differently, according to their response to Him. To the Pharisees, Jesus gave sharp rebukes. The multitudes who followed just for the loaves and fishes, Jesus chided. Those who would not forsake all, He rejected, but those who forsook all, He favored. Then He favored Peter, James, and John over the rest, and it was the disciple, John, who went down into history as the one *"whom Jesus loved"* (John 13:23).

Let us not get trapped in this false doctrine that Jesus treats everyone the same. He treats everyone fairly in their relationship and in their response to Him. And all those who are born of Him will also have their favorites, yet, without being cliquish. There are special relationships that are divinely ordained to accomplish God's special purposes.

Legalism Versus Discipline

Praying always with all prayer and supplication
in the Spirit, and watching thereunto with all
perseverance and supplication for all saints.

—Ephesians 6:18

Imagine the discipline it took for Paul to pray *"always."* Paul had to make time for prayer. He had to fight the battle against sleepiness, exhaustion, doubts, disappointments, human expectations, and coldness of spirit, just as you and I have to fight to get to prayer. If a man determines to stick to a diet, do not call it legalism—call it discipline and conquest. If a man determines to pray so many hours each week, let us not call it legalism—let us call it a yearning for Christ's kingdom to come. If a man witnesses at every opportunity—let us not call it legalism, but let us call it a passion for lost souls.

The difference between legalism and discipline is simply this: in legalism, you become a slave to a system, a method or a program. This was the problem with the Pharisees. But in sanctified, Christian discipline, you choose to become a slave to a Master. This kind of discipline, rather than imprisoning us, sets us free. Hence, George Matheson writes, "Make me a captive Lord, And then I shall be free; Force me to render up my sword, And I shall conqueror be."5 So in Christianity, we cannot choose whether we want to be slaves or not, but we can choose whether we want to be captive to systems and methods or to the King of kings. Hence, after Paul left the pharisaical system, he joined the armed services of the King of kings and admonished Timothy to do likewise, by saying, *"Thou therefore endure hardness, as a good soldier of Jesus Christ"* (2 Tim. 2:3).

Friend, only the disciplined become conquerors, and the discipline of prayer is the most noble, the most effective, and the most important discipline in the conquest of evil.

A Man Versus Men

*And I sought for a man among them, that
should make up the hedge, and stand in the
gap before me...but I found none.*

—Ezekiel 22:30

Men look for men, but God looks for a man. God looks for a man among men. God looked for a man who could make up the gap, a man who would prevent the unleashing of His wrath upon mankind—but He found none. That which could have prevented the destruction of Israel, the final deportation of the Jews from Jerusalem to Babylon, was one man. One man, the right man among the many wrong men.

The architects of religion and the institutions of religion of the sixth century B.C. could not produce one man who could stand in the gap to make up the hedge to save a nation. They could produce masses of worshippers but not one man good enough, holy enough, consecrated enough, to stop disaster. Just think of it, that in all of the over one million religious people, there was not one who met God's standards as intercessor, as a savior of a nation, whose heart was perfect toward Him.

Oh, can you see why I said religious leaders look for men, for masses of worshipers, but God looks for a man? *"And I sought for a man."* Think of the power that one man can have with God. We see this with Moses as he prayed and reasoned with God not to destroy Israel. And God did not destroy her. So, as Moses saved Israel in his day, God looked for another Moses in the days of Ezekiel, but He found none.

Let us volunteer to become the man God is looking for.

The Perish Theology

Shadrach, Meshach, and Abednego, answered...
If it be so, our God whom we serve is able to deliver us
from the burning fiery furnace, and he will deliver
us out of thine hand, O king.

—Daniel 3:16–17

Shadrach, Meshach, and Abednego are wonderful examples of the perish theology: willing to perish while upholding the truth. Whenever the church has an accommodation theology—compromising the truth to make one's life more comfortable—she is as salt that has lost its savor. God is looking for men who fear Him more than they fear bankruptcy, hunger, poverty, persecution, prison, and death. Shadrach, Meshach, and Abednego were such men.

These three feared God enough not to fear man. Oh, how great is such a fear of the Lord? The fear of the Lord is the beginning of wisdom. It is to depart from evil, and it is our strong confidence, a fountain of life, a great treasure, and our rock and salvation. If we fear man, we shall die spiritually; but if we fear God, we shall live forever.

Oh, how much fear of man lies within us? Among those large multitudes of Jewish worshippers in the days of Daniel, only three opted for the perish theology. The rest of them chose the theology of accommodation. The former was born out of the fear of God, and the latter born out of the fear of man.

How this reminds us of Jesus' days upon the earth. *"Howbeit no man spake openly of him for fear of the Jews"* (John 7:13). Many of the Pharisees believed on him, but they did not confess him, lest they be put out of the synagogue (John 12:42).

Oh, this dreadful fear of man. What all does it keep us from, and what awful things does it lead us to?

They All Murmured

—⊸◖◗⊷—

And when they saw it, they all murmured,
saying, That he was gone to be guest
with a man that is a sinner.

—Luke 19:7

The people of Jericho murmured because Jesus ate with Zacchaeus. The children of Israel murmured against Moses, and Paul attributes the premature death of these Israelites to a murmuring spirit when he warns us all from 1 Corinthians 10:10, *"Neither murmur ye, as some of them also murmured, and were destroyed of the destroyer."*

Then there were some that murmured against the woman who anointed Jesus for His burial, and, further, there were the Pharisees who murmured against the disciples because they associated with the publicans. Again, think of those strong words concerning the murmurers in the wilderness, of whom it is said that they *"were destroyed of the destroyer."* Or consider these words concerning them: *"...whose carcases fell in the wilderness"* (Heb. 3:17).

These murmurers were walking carcasses! They were dead before they fell to the ground. Because they ate manna from heaven and drank water out of the rock to the very last days of their lives, an autopsy would have revealed no malfunction of any of their vital organs. Yet, they fell in the wilderness as a result of their murmuring.

May we see how much God hates a murmuring spirit. All in Jericho murmured except for Zacchaeus, whom everyone thought to be the worst sinner. Yes, the murmuring spirit causes us to see the best man as the worst, and the worst as the best. No wonder Paul admonishes us to *"Do all things without murmurings..."* (Phil. 2:14).

Indeed, as murmuring turns us into spiritual carcasses, so a murmurless heart will bring Jesus into our homes and churches.

Rahab in the Abbey

*By faith the harlot Rahab perished not with
them that believed not, when she had
received the spies with peace.*
—Hebrews 11:31

How this harlot ever got to be in the eleventh chapter of Hebrews is a wonder to many scholars. After all, the well-known and oft-quoted Hebrews 11 is called the Westminster Abbey of the Bible. In Westminster Abbey, the English buried their famous ones, such as their kings, and their finest playwrights, poets, and warriors.

I believe Rahab entered the Westminster Abbey of the Bible because she had a rock-solid faith. This pagan harlot was the only Canaanite of her time who, upon hearing the reports about Israel, believed them enough to risk her life to help and encourage God's messengers. The moment that Rahab took these messengers into her house, she counted her life less than theirs. Hence, Rahab followed Queen Esther in her thinking when she said, *"if I perish, I perish"* (Esther 4:16). This perish theology seeks nothing for itself but everything for God.

All the Canaanites fainted because of what God had done to Israel's enemies. But fainting without repentance is of no avail with God. We must repent, for the fear of God without repentance is incomplete and fruitless. To fear God and His judgment without a willingness to surrender to His will, even "fearing unto fainting," is a fear without faith, and it leaves God no option but to execute His wrath as He did on Jericho.

Let us "fear unto repentance," and there will be a place for us in God's Westminster Abbey.

145

Glory!

But we all, with open face beholding as in a
glass the glory of the Lord, are changed into the
same image from glory to glory, even as
by the Spirit of the Lord.

—2 Corinthians 3:18

Glory is that which causes to you say, "I'll know it when I see it." We know glory when we see it because glory has many faces, and it is always altogether "other." Glory has one face in the golden twilight of a sunrise and another in the crimson red of the sunset. It has one face in the sound of Händel's Messiah, and it has yet another in the cricket's violin concert. Glory is beauty, and if it doesn't cause you to be stunned or to lose your breath or to shout "Glory!" in your heart or aloud in praise, it is not glory.

Glory is the greatest weapon the church has against unbelief. The early church, as seen in the book of Acts, had glory. The virgin church convinced the pagan world that God was in Christ, reconciling sinful man with God. For the Jew and Greek to believe that, they had to see the glory in God's people, and they did.

But this glory soon left the infant church because the doctrinal pillars of self-denial and childlike trust were broken down. When these pillars were lost, men no longer saw the glory in the church, and the church became disgusting to them.

Jesus will come for a glorious church, a church that does not have a wrinkle, spot, blemish, or any such thing. When He comes, He will come with a shout of the Archangel that will resound around the globe. Glory!

To behold God's glory is the end of all of man's searching. It will resolve all his questions, longings, and fears. It is the fulfillment of all his desires.

United Prayer

*For where two or three are
gathered together in my name, there
am I in the midst of them.*

—Matthew 18:20

From personal experience, I know of nothing more difficult to conduct successfully than a corporate prayer meeting.
Yet, on the other hand, nothing is more important than
corporate prayer for the church, for the growth of the
believer, and for the coming of the kingdom of God.

It was not 120 persons, each praying individually in their
prayer closets, that brought the outpouring of the Holy Spirit
on Pentecost. Rather, it was 120 persons praying together
in one place and in one accord, for ten straight days, that
caused the Spirit to come from the throne of our glorified
Lord.

To have prayer in one place and in one accord is the goal
every pastor should strive for. Without it, his church will
be as a severely stunted tree, barren of most of the fruit it
would otherwise bear.

The devil does not want united prayer. He knows that
there is power when two or three come together in Jesus'
name. This united "prayer power" that brought Pentecost
is the same power that made the lame man to walk at the
gate Beautiful, that caused hundreds to be healed in the
shadow of Peter, and that delivered the apostles out of
prison. Now, can you see why Jesus and the Holy Spirit
always sent out two men together that there might be two
or three praying together with power?

Oh, friend, the devil would much prefer that we preach,
conduct Bible studies, and hold missions conferences, rather
than that we pray together. Let us renew our effort to meet
with someone regularly for prayer. Jesus will be right there
with us.

May 25

Let God Choose

*And the rib, which the Lord God had taken
from man, made he [built He into] a woman,
and brought her unto the man.*

—Genesis 2:22

Genesis is the book of beginnings, and Genesis is the book of patterns. In this book, God lays down the pattern for worship, for work, for rest, for morality, for love, for marriage, and for the family.

Let me ask you, how many dates did Adam have with Eve before he knew that she was the right one for him? Again, let me ask, how much input did God request from Adam as to what he wanted in a woman? Did God ask Adam what type of disposition, hair color, personal interests, height, and weight he wanted in a wife?

God made Eve, and He brought her unto Adam! That is the first symphony in man's history of the marriage song. Could it be any more beautiful than that? Isn't God still able to do this, and to do it right? Can't God still be trusted to bring a faithful soul a mate? Or has He lost His touch and interest in bringing a man and woman together?

Indeed, God still has an interest in choosing a wife for a man, but man so often makes his own choice out of personal interests, physical attraction, and worldly wisdom. How pitiful is this dating process in America; a young man trying this girl and that girl, and then another girl, to see which best pleases the dreams and aspirations of his Self-life; always leaving behind tears of disappointment and a broken heart.

Since we are born of the Spirit, and if we walk in the Spirit, indeed, we will do as Adam did: we will wait for God to choose for us. We will stop dating relationships that lead nowhere, and we will trust God that He will do as He did at the first with Adam, that He will bring the right one to each of us.

Higher and Wider

*For my thoughts are not your thoughts,
neither are your ways my ways, saith the Lord.*
—Isaiah 55:8

We know that Jesus took on human nature, but His Father never did and never will. Therefore, because the Father is void of humanity, His thoughts are not our thoughts, neither are His ways our ways. *"God is a Spirit: and they that worship him must worship him in spirit and in truth"* (John 4:24). All of God's ways spring out of the Spirit.

God has no limits in space, time, or power. He is everywhere. He can do all things. To Him, yesterday and tomorrow are today, because He is the great I AM. God knows everything that ever happened and that will ever happen. So, all God's judgments and thoughts reach beyond the realm of the human, the earthly, and the transient. Surely, the Psalmist was right when he said, *"thou art from everlasting"* (Ps. 93:2).

So, dear ones, don't fret; don't become impatient. God is God. He is Lord over all. He is eternal, knowing and seeing all things. He is all-powerful, the ever present friend. How beautiful the words of Walter C. Smith in the hymn *Immortal, Invisible, God Only Wise.* The second stanza reads:

Unresting, unhasting, and silent as light,
Nor wanting, nor wasting, Thou rulest in might;
Thy justice like mountains high soaring above
Thy clouds which are fountains of goodness and love.[6]

Yes, indeed, God's ways and thoughts are higher than ours, yea, much higher than the heavens above.

He Can Be Touched

———⟨⟨⟨⟨∫⟩⟩⟩⟩———

*For we have not an high priest which cannot be
touched with the feeling of our infirmities; but was in
all points tempted like as we are, yet without sin.*

—Hebrews 4:15

As we learned yesterday, God the Father is Spirit, He has
never experienced humanity, and He never will. But Jesus
took on our bone, flesh, and blood. He became all man,
although always remaining all God.

Jesus became our High Priest, who was and is touched
to this very day by our infirmities. Being omniscient, God
can know how we feel, but Jesus can feel how we feel, having been human. That is the difference between the Father
and the Son.

God knows our temptations, but Jesus has experienced
them to the innermost depth of His being. He was tempted
in all things such as we are. For, you see, divinity does not
get tempted, but humanity does.

God has never experienced physical pain, but His Son
felt the thorns in His brow, the whip upon His back, and the
nails in His feet and hands. God never tasted death, but
Jesus did. The Father never experienced loneliness, but
Jesus did. God has always been surrounded by the praises
of the angels, but Jesus felt forsaken and cried on the cross,
"My God, my God, why hast thou forsaken me?" (Mark 15:34).
God was never tired, weary, or hungry, but Jesus experienced all of these lassitudes.

Aren't we grateful for this great High Priest, Jesus? For
He knows our infirmities, and we can touch Him with them,
and He, then, will touch the Father on our behalf.

Fiery Trials

⎯⎯⎯⎯⎯

*Beloved, think it not strange concerning
the fiery trial which is to try you, as though
some strange thing happened unto you.*

—1 Peter 4:12

The mature Christian thinks *"it not strange concerning the fiery trials."* He knows he must go through much tribulation to enter the kingdom of God. To him, as to Job, *"affliction cometh not forth of the dust, neither doth trouble spring out of the ground; Yet man is born unto trouble, as the sparks fly upward"* (Job. 5:6–7).

Whether our tribulation is set in motion by God, man, or the devil, the saint has learned to glory in it, *"knowing that tribulation worketh patience; And patience, experience; and experience, hope: And hope maketh not ashamed; because the love of God is shed abroad in our hearts by the Holy Ghost which is given unto us"* (Rom. 5:3–5). The consecrated heart can say, *"Nay, in all these things we are more than conquerors through him that loved us"* (8:37).

The Christian warrior lives under the protective umbrella of God's care where all things always, in His time, work together for good. In that place, no tribulation will ever come his way without divine consent or hidden blessing, whether it be cancer, accidents, poverty, or whatever.

So, nothing, absolutely nothing, can happen to God's true servant unless it is God's permissive or directive will. Hence, for him, every suffering redounds to God's glory. Every tribulation for him will work to the refining of the soul so that it might be more like Jesus.

Therefore, my dear friend, if you suffer, don't let the devil buffet you. Don't think it a strange thing. God is in it, as He was with Christ in His sufferings. And when the last page of your life is closed, He will meet you at heaven's gate with, *"Well done, thou good and faithful servant...enter thou into the joy of thy lord"* (Matt. 25:21).

Two Opinions

*But Joshua the son of Nun, and Caleb
the son of Jephunneh, which were of the
men that went to search the land, lived still.*

—Numbers 14:38

*Behold, the Lord thy God hath set the land
before thee: go up and possess it.*

—Deuteronomy 1:21

At Kadesh-barnea, where Israel was to enter Canaan, God separated those who would go by opinion from those who would go by revelation. Ten of the men who were sent to spy out the land came back with the opinion that the conquest of Canaan by Israel was impossible. Two of the twelve spies came back, reminding Israel of the revelation of God, *"go up and possess"* the land.

The viewing of the land by the twelve was not to discourage Israel but to encourage them concerning that which the Lord their God would do if they would only believe. But the majority of the Jews sided with the ten spies who made the condition of entering or not entering a matter of their own personal opinion.

Oh, how dangerous is man's opinion. Because opinion triumphed over revelation at Kadesh-barnea, more than six hundred thousand Israelites were buried in the sands of the wilderness on the wrong side of Jordan. They were buried there because of their unbelief. The book of Hebrews called them "carcasses" even before they were dead.

Dear ones, Jesus wants you to enter into sanctification and the victorious life. He desires that you overcome as you look upon the giants and the walls in your path. Don't faint. Don't be unbelieving. Remember that your "giant," the omnipotent God, is greater than all the giants of the world put together. Don't go by the opinions of man but by the revelation of God.

A Common Root System

And there went great multitudes with him:
and he turned, and said unto them, If any man
come to me, and hate not his father, and mother,
and wife, and children, and brethren, and sisters,
yea, and his own life also, he cannot be my disciple.
And whosoever doth not bear his cross, and
come after me, cannot be my disciple.

—Luke 14:25–27

Here, we learn that Judaism and Christianity have the same root system. This is not surprising since both faiths were born out of the same divine light.

When God called Abraham to be the father of Israel, He asked him to forsake his country and all his kindred. He would take him to a land he knew nothing of. Jesus asked the multitude to do the same—to forsake all earthly attachments and enter into a new country, the country of the kingdom of God. What marvelous parallels, and what profound principals are in the making of His people that would fully belong to God.

Furthermore, God told Abraham *"Get thee out of thy country, and from thy kindred...unto a land that I will shew thee"* (Gen. 12:1). Abraham could only find this country as he followed the Lord step by step. So we, too, as the redeemed by the blood of the Lamb, can only find our country of God's perfect will by following Jesus, step by step.

Yes, the Jew and the Christian may have grown far apart in their many "add-on" doctrines, but it was not so in the beginning of their faith.

Radical, Yet Righteous

*The judgments of the Lord are
true and righteous altogether.*

—Psalm 19:9

We must abandon our false, wishful perception that God is a smooth, political operator. God is righteous and true, and so are His judgments. That God can be "smooth" is not in question, but that God can be radical in His righteousness is also displayed clearly on the pages of the Bible.

Just consider the following dealings of God, and be amazed with His radical nature. God destroyed a whole civilization in Noah's day by drowning (Gen. 6–7). That was radical. God's plan to destroy the righteous with the wicked at Sodom was only amended by the intercession of Abraham (Gen. 18:16–33). That was radical. The earth opened up and swallowed those who opposed Moses (Num. 16). That was radical. God commanded that Achan and his family be stoned for having taken Babylonian loot (Josh. 7). That was radical. The waters churned and roared, putting many souls in jeopardy just because one man, Jonah, disobeyed God (Jonah 1). That was radical. Jesus said, if thy right hand offend thee, cut it off, and unless we forsake all we have, we cannot be His disciples (Matt. 5:30; Luke 14:33). That is radical!

All of these passages indicate that God in His righteousness is also radical. And the word "radical" comes from the Latin *radic*, meaning center or root. A radical person is centered or rooted in something. Hence, all those centered in God through Christ will also have a radical mindset. As the plan of redemption was radical, necessitating the murder of the Son of God, so will be the consummation of the age. God is indeed radical, yet His judgments *"are true and righteous altogether."*

A Line in the Sand

*...so shall we be separated, I and thy people, from
all the people that are upon the face of the earth.*
—Exodus 33:16

Here, Moses speaks of a great separation. God can do nothing without separation. While man compromises and accommodates, God is the great separator.

Some of God's first deeds were deeds of separation. He separated the light from the darkness and the water from the land.

As He began the creation of the universe with separation, so He began the creation of a nation unto Himself with separation. He said to Abraham, *"Get thee out of thy country, and from thy kindred"* (Gen. 12:1).

God placed the principle of separation in the middle of the Bible, in the first lines of our best devotional literature, *"Blessed is the man that walketh not in the counsel of the ungodly, nor standeth in the way of sinners, nor sitteth in the seat of the scornful"* (Ps. 1:1).

Jesus came, turned to the multitudes, and said, *"If any man come to me, and hate not his father, and mother, and wife, and children, and brethren, and sisters, yea, and his own life also, he cannot be my disciple"* (Luke 14:26).

The Bible ends with separation of the just from the unjust. All of God's judges, prophets, and apostles were called to be watchmen over this separation. And whenever the lines of separation became blurred, the church lost purity and power. Indeed, there is a line of separation drawn into the sands of time from Genesis through Revelation. Whenever that line is erased, God's people lose their vision of the knowledge of the holy, and the watchmen begin to give forth an uncertain sound.

Surely, the doctrine of separation is the first doctrine of God, and any theology not based upon this premise is as salt that has lost its savor.

Burdens Become Blessings

———⟨≈⟩———

*Unto the woman he said, I will greatly multiply thy
sorrow and thy conception; in sorrow thou shalt bring
forth children; and thy desire shall be to thy
husband, and he shall rule over thee.*

—Genesis 3:16

"...he shall rule over thee." There is always a consequence
of sin. Sin always produces losses, scars, and regrets, and
never makes a winner. Prior to the Fall, man did not rule
over woman, neither did woman rule over man. There was
perfect love and understanding.

Using Paul's words, we can assume that Adam and Eve
were *"perfectly joined together in the same mind and in the
same judgment"* (1 Cor. 1:10), but then, with sin, there came
division and disorder. Adam wanted one thing and Eve
another. And so, to prevent anarchy, God said to Eve, *"and
he shall rule over thee."* So here we have the first call to
submission of one person to another. Eve's submission to
Adam became a constant reminder of her having been
deceived (1 Tim. 2:14). It became a burden to be borne by
the woman.

But then, finally, through the work of Christ, what had
been a negative picture and curse on the woman, now
became a beautiful picture of blessing. Through Christ, the
woman's submission to her husband has come to be a
picture of the church's submission to Christ.

Now, a wife obeying her husband in everything is a glorious picture of Christ's bride submitting joyfully to the
lordship of Jesus. Oh, praise the Lord for our wonderful
Savior who can turn night into day, disgrace into grace,
shame into blessing, sorrow into joy, and loss into gain.

Yes, sin has its consequences, but Jesus can take the bitterness and stain out of it and liberate you from the failures
of the past *"to present you faultless before the presence of
his glory with exceeding joy"* (Jude 24).

Too Many Questions

Master, we have toiled all the night,
and have taken nothing: nevertheless
at thy word I will let down the net.

—Luke 5:4–5

During His earthly ministry, Jesus did not choose one single Pharisee to be an apostle. Most Pharisees, no doubt, had godly, honest aspirations as they entered their religious training, but upon graduation, they had become specialists in the fine art of analyzation. Every time they met Jesus, they confronted Him with questions. "Who gave you authority?" "Why do you break the Sabbath?" "Why do your disciples not wash themselves?" "Why did Moses allow a writing of divorcement?" "Why?" "Why?" "Why?"

If we have too many questions, we will never *"become as little children"* (Matt. 18:3). A questioning and reasoning heart will have no place in the kingdom of heaven. Only a trusting, childlike, and obedient heart will keep Christ indwelling. Jesus found such a heart in Peter, a man uneducated, uncultured, and unseasoned.

Peter was exhausted and discouraged after a long night of unsuccessful fishing. He was in one of his first meetings with Jesus, who asked him to go out again and to cast his net on the right side of the boat. It is a marvel that there was no question with Peter of his new acquaintance, such as who are you and what do you know about fishing. There was only a childlike trust which brought in the catch of his life. Oh, what the Pharisees could have caught had they only reduced their "whys" to the bare necessities!

God always works through trust and obedience, for the kingdom operates not by reason nor by intellect. No wonder Jesus said, speaking of His simple, uneducated apostles, *"I thank thee, O Father,...because thou hast hid these things from the wise and prudent, and hast revealed them unto babes"* (Matt. 11:25).

Coming to the Last "Why?"

*And it came to pass on a certain day, as he was
teaching, that there were Pharisees and doctors of
the law sitting by, which were come out of every town
of Galilee, and Judea, and Jerusalem: and the
power of the Lord was present to heal them.*

—Luke 5:17

Peter, on his first day alone with Jesus, had come to the last "why" concerning who this Nazarene was. It brought him to the catch of his life. He caught so much fish that the nets began to break, and the ship began to sink.

The Pharisees and lawyers never came to their last "why" concerning this Galilean carpenter. Consequently, they never came to the catch of their lives. In fact, they never caught a single "fish" because they continued to question the Son of God. Oh, what could they have received had they only turned their doubts into childlike faith?

Here, in Capernaum, for example, the power of the Lord was present to heal them all. For some of them, the catch of their lives was waiting here. But none of them were healed because they came to question Him rather than to believe in Him.

Dear questioner, what all have you missed in your life because you were never satisfied with the answer Jesus gave you? You have too often said, "This is my last question. When this is answered, I shall rest and believe," but you, up to this day, are neither resting nor believing—you continue to question.

Oh, what misery, what loss of blessings and loss of abounding fruits is theirs who never come to their last "why." Could you get on your knees today and just come to your last "why" and believe and follow from henceforth? Do it, and you, too, shall have a good catch.

A "We" Religion

*And hath put all things under his feet, and gave him
to be the head over all things to the church, Which is
his body, the fulness of him that filleth all in all.*
—Ephesians 1:22–23

Here, we have the head to body relationship as it relates to Christ and the church. One of the historical divisions between Roman Catholicism and Protestantism is that the former has always emphasized that there is no salvation outside the body (the church), and the latter that there is no salvation outside of Christ. Of course, both are right, and both are so much the more right when they accept each other's theology. Theologically speaking, as there is no bodiless Christ, there is no headless church.

Therefore, my friend, if you belittle the body, you belittle the head. If you separate yourself from the body, you separate yourself from the head. If you don't love the body, you don't love the head, for John said, *"By this shall all men know that ye are my disciples, if ye have love one to another"* (John 13:35).

Christ's body is the only visible expression of Him in the world. It is both our acting alone and in concert with other Christians that paints a picture of Christ on the canvas of the human mind and heart. Now, is the picture our lives paint of Jesus a true or distorted image of Him?

At conversion, when we receive Christ, we are all grafted into His body. Therefore, our Lord taught us to pray, *"Our* Father" instead of *"My* Father"; "Deliver *us* from evil" instead of "Deliver *me* from evil"; and "lead *us* not into temptation" rather than "lead *me* not into temptation." From the beginning of the Christian life, we learn that Christianity does not and cannot exist in isolation. All those who belong to Him also belong one to another. So, true Christianity is never an "I" but always a "we" religion firmly joined to Christ the Head.

Spirit over Body

*For we must all appear before the judgment
seat of Christ; that every one may receive the
things done in his body, according to that he
hath done, whether it be good or bad.*

—2 Corinthians 5:10

It is impossible to come to spiritual maturity without mastery over the body, for the body controlled by its lust is enmity against God. Only the disciplined are conquerors. All men who succeed in any endeavor must first gain mastery over their bodies. This requires self-denial and discipline. There are no easy roads.

Those who lack self-control will be weak and irregular in prayer, in worship, in witnessing, in the control of the tongue, in the keeping of the heart, and in resisting temptation. The mastery over the body also includes restraint with food and money. Mastery gives us courage to say yes and no at the right times.

Those who lack self-control will be full of excuses, and they will have difficulty keeping promises to men and to God. The more we become acquainted with Christ in the school of prayer, the more we see that subduing the body is part of the way to freedom. That is why Paul said, *"But I keep under my body, and bring it into subjection"* (1 Cor. 9:27). Think of it!

We shall be judged by the things done in the body! For the body is the temple of the Holy Spirit, and he who defiles this temple shall himself be destroyed. Therefore, victorious Christian living is simply—spirit over body.

The World Is Not Fair, but God Is Good

———⚭⚭⚭———

And they took him, and cast him into a pit:
and the pit was empty, there was no water in it.
—Genesis 37:24

Now, in this passage, we find Joseph, the boy, being cast into a pit. From man's perspective, it was a pit of rejection, of loneliness, of despair, of punishment, and of darkness. But from God's perspective, the picture looked different. From God's view, this was a pit of preparation and deliverance. From God's view, it was the first steppingstone into a bright future for a young boy.

The pit for Joseph became God's means to get him to Egypt to deliver both Egypt and Israel from physical famine, and, in the end, the world from spiritual darkness and despair. Israel was saved from extinction by starvation through Joseph's trip to Egypt, and because Israel was spared, a Savior for all men could be born into the world 1,700 years later. Joseph had to go through a pit experience 3,700 years ago so that you and I might come to know the Savior.

Yet, when Joseph was in the pit, he knew nothing of all this. All he knew was darkness, coldness, and rejection. But, in the midst of this, Joseph had an unfaltering faith to believe that, although the world was not fair, God is good. He held on to the unseen God that rules the universe, even against all the visible and invisible odds stacked against him.

Yes, indeed, it would be easier if God would tell us each time why we are in a pit. But His ways are higher than our ways, and He knows that our faith grows more quickly and stronger in the darkness and in the fire of affliction than in the light and in days of ease.

Sent and Sold

━━◅◦◦▹━━

He sent a man before them, even Joseph, who
was sold for a servant: Whose feet they
hurt with fetters: he was laid in iron.

—Psalm 105:17–18

Sent, sold, and placed in fetters is the commentary on the life of Joseph. There is so much that could have been said about the rise of this country boy to one of the most powerful dynasties of his time.

God looks at a man's success by looking at the inner development of that man rather than at his outward accomplishments. Success to God is not so much measured by what you do on the outside but what you let God do on the inside.

The first reason why Joseph was sent, then, was because he was a pure man. Sent men are pure men. Sent men are surrendered men. Sent men are tempered men. The fact that Joseph was sent is an indication that his inner spiritual constitution was right. So, Joseph was sent. No man could have delivered Egypt and Israel but a sent man whose inner life was pleasing to God.

Second, notice that Joseph could be sold by man and yet remain God's property. Joseph had the quality to become a slave without being enslaved. Joseph could become a slave in a pagan, idolatrous, and adulterous court without losing his vision and his intimacy with God.

Third, Joseph was laid in iron, but the chains on his feet and hands only put more iron into his soul, never to abandon his mission. He patiently waited upon God until his dreams were fulfilled.

Joseph was sent to be a deliverer for Israel. In order to reach that divine purpose, he had to be molded on the road of affliction. You may appear ready on the outside to be a deliverer, but are you fit on the inside to be one? Sent, sold, and placed in fetters was Joseph's story. Now, what is yours?

Sources of Power

—⊸⟪⟫⟫⟫⊶—

The king sent and loosed him; even the ruler of the people,
and let him go free. He made him lord of his house,
and ruler of all his substance: To bind his princes
at his pleasure; and teach his senators wisdom.
—Psalm 105:20–22

Joseph's journey to power came through God's highway of suffering. Pharaoh also had power, but his power was handed to him on a silver platter from his ancestors.

There is a difference between power that comes through man and power that comes from God. There is a difference between power that comes by self-assertion and power that comes from self-surrender. There is a difference between power that comes through manipulation and power that comes through the way of the cross. The former power is of the earth and is soon forgotten. It is full of glitter and pomp. But because it does not come from God, the persons exercising it are soon lost in the dust of history.

Notice that this pharaoh's name was never mentioned in the Bible. Well, what pharaoh's names are ever mentioned in the Bible? It is always pharaoh, pharaoh, pharaoh, but which pharaoh? Pharaoh is just the Egyptian name for king. In God's book, this pharaoh was *King Nobody*.

Friend, if we don't move in divine history, which is the road of suffering, the Calvary road, our names will be blotted out by the shifting sands of time. We will become nobodies. But if we are willing to suffer for Christ's sake and die, that Christ may be all in us and through us, our names will become new names, written on white stones in the Book of Life and on the twelve gates of the temple. Praise the Lord!

The Country Boy Becomes a Professor

...and teach his senators wisdom.

—Psalm 105:22

We learned yesterday that the power that Joseph had was of God, and the power that Pharaoh had (whichever pharaoh it was) was of man. Everything of man perishes with man, but everything of God lives on forever. Joseph's power over all of Pharaoh's substance (v. 21) came through suffering, and so did Joseph's wisdom.

Here, a slave, a foreigner, a country boy, came to teach Pharaoh's senators! No doubt, these senators had all gone to the top universities of Egypt. They were all *cum laude* graduates with doctor of philosophy minds. Yet, Joseph, the man from the wilderness, the man from the pit, the man who once was laid in iron, taught these senators wisdom.

He set up a classroom for them and gave lectures. What did he teach them? What was his textbook? What were his credentials? What degree had he earned, and what university had he attended? Well, my friend, he taught them about suffering, self-denial, and self-surrender as the road to wisdom, the wisdom that locks into the omniscient God. His textbook was life. His credentials were the scars on his back. His degree was the invisible smile of God's favor. His university was the school of obedience where he sought first the kingdom of God, keeping his heart with all diligence.

There he was, a slave in the beautiful lecture hall of Pharaoh's palace, teaching pagan senators the wisdom of Almighty God. Oh, what a picture.

OBEDIENCE: the Measure of Love

If ye love me, keep my commandments.

—John 14:15

Love and obedience are inseparable in the mind of God. Our love is measured by our obedience to a specific command of God. The rich young ruler knew the first and greatest commandment, yet, without a specific order, he could not measure himself against it. Jesus gave him that specific order when He said to him, *"sell whatsoever thou hast, and give to the poor"* (Mark 10:21).

It is easy for all of us to live under the illusion that we love God. However, it is the specific orders, the specific "thou shalts" that pull us out of our fantasies and make us face the real person that is inside of us. God gives "thou shalts" in the Ten Commandments. If we don't keep these laws, and what Jesus tells us in our hearts, we don't love God. Love revolves around the laws of obedience.

So, Jesus also measured the rich young ruler's love by the law, *"Do not commit adultery, Do not kill, Do not steal, Do not bear false witness, Defraud not, Honor thy father and mother"* (Mark 10:19). When the young man said that he had kept all these, Jesus measured him against the last of the Ten Commandments, *"Thou shalt not covet"* (Ex. 20:17). It is here where the young man fell, for he had many possessions. Love without obedience is not love. Again, it is our response to the specifics that are the measure of our love to God and man.

Let us stop measuring our love to God by attitude or feeling alone, for that can be deceptive. Instead, let us ask, "Did I obey God the last time He asked me to do something?" If I did, I know I love my Lord indeed.

OBEDIENCE: the Ultimate Sacrifice

*And Samuel said, Hath the Lord as great delight
in burnt offerings and sacrifices, as in obeying the voice
of the Lord? Behold, to obey is better than sacrifice,
and to hearken than the fat of rams.*

—1 Samuel 15:22

Obedience is better than sacrifice. Obedience is the ultimate in sacrifice. Obedience is the consistent crucifying of my Self-life so that the life of Christ may show forth, forever resounding to the glory of God.

The apostle says in Romans, *"I beseech you therefore, brethren, by the mercies of God, that ye present your bodies a living sacrifice, holy, acceptable unto God"* (12:1). That is obedience at its best. It is the presentation of one's whole being to God without vacation or variation.

But Saul became a classical demonstration of partial obedience, of a partial giving of oneself to God. God told Saul to utterly destroy all oxen, sheep, camels, and asses. However, Saul kept the best of the sheep and oxen. God did not want the best of the sheep and oxen; God only wanted the best of Saul. And because God never received Saul's best—his whole heart, soul, mind, and strength—he was rejected by God.

So also, the rich young ruler made a sacrifice of obedience unto the Lord (Matt. 19:16–24). But again, it was a partial sacrifice of obedience, translating only into a partial self-surrender. He kept five of the commandments and thought that would do, but Jesus took him to the tenth commandment. When examined by Jesus, the young man, like Saul, found himself unfit to be used of God.

Yes, indeed, obedience is better than sacrifice. Obedience is the ultimate sacrifice without which all other sacrifices become meaningless.

OBEDIENCE: the Key to Unity

If any man desires to do His will (God's pleasure),
he will know (have the needed illumination to recognize,
and can tell for himself) whether the teaching is from God
or whether I am speaking from Myself and of My
own accord and on My own authority.

—John 7:17 AMPLIFIED

Hallelujah! The only way the doctrinal confusion amongst the hundreds of denominations will be cleared up is by obedience to the will of God. For two thousand years, the church has had councils, seminars, workshops, and conferences to come to doctrinal unity. Yet, there are now more different doctrinal positions than ever before. When are we going to learn that consultations on church doctrine do not lead to oneness of belief?

Jesus said that *"If any man will do his will, he shall know"* (John 7:17), that is, he will know whether a doctrine is of God or of man, of the flesh or of the Spirit. Obedience is the key to divine truth. Without that key, it is as difficult to get to truth as it is to get into a bank vault. You take a Methodist, a Baptist, a Pentecostal, and a Lutheran and have them all do the will of God in perfect submission, and it won't be long until they will all preach the same message. This was the dream of Paul, and had he not believed it was possible, he would not have admonished his brethren that there would be no divisions among them and that they would be perfectly joined together in the same mind and spirit (1 Cor. 1:10).

Eternity will prove that nothing matters but the will of God. Therefore, finding and doing the will of God is our only obligation in life. That is the essence and the substance of Christianity. And doing the will of God will bring us into the unity that Jesus is praying for us to experience.

Cry Aloud!

...ten men that were lepers...stood afar off:
And they lifted up their voices, and said,
Jesus, Master, have mercy on us.

—Luke 17:12–13

So, the *"lepers...stood afar off."* That is what they had to do. It is not what they wanted to do. Leprosy is a heinous disease. It eats away at the extremities of the body, such as at the fingers, the toes, the nose, and the ears. It is infectious; hence, Jewish law demanded isolation from the community for anyone who was a leper. Lepers had to cup their hands over their mouths and shout, "Unclean, unclean, unclean" when someone was about to approach them.

Let me ask you, have you ever felt yourself standing afar off? Perhaps, for some of you, it is your sin that separates you from God; some terrible sin, such as fornication, adultery, or homosexuality. These are terrible sins, certainly causing man to stand afar off from God until repented of and forsaken.

Perhaps you are a praying saint, you have done all you know to do, but it seems it has been weeks and months since you felt God near and dear. You have prayed and fasted and wept, and yet heaven has remained like gates of brass to you. Oh, is there anyone among us who has not felt, at one time or another, *"afar off"*?

Well, my friend, I offer you this wonderful medicine that worked for the ten lepers: crying out aloud, or "hollering," again today. Lift up your voice and cry aloud for the mercies of God. As Jesus heard the earnest cry of the lepers and of blind Bartimaeus, so your Savior will surely hear you, if you do likewise.

Cain Had Nothing against God

*If a man say, I love God, and hateth his brother, he is
a liar: for he that loveth not his brother whom he hath
seen, how can he love God whom he hath not seen?*

—1 John 4:20

Getting along with God was no problem at all, as far as
Cain was concerned. Cain built an altar. Cain provided a
sacrifice, and Cain worshipped God. Cain had nothing
against God. His attitude toward God was entirely positive; however, it was his brother whom he resented.

Yet, it was partly this unloving attitude toward his
brother that caused God to reject his sacrifice. And since
his sacrifice was rejected, sin continued to dwell at Cain's
door (Gen. 4:7). His resentment turned into hate, and hate
turned into murder. The first sin committed outside of Paradise was man sinning against man, and God would not have
it. Consequently, God cursed Cain from the earth (Gen. 4:11).

Yes, you may think that there is nothing between you
and God, yet, if there is something between you and your
brother, behold God's attitude toward you. We need to seri-
ously examine our relationships with our fellow man. *"Leave
there thy gift before the altar, and go thy way; first be reconciled to thy brother, and then come and offer thy gift"* (Matt.
5:24).

The first sin in the garden was man getting into a wrong
relationship with God. The first sin outside the garden was
man getting into a wrong relationship with his brother. The
first sin made man a rebel, the second a murderer.

Be ye reconciled, one with another.

A Glaring Neglect

━━◦⊸☰☰\☊☰☰☰◦━━

*There was a certain rich man, which was clothed in
purple and fine linen, and fared sumptuously every day:
And there was a certain beggar named Lazarus, which was
laid at his gate, full of sores, And desiring to be fed with
the crumbs which fell from the rich man's table.*

—Luke 16:19–21

This story stands out because it is the only story in the
Gospels where we read about a specific man literally having gone to hell. Were this a parable, Jesus would not have
said a *certain* rich man, nor would He have given the poor
man a name. This story in the Bible tells us what hell is
like, and what may get us there.

No doubt, this certain rich man, having lived in a highly
religious society, had most of his religious pieces in the right
places of life's puzzle. But there was a glaring neglect, and
that neglect sent him to hell.

Some people have said that when we get to the gate of
heaven, the apostle Peter will ask us why he should let us
into heaven. If we give the right theological answer, we are
in; if not, we are out. But this story of the rich man and
Lazarus clearly suggests to us that on Judgment Day, practical, sacrificial compassion in Christianity is far more likely
to be tested than the right theological answer.

Perhaps we had best pay more attention to how we live;
for since this man went to hell because he neglected a poor,
righteous man, what makes us think that we can get into
heaven if we make the same mistake?

In this context, let us also remember Jesus' words of judgment in Matthew 25, *"Depart from me, ye cursed, into
everlasting fire...For I was an hungred,...I was thirsty,...I was
a stranger,...naked,...sick, and in prison...Verily I say unto
you, Inasmuch as ye did it not to one of the least of these, ye
did it not to me"* (vv. 41–46).

You Can Fly

————

*And said, Verily I say unto you, Except ye be
converted, and become as little children, ye shall
not enter into the kingdom of heaven.*

—Matthew 18:3

There are two wings that we need in salvation theology in order to fly into the kingdom of heaven. The long lost message of *conversion* was rediscovered during the great Reformation period. That takes care of wing number one: *"Except ye be converted."* There is another wing that takes us into the kingdom of heaven, and that is, *"become as little children."* We are born again to fly, and it takes two wings to do it.

One wing on a bird only leads to circular movement, going nowhere, no matter how much that bird thrashes about. It is impossible to get airborne into God's kingdom—into righteousness, peace, and joy; into that perfect and acceptable will of God—without the second wing.

Unfortunately, too many have hung their whole salvation doctrine on the conversion experience. Oh, my friend, there is so much more to go after and to discover. Conversion is a crisis experience, and a good one at that. It is an event of the moment, but it becomes history thereafter. However, "becoming as a little child" is an endless, ongoing process toward humility and dependence on God.

Oh, how very much becoming a little child goes against the grain of human nature, against our pride, which continually pushes us to be somebody, to accomplish something. Most likely, you have been converted, but have you learned to fly?

Socrates Was Looking for Christ

---

*Whosoever therefore shall humble
himself as this little child, the same is
greatest in the kingdom of heaven.*

—Matthew 18:4

Once the new life in Christ has begun at conversion, it is vital that the new convert start toward utter dependence upon God. This is the heart of the process of becoming *"as this little child."* We must come to that point as Jesus did when He said, *"The Son can do nothing of himself"* (John 5:19).

Socrates traveled throughout Greece looking for a man who knew he was nothing. It would seem that surely Jesus was the One for whom Socrates was searching, for he found that all other men thought themselves to be something. Yet, it is in nothingness that we touch the depths of the heart of God.

Yes, the greatest in the kingdom of God is the one who is the most childlike in trust, humility, and dependence. This is why Jesus said, *"he that is least among you all, the same shall be great"* (Luke 9:48).

Moses, the great statesman, educator, and scholar, needed forty years to travel from the point of thinking himself to be something to thinking himself to be nothing. It was when he reached that point of utter dependence upon God, that God could hire him and do anything and everything He wanted to do through his life. The chapter on Moses' life closes with the Lord speaking unto Moses face to face as a friend speaks unto a friend, and with the testimony that Moses was the meekest man on the face of the earth (Ex. 33:11; Num. 12:3).

Such testimony should inspire all of us to pursue childlike dependence and humility.

The Common Denominator

*And he gave some, apostles; and some, prophets;
and some, evangelists; and some, pastors and teachers;
For the perfecting of the saints, for the work of the
ministry, for the edifying of the body of Christ.*
—Ephesians 4:11–12

This verse refers to what is commonly called the fivefold ministry of the church: apostles, prophets, evangelists, pastors, and teachers. First, notice that there is diversity in this ministry, as Paul also states in 1 Corinthians 12:4–6. There are diversities of gifts, diversities of administrations, and diversities of operations. A teacher has a different function from a pastor. An evangelist has a different ministry than a prophet. Yet, despite these diversities, there is a common denominator. All of them, from apostles to teachers, are called for the purpose of perfecting the saints for the ministry.

Now, how hard do we work on perfecting the saints before we send them forth to minister? How well do our Bible colleges and seminaries prepare our ministers for the perfecting of the saints? Do we truly believe that it is possible to perfect a saint? These are questions to ponder. And perhaps, we are in such a hurry to save the world that the perfecting of the saint is only a theological afterthought.

Or perhaps we believe that once a person is saved that there is nothing left in him to be perfected. Oh, my friend, every minister in the fivefold ministry is called for the perfecting of the saints so that Christ might *"present it to himself a glorious church, not having spot, or wrinkle, or any such thing; but that it should be holy and without blemish"* (Eph. 5:27).

Prayer Is the Goal

————————

And he taught, saying unto them, Is it not written,
My house shall be called of all nations the house
of prayer? but ye have made it a den of thieves.

—Mark 11:17

Here, Jesus brings into focus the primary reason for the temple; not sacrifice or religious education, but prayer. That is not to say that the temple was not to be associated with education or sacrifice. Many times the Word of God was read and taught in the temple, and Jesus Himself frequently went into the temple to teach (Matt. 21:23). And sacrifices were to be made in the temple.

Yes, education and sacrifice were important, divinely ordained temple activities. However, both of these things must never overtake the place of prayer. Sacrifices and the reading of the Word were only means to get men into intimacy with God, but never ends in themselves. You hear the Word, and you meditate upon its truth. Then, you sacrifice in order to enter the Holy of Holies to commune with God. Yes, communion with God, coming into the presence of God, was the ultimate purpose of the temple. All else was the means to the end.

But Israel, like the church throughout the centuries, had made the means the end. She had made the Word and the atonement primary and put prayer and communion with God into the last place.

Is it not wonderful that when Jesus died on the cross, the veil of the Holy of Holies was rent in two, symbolizing the fact that from now on, all who love the Word and accept the sacrifice will have intimate communion with God, and even better and closer communion than the high priest had in the days of old?

The Word and the sacrifice are means, but prayer—intimate communion with God—is always the end goal.

Make Your Plans Tentative

*By faith Abraham, when he was called to go out into
a place which he should after receive for an inheritance,
obeyed; and he went out, not knowing whither he went.*

—Hebrews 11:8

When you enter the Spirit-filled life, you will become a
true child of Abraham. You will no longer know where you
are going. All your personal plans will become tentative,
for you are ever ready for the Master's bidding.

Abraham went out. He went out of a life governed by
Self and by circumstances into a life governed by obedient
faith in God. He surrendered "Self-government" for "God-
government." He surrendered his plans for God's plans. He
surrendered his will so that he could receive that *"good,
and acceptable, and perfect, will of God"* (Rom. 12:2).

Like Abraham, true saints of God operate by the inner
voice. *"For as many as are led by the Spirit of God, they are
the sons of God"* (Rom. 8:14). Being led by the Spirit is one
of the tests of our divine sonship. Religious institutions carefully and thoughtfully plan far ahead, but the early apostles
did not know where they would lay their heads the next
night. Their assignment to bring salvation to the world was
revealed just one step at a time.

So, the more closely we follow Jesus, the more unpredictable we are. Oh, it does not mean that we don't plan at
all. Yes, it is valid to plan to try out our oxen just bought or
our land just purchased. And it is good to plan to bury our
father. *But, whenever His invitation comes,* we must be
prepared to forget the oxen, the land, and the funeral to
enter into a feast with our Lord, which is His perfect will.
Abraham did not know where he was going, but he certainly
knew Who he was following, and that was good enough for
him. May it also be so for us.

The Fulness of God

*For out of His fullness (abundance) we
have all received [all had a share and we were all
supplied with] one grace after another and spiritual
blessing upon spiritual blessing and even favor
upon favor and gift [heaped] upon gift.*

—John 1:16 AMPLIFIED

Oh, the blessing of the incarnation! This is one of the greatest truths of the redemption story. How much richer are we now than Abraham, David, and Elijah ever were.

But this is not all. Not only does the fullness of our Lord spill over on us, but the same fullness that filled Jesus while in His earthly tabernacle can also fill our mortal bodies. Hence, Paul prays, *"And to know the love of Christ, which passes knowledge, that ye might be filled with all the fulness of God"* (Eph. 3:19).

What shall we say about this breathtaking prayer? Shall we say Paul was a madman or a dreamer? Or, shall we believe that it is truly a divine possibility that we, too, can be filled with all the fullness of God?

I believe that Paul's words are God's words. I believe that Paul's words here reflect God's desires and real possibilities. Yes, this does surpass knowledge. It is incomprehensible to the finest of minds for us to be filled with all the fullness of God. But by faith we understand, we believe, and we reach for it. And, by so reaching for it, we shall receive it.

May it be even so, Lord Jesus.

Jesus Marveled

*When Jesus heard these things, he marvelled at
him, and turned him about, and said unto the people
that followed him, I say unto you, I have not found
so great faith, no, not in Israel.*

—Luke 7:9

In Nazareth, we find Jesus marveling at the unbelief of the people (Mark 6:6). But here at Capernaum, we find our Lord marveling at belief. These are the only two recorded instances where we find Jesus marveling. Imagine the Son of God *marveling* at anything!

Indeed, the faith of the centurion was something about which to marvel. Perhaps it was the only faith that Jesus found which was equal to mustard seed faith. *"If ye have faith as a grain of mustard seed, ye shall say unto this mountain, Remove hence to yonder place; and it shall remove"* (Matt. 17:20).

Think of it, this Roman officer had that kind of faith! Now observe that such faith is deeply rooted in obedience to authority. The centurion would never have become an officer had he not learned absolute obedience. Only those people who have consistently lived in obedience under authority are likely to have such faith.

To this centurion, it was obvious that when a superior officer spoke, his word became flesh. So, to him, Jesus was the highest officer on earth, vested with absolute authority from heaven. Hence, when he said to Jesus, *"but say in a word, and my servant shall be healed"* (Luke 7:7), he was acknowledging that Christ's word was equal to Christ's deed.

So, faith has more to do with obedience than with religious upbringing or knowledge. According to our obedience, so shall our faith be. The degree to which you obey is the degree to which you believe.

Say No to the Juniper Tree

─────⊰⊱─────

But he himself went a day's journey into the wilderness,
and came and sat down under a juniper tree: and he
requested for himself that he might die; and said,
It is enough; now, O Lord, take away my life;
for I am not better than my fathers.

—1 Kings 19:4

God did not speak directly to Elijah under the juniper tree, but through an angel, and that was only to tell him to get up and get away from it.

God does not want any one of us under a juniper tree. The juniper tree was a place of self-pity, bitterness, discouragement, hopelessness, loneliness, disorientation, unbelief, and darkness. Juniper tree experiences have weakened and shortened many a servant's ministry. Elijah was not a failure. He was as good as or better than his fathers. He had courageously brought revival to the whole nation of Israel. But the devil is a liar.

Oh, how we need to guard against juniper tree experiences, where we get nothing better than the lies and accusations of the devil. Juniper tree experiences are not to be sought out but avoided at all costs.

Joshua tried to have a juniper tree experience after the battle of Ai; in fact, he even dressed for it. But God would have none of it. God told Joshua, *"Get thee up; wherefore liest thou thus upon thy face?"* (Josh. 7:10).

God did not want Elijah to quit; the devil did. Friend, God never wants you to quit or be discouraged. He never wants you to compare yourself to others. Elijah had obeyed God, and that is success. The God that was able to deliver Elijah from the hands of Ahab was also able to deliver him from the hands of Jezebel.

Oh, I wish to God that his servant had been there to tell him that the devil was wrong.

The Strategy of Isolation

*And when he saw that, he arose, and went for his
life, and came to Beersheba, which belongeth
to Judah, and left his servant there.*

—1 Kings 19:3

We learned yesterday that we need to say *no* to juniper tree experiences. Elijah's greatest mistake was that he left his servant at Beersheba and ended up under a juniper tree.

Now, how long did it take Elijah to get to utter despair without his servant? One day! Have you ever wondered why Hebrews 3:13 says, "*exhort one another daily*"? Scriptures also tell us that we ought to pray daily and take up our cross daily (Matt. 6:11; Luke 9:23). Miss one day of that, and you get into trouble. The one who was called and equipped to exhort Elijah was left behind. The very thing the prophet needed was the very thing he rejected: fellowship with another man of God. Isolation from God's people will almost certainly lead to juniper tree pity parties.

One of the first strategies of the devil to get us into trouble is the strategy of isolation. When he gets us by ourselves, there is sometimes no other voice we may hear but his. Oh, how Elijah needed his servant now to say, "Come on, master, look to God. Have faith! The devil is a liar. God will carry you through." But Elijah rejected his servant's company, and so the devil did the only talking.

So, please, my friend, never, never separate yourself from the fellowship of the saints, and you will stay clear of juniper tree experiences. Remember, therefore, the Hebraic admonition, "*Not forsaking the assembling of ourselves together...*" (Heb. 10:25). Yes, we may get alone by ourselves to pray, but never, ever to sob and feel sorry for ourselves.

The Cost of Sulking

*And Jehu the son of Nimshi shalt thou anoint to be king
over Israel: and Elisha the son of Shaphat of Abelmeholah
shalt thou anoint to be prophet in thy room.*

—1 Kings 19:16

The juniper tree syndrome, as we have discussed the last two days, causes even God's best to be confused. Elijah thought he needed sleep, but God knew he needed travel. Elijah thought he was the only one left, but God had reserved for Himself seven thousand men of righteousness. Elijah prayed fire down from heaven that destroyed all the false prophets and ended the long drought. But even this success was perceived to be a failure by the prophet.

When we are depressed or discouraged, we are at our worst in the art of discernment. As we proceed in our story, we observe that God made Elijah pay for his trip to the juniper tree, for the next time God talked to Elijah, God announced His replacement for him. Consequently, this juniper experience cost Elijah his ministry.

Oh, the price to be paid for discouragement! Discouragement led to the replacement of Elijah. God had to appoint a new prophet. Yet, how marvelous it is that Elijah obeyed in order to train Elisha and to prepare him for his new office. This time, Elijah's attitude was devoid of sulking, self-pity, or resentment. Thank God, Elijah was a man of only one mistake. And God loves us so much to have published Elijah's juniper tree mistake that we may never fail in like manner.

God also published this experience to let us know that forgiveness seldom cancels the consequences of foolish choices. Yet, how marvelous it is that the two great men who each made a mistake, Moses and Elijah, were both found rejoicing with Jesus on the Mount of Transfiguration.

The Problem of Doubt

*And John calling unto him two of his disciples
sent them to Jesus, saying, Art thou he that
should come? or look we for another?*

—Luke 7:19

Today, let us consider the problem of doubt. First, let us agree that we don't want to doubt the things of God. Doubt is faith damaged, assurance shaken, and loyalty weakened. Doubt is uncertainty, and it leads to moral fumbling. Therefore, we shall pray, "O Lord, our God, deliver us from doubt."

Yet, the reality of the matter is that even some of the greatest biblical characters have at times found themselves in the shadows of doubt. Elijah doubted his self-worth. Joshua doubted God's favor when he lost the battle of Ai. Job had his doubts about the goodness of God. Sarah doubted that she could conceive in her old age. Ten of the twelve spies doubted that they could conquer Caanan. John the Baptist doubted, and he was the greatest man born of woman. The early Christians doubted the genuineness of Saul's conversion. Satan introduced doubt to Eve when he said to her, *"Yea, hath God said...?"* (Gen. 3:1). Yes, ever since Eve's time, man has wrestled with doubt!

Hence, there is the problem of doubting God, His love, His benevolence, His mercy, His forgiveness, etc. Furthermore, there is the problem of doubt in reference to others. Sometimes, pastors doubt the sincerity of their parishioners, and often parishioners doubt the integrity of their pastor. Husbands doubt the love of their wives, and wives doubt the faithfulness of their husbands. Sometimes, brother doubts brother, and sister doubts sister.

Doubt is a transition zone from belief to unbelief, from assurance to uncertainty. Tomorrow, we will see a solution to this problem.

Doubt Your Doubts

*When the men were come unto him,
they said, John Baptist hath sent us unto
thee, saying, Art thou he that should
come? or look we for another?*

—Luke 7:20

To doubt is human. Even Jesus fought doubt in the Garden of Gethsemane, and He was tempted in all things such as we are. But what we do with our doubt reveals the condition of our heart. When we doubt, do we go to those who will confirm our doubts or to those who will destroy them?

Jesus called John the Baptist the greatest man born of women, and how he handled his doubts about Jesus confirms his greatness. Rather than taking his doubts about Jesus to the Pharisees, he took them to Jesus and His disciples. He did not want his doubts confirmed, but destroyed.

When you doubt, do likewise: go to Jesus and to the most faithful and loyal to Him. Go to the prayer warriors, the obedient ones, and say to them, "Tell me again of the wonderful things of God." Hear it again that *"the blind see, the lame walk, the lepers are cleansed, the deaf hear, the dead are raised, to the poor the gospel is preached"* (Luke 7:22).

Oh, my friend, do not fall in love with your doubts. Do not nourish them. Doubt your doubts, and review how wonderful your walk with Jesus was before you entertained them.

Intimacy Overcomes Doubt

*Now when they saw the boldness of
Peter and John, and perceived that they
were unlearned and ignorant men, they
marvelled; and they took knowledge of
them, that they had been with Jesus.*

—Acts 4:13

What is the greatest preventative of doubt? What is it that will stop the seeds of doubt from springing up in the first place? Oh, my friend, it is intimacy.

Intimacy was what John the Baptist lacked, but Peter and John had it. As soon as John had baptized Jesus, he was never seen in His presence again. Whether that was out of John's sense of unworthiness, or otherwise, I do not know. But the fact is, separation from the One we are called to serve and to help always leads us to the treacherous path of doubt.

Peter and John were never found to be on that road. Their early life after Pentecost reads, *"Now Peter and John went up together into the temple at the hour of prayer, being the ninth hour"* (Acts 3:1). These apostles were in regular, daily contact with Jesus. To deliver yourself from doubts about Jesus, meet with Him every morning. Stay in touch with Him all day long.

Unfortunately, many ministers and busy Christians often spend too much time with the mission of God rather than the God of the mission. This will always, in time, lead to wedges of doubt between God and man, and man with fellow man.

How essential that we heed Jesus' words to Martha, *"Martha, Martha, thou art careful and troubled about many things: But one thing is needful: and Mary hath chosen that good part, which shall not be taken away from her"* (Luke 10:41–42). Yes, intimacy prevents the seeds of doubt from sprouting.

Thank You, Mary!

Peter therefore was kept in prison:
but prayer was made without ceasing
of the church unto God for him.

—Acts 12:5

First of all, notice that the Christian life is not easy sailing. If we earnestly go all out for God, we find the winds of life rather contrary. This chapter begins by saying, *"Now about that time Herod the king stretched forth his hands to vex certain of the church"* (v. 1). Doesn't that make cold chills go down your spine? And consider the next two verses, *"And he killed James the brother of John with the sword. And because he saw it pleased the Jews, he proceeded further to take Peter also"* (vv. 2–3).

So, Peter ended up in prison, but hallelujah, *"prayer was made without ceasing of the church."* United prayer is the greatest weapon of the church, and the devil will do everything he can to prevent church prayer meetings from getting started and from continuing once they have begun.

At the core of every prayer meeting, there is one or there are several saints who have a great vision for prayer, who will not let go until others in the church join them in prayer. In this case, the saint who had the vision for prayer more than any was probably Mary, the mother of John, who had a prayer meeting in her house, for the Word reads, *"And when he had considered the thing, he came to the house of Mary the mother of John, whose surname was Mark; where many were gathered together praying"* (Acts 12:12).

Thank you, thank you, thank you, Mary, for opening your house for prayer! And thank you to all others who since have opened their houses for the prayers of the saints.

Rhoda

And all things, whatsoever
ye shall ask in prayer, believing,
ye shall receive.
—Matthew 21:22

There is praying with believing and praying without believing. In the story of the church praying to get Peter out of prison, as we observed yesterday, we see both faithless praying and faith-full praying.

When Peter came to the home of Mary after his escape from prison, Rhoda believed that her prayer was answered, but the rest of the congregation believed not. All it took for Rhoda, a servant girl, to believe was just to hear Peter's voice on the other side of that yet-locked door. Our text says, *"she opened not the gate for gladness..."* (Acts 12:14). Rhoda had been anticipating the answer to her prayers every minute throughout the night. Yet, when Rhoda told the rest of the prayer warriors that Peter was delivered, none of them believed. Yes, they all prayed without ceasing, earnestly—but they did not believe (vv. 5, 15). We see the depth of the unbelief of these seasoned, praying saints when we read that they called Rhoda *mad*, and then after her further pleading with them to believe, they said, *"It is an angel"* (v. 15). When Peter was finally let in, *"they were astonished"* (v. 16).

Oh, how can we be effective at prayer, how we can be so quick at seeing the need for prayer, how can we be so good at praying fervently, perseveringly, and regularly, if we don't truly believe God for the answer? What good does it all do, if we do not believe as earnestly as we pray? Who, then, got Peter out of prison: the many who prayed and did not believe or the one who prayed and did believe?

Again, thank you, Mary, and now also Rhoda, for without the two of you, we would not have Peter's epistles.

What Kind of Faith?

⸺⚬⚬⚬⸺

*But as many as received him, to them
gave he power to become the sons of God,
even to them that believe on his name.*

—John 1:12

What is this thing about believing in His name? What does it mean? What does it include? Oh, that word *believe* is such a broad word in our everyday vocabulary, isn't it?

What kind of belief does it take to be saved and to become a son of God? James says that the devils also believe and tremble (James 2:19). And he also says, *"My brethren, have not the faith...with respect of persons"* (James 2:1).

So, there is a right faith and a wrong faith. A wrong faith may be a believing faith, but it is a faith in the Lord Jesus Christ that does nothing to get us to heaven, a faith that is despicable in the sight of God. What marks the faith of the devil is that it is a faith without surrender. Hence, we can call any faith without surrender "devilish faith."

Then, there is a faith James refers to that favors the rich over the poor, a faith that is mixed with prejudice. Neither is that faith the faith of our Lord Jesus Christ, for it, too, comes short of making us sons of God. There is also the faith of King Saul, a faith that was willing to sacrifice, yet had the seeds of rebellion within it.

Oh, may we have the faith that saves to the uttermost, making us true sons and daughters in the likeness of our dear Savior.

The Primacy of Love

*Nevertheless I have somewhat against
thee, because thou hast left thy first love.*
—Revelation 2:4

The first church that Jesus addresses in the book of Revelation is the Ephesian church. Jesus has many good things to say about this church. He commends her for her patience, for her doctrinal purity, for her industry, and for her courageous witness. Shouldn't that have been enough to win the Ephesians a gold medal in the spiritual Olympics?

But such is not the case. The Ephesian Christians had lost their first love, which was the love they first had for Jesus. Because of that, Jesus was considering removing His candlestick from their midst. Unless the church repented and returned to love God as at the first, He would withdraw His light and gracious anointing.

So, how important is love to Jesus compared to doctrinal purity, evangelical missionary zeal, patience, and hard work? Very important! For we learn here that doctrinal purity, missionary zeal, patience, and hard work, without first-class love, will make us a church without Jesus.

Hence, anything that is not done in or out of our love to Jesus will come to nothing. When our love to Jesus ceases to be first-rate love, our love to our brothers dies, and God ceases to abide in us. Therefore, let us consider these Scriptures: *"He that loveth not knoweth not God; for God is love"* (1 John 4:8); *"By this shall all men know that ye are my disciples, if ye have love one to another"* (John 13:35); *"But now abide faith, hope, love, these three; but the greatest of these is love"* (1 Cor. 13:13 NASB).

The best churches cease to be God's churches once first love is abandoned. So, let us repent if we need to, that the love of God may be shed abroad anew in our hearts by the Holy Ghost which has been given unto us (Rom. 5:5).

Full Mercy

Blessed are the merciful:
for they shall obtain mercy.

—Matthew 5:7

To be merciful means to be full of mercy. And when we are full of mercy, there is no room left for criticism, faultfinding, or a judgmental attitude within our hearts. So, it is one thing to have a measure of mercy toward certain persons in reference to certain matters, but it is another thing to have a heart that is full of and overflowing with mercy toward everyone.

Hence, we see that there are degrees of mercy. Some have mercy toward their friends but not toward their enemies. Some have mercy toward their employees but not toward their spouses. Some have mercy toward their children but not toward their parents or their pastor. Some have mercy when they feel good but not when they are distressed. How many are merciful with all people and in all circumstances, even when they are in need of mercy?

The blessings that come with the mercies of God do not come to us if we are selective in our mercies. We will receive the blessings of mercy only if we are full of mercy, for only the heart with mercy to all and at all times reflects the Spirit of our Lord.

So, let us do even as Jesus did and does today: extend full mercy to both friend and enemy, and the Lord will give us full mercy on Judgment Day.

An Extravagant God

It is more blessed to give than to receive.
—Acts 20:35

The heavens declare the glory of God;
and the firmament sheweth his handywork.
—Psalm 19:1

My friend, God is a God of extravagance. When He made the sun to rule the day, He made the moon and stars to light the night, also. God's deeds are never without extravagance. He created thousands of marine species, billions of them living out their splendid glory, going from birth to death in the depths of the seas without ever having been seen by man. Oh, what extravagance!

Consider the diversity of the many brilliantly created species of birds, from the hummingbird to the eagle to the pelican! Extravagance! Ponder the abundance and individuality of lakes, streams, forests, plains, mountains, and flowers. Extravagance!

Finally, notice God's redemption: His marvelous plan of atonement, His generous mercies, forgiving and forgiving again, and the giving of His best, His own Son, on Calvary's tree. Extravagance!

Not only does He forgive us, but He cleanses us. Not only does He cleanse us, but He renews us. Not only does He renew us, but He resides in us. Not only does He reside in us, but He communicates with us. Not only does He communicate with us, but He empowers us. Not only does He empower us, but He keeps us. Not only does He keep us, but He will present us *"faultless before the presence of his glory with exceeding joy"* (Jude 24).

Yes, our God is a God of extravagance. Let us also be extravagant in our love toward Him and all of mankind.

The Stewardship of the Heart

———⚙️———

Now when Jesus was in Bethany. ...There came unto
him a woman having an alabaster box of very precious
ointment, and poured it on his head, as he sat at meat.
But when his disciples saw it, they had indignation,
saying, To what purpose is this waste?

—Matthew 26:6–8

To the disciples this action was a waste, but to Jesus it was a blessing. No doubt the disciples called this "terrible, irresponsible stewardship," but Jesus called it the will of God. The disciples were indignant, but Jesus was glad. The disciples' eyes were focused on the value of the ointment, but Jesus was focused upon the value of the woman and the deed she had done. Jesus understood that her need to give to glorify Him was as important as whatever the disciples would have chosen to do with the money. Hence, the disciples' attitude was one of condemnation, but Jesus' was one of accommodation.

Oh, what is the distance between condemnation and accommodation? The Lord says, *"For as the heavens are higher than the earth, so are my ways higher than your ways, and my thoughts than your thoughts"* (Isa. 55:9). Again, consider that Jesus had an attitude of commendation, and the disciples had an attitude of judgment. So, Jesus applauded this woman's generosity, worth one year's salary, poured upon His sacred head.

Now, my dear friend, ask the Lord to deliver you from the disciples' cold-blooded, mathematical concepts of stewardship. Learn from the woman of Bethany that the best stewardship does not come from the calculator but from a generous, loving heart. Extravagant giving of worship is never a waste to an extravagant God.

Take Your Demotion like Moses

And the Lord spake unto Moses and Aaron,
Because ye believed me not, to sanctify me in
the eyes of the children of Israel, therefore ye
shall not bring this congregation into the
land which I have given them.

—Numbers 20:12

After having obeyed God for thirty-nine years, Moses, in a moment of weakness and provocation by the people, overstepped his territory: he struck the rock when he should have spoken to it. Because of this sin, Moses was not allowed to lead Israel into the Promised Land.

Did Moses sulk, quit, or take downtime for his failure? No! Moses knew that he was not fired, but only demoted. And since his heart was the meekest heart on the face of the earth, he could handle a demotion.

Oh, what a wonderful man Moses was. He was able to be as gracious in his demotion as in his promotion. Moses, because of the greatness of his heart and his love for God, was able to settle for less than he had been accustomed to. In all of this, he was able to maintain a close walk with God, to be the rare man to whom God could talk face to face. In spite of his own lowered status, Moses never once ceased to give his job his best effort.

In those remaining months before Moses met God at Mount Nebo, he continued to courageously and skillfully lead God's people. Is it any wonder, then, that Jesus wanted to meet him on the Mount of Transfiguration to be one of the first mortals to see his celestial glory?

Indeed, at first glance, Moses teaches us to remain humble in moving up. But how much greater is the lesson he has taught us in moving down without ever missing a step with God? Bitterness and sulking were just not in his inventory.

The Man Inside

*That he would grant you, according to
the riches of his glory, to be strengthened with
might by his Spirit in the inner man.*

—Ephesians 3:16

Paul's concern was for the inner man. The inner man is that man that will live forever and ever either in eternal darkness or everlasting light.

The inner man had its beginning when God breathed into Adam's body, and he became a living soul. The inner man was corrupted when Adam sinned, and ever since, the inner man's *"heart is deceitful above all things, and desperately wicked"* (Jer. 17:9).

Christ, the second Adam, came. And through Christ, we have a redeemed inner man, and we have become a new man in Christ Jesus. But the inner man must be strengthened with might by His Spirit. Unless the inner man is strengthened each day, even though redeemed, he will not be able to resist temptation.

Believers who do not let the Holy Spirit feed them by His daily Word, daily communion with God, and fellowship, will easily succumb to temptation, to the lust of the flesh, to the lust of the eyes, and to the pride of life. They will not be able to resist criticism, jealousy, carnal analyzation, selfishness, and jesting for long.

If we do not wait upon God for the strengthening of the inner man, we will be unfit to conquer the land of milk and honey, and we shall die in the sands of murmuring and unbelief as Israel did in days of old.

Let your inner man feast on the fresh manna of heaven each day, for the manna of yesterday will not do for the needs of today.

Jesus Invited Himself

*And when they saw it, they all
murmured, saying, That he was gone to
be guest with a man that is a sinner.*

—Luke 19:7

There are two things which immediately prejudice people
against Zacchaeus. The first is that he was a tax collector,
and the second is that he was rich. But, oh, how we need to
be so careful in our judgment of all men. Man looks at the
outward appearance, but God looks at the heart. Both tax
collectors and rich men can have wonderful hearts.

So, Jesus invited Himself into Zacchaeus' house. In fact,
it is the only house, as far as the gospel record tells us, into
which Jesus ever invited Himself. But when this was done,
all the people murmured.

It is this murmuring spirit that too often causes us to
judge good men as bad men and bad men as good men.
Because of this murmuring spirit, the multitude was
deceived as to the true value of Zacchaeus. We may be "followers" of Jesus, we may enjoy His teachings, be blessed by
His miracles, and spend precious hours with Him in prayer;
but if we murmur, we are deceived and prejudiced.

May God help us to search our hearts for any evidence of
a murmuring spirit. And may we know that if we have a
heart like Zacchaeus', who gave half of his goods to the poor
and who made all things right with his fellow man, Jesus
will also invite Himself into our hearts to abide within us
forever.

A Mission Greater than Your Problem

*And there came thither certain Jews
...and, having stoned Paul, drew him out of the
city, supposing he had been dead.*

—Acts 14:19

The apostle Paul had many problems. He gives an abbreviated list of them in 2 Corinthians 11:24–27: *"Of the Jews five times received I forty stripes save one. Thrice was I beaten with rods, once was I stoned, thrice I suffered shipwreck, a night and a day I have been in the deep...In weariness and painfulness, in watchings often, in hunger and thirst..."*

Yet, the remarkable thing is that no problem whatsoever, whether it was physical, emotional or spiritual, could ever divert Paul from his mission, because every problem was always smaller than his mission.

And is not this the principle of success of all great men and women in history? They were so focused on what they felt called to do that nothing could get them off course or to quit. They had no time to get into self-pity or hurt feelings, to pay attention to the slanderous remarks of friends and enemies. They would not allow sickness, family problems, and financial ruin to stop them in their hot pursuit of the prize which was before them. They, as Job and Paul, could afford to lose everything without losing anything, ever focusing on the mark that was set before them. So it was that Paul, supposedly dead, when surrounded by the disciples, arose and went into the next cities, confirming the souls of the disciples, exhorting them to continue in the faith (Acts 14:21–22).

Oh, how pitiful that the problems of too many of God's children have taken them away from their mission, because their mission was smaller than their problems. Dear friend, if you do not have a mission greater than any problem that you can possibly face—ask the Lord to give you one, and never, never leave it!

Hidden Gods

*Now Rachel had taken the images,
and put them in the camel's furniture,
and sat upon them.*

—Genesis 31:34

In Genesis 31:22–35, we have the story of a young lady who is supposed to be a type of the bride-elect. Unfortunately, she was sitting on some gods that should not have been there. Since all of us are riding with the Bridegroom, let us ask whether we have any hidden gods under our saddles.

Some believers, upon leaving the worldly system, take some of the old gods with them. We can have hidden gods in the depths of our hearts, and we can have them in our homes. These gods are things of the world. They may be love affairs we carry in our hearts, pictures or magazines we look at when no one is around. These gods may be sounds we listen to on the radio, or movies we watch on television when we are alone.

We know we are not supposed to have these gods, and we are ashamed about that. We are convicted that we should not have them, but we have them because we think we cannot do without them. We try to hide them from Christ and our fellow Christians, just as Rachel hid her idol from Jacob and her servants.

Rachel covered her gods by a lie and an excuse. We never hear of her giving them up. These gods of hers were passed on from generation to generation in one way or another, and they remain with the bride-elect today.

Finally, Rachel died while giving birth to Benjamin. Her gods had made her weak, having lost favor with the Almighty. She was strong enough to bear, but too weak to raise up. Isn't that a picture of many a church today?

May we, this day, examine our hearts for hidden gods.

We Need an End-Time Mentality

*Therefore, my beloved brethren, be ye
stedfast, unmoveable, always abounding in the
work of the Lord, forasmuch as ye know that
your labour is not in vain in the Lord.*

—1 Corinthians 15:58

If that admonition was appropriate at the beginning of the church age, how much the more do we need to heed it as end-time Christians? Jesus' warning concerning the last days is: *"...because iniquity shall abound, the love of many shall wax cold"* (Matt. 24:12). As iniquity is abounding, it requires a higher and higher level of vigilance, prayer, devotion, and zeal to remain pure for the coming of the Bridegroom.

Yet, many a Christian is not acting like an end-time Christian at all. Prophecies concerning His coming abound, but preparation is woefully absent. The signs of the Lord's coming are all about us, but it is difficult to detect an increase in effort or energy expended in preparation for the sound of the great trumpet.

Too many believers entertain themselves with too much television and pastimes, calling the pastor only when anything hurts, rather than also calling for sanctification and confession. Most believe that their rebirth alone will carry them through the golden gates. Oh, may there be within us an enduring spirit, a steadfast spirit that will not quit when the blessings stop, when the benefits dry up, when the feelings are gone, when other Christians abandon their posts, when the winds become contrary, and when pressures increase.

More than ever, we must quit ourselves like men, for only he that endures to the end shall be saved (Matt. 24:13).

Suffer with Me

━━◄◈►━━

Thou therefore endure hardness,
as a good soldier of Jesus Christ.

—2 Timothy 2:3

"Thou therefore endure hardness." On this text, Martin Luther says, "suffer with me." The Amplified Bible also says, *"Take* [with me] *your share of the hardships and suffering."* Observe that there can be no walk with God without suffering. Suffering is inextricably linked to Christianity. The symbol of our faith—the cross—is a symbol of suffering.

Jesus came into the world to suffer and to die (Matt. 16:21). Paul said, *"For unto you it is given in the behalf of Christ, not only to believe on him, but also to suffer for his sake"* (Phil. 1:29). And James pointed to the prophets as *"an example of suffering affliction, and of patience"* (James 5:10).

We learn from Paul that if we suffer with Christ, we shall also reign with Him (2 Tim. 2:12). The cross and the crown go together. From this we learn that suffering is often more pronounced for those who stay close to God and to His servants. So, Luke and Timothy, for having followed Paul, suffered more than the rest. Mark, for having traveled with Peter, also suffered more than he would have had he not followed Peter. Many apostles, for staying close to Jesus, became martyrs.

Yes, the church's great lessons have come through suffering. There is a suffering that comes to us by virtue of wrong and selfish choices. There is no glory in that kind of suffering. But there is a suffering that comes by our casting our lot with Jesus. That suffering, if endured with patience and joy, becomes the seed bed of the kingdom of God in power and great glory. For *"if any man suffer as a Christian, let him not be ashamed; but let him glorify God on this behalf"* (1 Pet. 4:16).

Spiritual Arrogance

⎯⎯⎯⎯⎯⎯⎯⎯⎯

*That I may know him, and the power of his
resurrection, and the fellowship of his sufferings...*
—Philippians 3:10

We live in a Christian society that is infected with a pride
that "knows it all" and that has, theologically speaking, found
all there is to find. The "I've got it," arrogant type of doctrine, this lazy armchair theology pales next to the humble,
racetrack theology of the apostle Paul.

Look at these phrases from Philippians 3, for example,
and see what they do to the popular "I have arrived"
doctrine of the masses: *"...that I may win Christ"* (v. 8); *"That
I may know him..."* (v. 10); *"If by any means I might attain..."*
(v. 11); *"I count not myself to have apprehended"* (v. 13);
"...reaching forth unto those things which are before" (v.13);
"I press toward the mark" (v. 14).

Paul's lifestyle is little found in today's "know it all" theology and in the complacent attitude in the church that
"there is no more to get than what we already have." Rather, Paul was continually reaching, stretching, and pressing
for the mark. His eternal security was not in his *knowing*,
but rather in his pursuing that he *might know*; not in that
he *had attained*, but rather in the sure hope that he *might
attain*; not that he *had apprehended*, but that he *may ap-
prehend*. Wisely, therefore, does Paul warn the church about
thinking we have made it when he says, *"Wherefore let him
that thinketh he standeth take heed lest he fall"* (1 Cor. 10:12).

Is there any assurance, then, that we shall be able to make
it? Of course there is. If we are in the race, we can say with
Paul, *"...for I know whom I have believed, and am persuaded
that he is able to keep that which I have committed unto him
against that day"* (2 Tim. 1:12). It is the arrogance of com-
placency that deceives us. But in humble reaching toward
God, we find His Spirit witnessing with our spirit that we
are the sons of God.

Education Is Not Training

Train up a child in the way he should go:
and when he is old, he will not depart from it.
—Proverbs 22:6

Notice today that there is a vast distinction between educating and training. Education is the acquisition of knowledge, but, generally speaking, it has nothing to do with character building, which we call training.

Training a child to prepare him to walk with God is accomplished first and foremost by subduing and conquering the Self-will of that child. Indeed, this is what Jochebed did with her son, Moses. Susanna Wesley, mother of John and Charles Wesley, said that "self-will is the root of all sin and misery...[It is] the one grand impediment to our temporal and eternal happiness."[7]

We can take our child through every Sunday school class, through hundreds of sermons and prayer meetings, yet that child will never become a follower of Jesus unless his Self-will is broken, denied its way, and subdued to bring him into obedience with God. Until religious training becomes an integral part of religious education in the up-bringing of our children, the church will continue to have *"a form of godliness, but denying the power thereof"* (2 Tim. 3:5).

So, to train up a child in the way he should go involves helping our children to develop God-pleasing behavior patterns. It involves teaching them to take disappointment in stride, and to develop within them fortitude that will keep them on the narrow path in the face of great difficulties and temptations. Education is the acquisition of knowledge, but training is the shaping of character. Remember the difference.

The school and church can do the educating, but mother and father, you need to do the training. *"Train up a child in the way he should go."*

Water Is Thicker than Blood

*And he answered them, saying, Who is
my mother, or my brethren? For whosoever
shall do the will of God, the same is my
brother, and my sister, and mother.*

—Mark 3:33, 35

In this passage, Jesus taught the multitude that *"sat about him"* (v. 32). Suddenly, during His beautiful discourse, as thousands of eyes were fixed upon Him in expectant suspense, a messenger made his way carefully through the crowd, drawing attention away from our Lord. As he stood before the Son of God, interrupting His discourse, he said in essence, "Your mother and brothers would like for you to stop the meeting, send the people home, and come with them to attend a family gathering."

Imagine the audacity, the shortsighted vision, of Jesus' family to think that family affairs were more important than for Jesus to fulfill His calling—for, as yet, His brothers did not believe on Him.

Jesus took advantage of this strange interruption to give the whole world of believers one of the greatest lessons of the kingdom, namely that water is thicker than blood. Those who are baptized into the Lord Jesus Christ and do His will constitute the new family of God. And they must never allow earthly family ties to take precedence over what God is doing in their midst. This new family of God is indelibly tied to Jesus through the bond of obedience.

My friend, does that not tell us that it is time for us to have a new look at how we respond to our earthly family's demands to attend reunions, weddings, graduations, and parties? From here on, don't let the old family traditions stand in the way of your new family's calling. As you do so, you will be a true follower of Jesus. Indeed, in the kingdom of God, water is thicker than blood.

Look and Live

*And as Moses lifted up the serpent in
the wilderness, even so must the Son of man
be lifted up: That whosoever believeth in him
should not perish, but have eternal life.*

—John 3:14–15

Looking to Jesus is at the heart of this message. Looking to Jesus was at the heart of Paul's life when he said, *"Looking unto Jesus the author and finisher of our faith"* (Heb. 12:2). Looking to Jesus requires looking away from the troubles, the trials, the disappointments, the negatives, and the unbearable, unfair, and hurtful things of life which constantly clamor for our attention.

The bearers of bad news, of gossip, of criticism, of fault-finding, and the prophets of doom are ever about us. The serpents of hate, resentment, pride, jealousy, impure thoughts, self-pity, and anger are always ready to bite us in order to infect us with their deadly venom. But as Moses lifted up the serpent, so we must lift up Jesus.

There is a call of God upon our lives to abandon all sinister and wrong things and to employ heart, soul, mind, and strength to look to Jesus. The call is to praise Jesus; to praise Him long enough, to praise Him sincerely enough, to praise Him fervently enough so that His Spirit will inspire our spirit and lift us above the earthly to the heavenly; to cause us to sit with Him in heavenly places, to begin to think about the things which are honest, just, pure, lovely, and of a good report (Eph. 2:6; Phil. 4:8).

So shall we live with that wonderful and sweet name—Jesus, Jesus, Jesus—ever before us. And if that is our manner, there shall be nothing that shall separate us from the sweet fellowship of our Lord Christ Jesus.

Go for the Bread

━━◁◖◗▷━━

*And there went forth a wind from the
Lord, and brought quails from the sea, and
let them fall by the camp...And the people stood
up all that day, and all that night, and all the
next day, and they gathered the quails.*

—Numbers 11:31–32

The quails that Israel thought would bless and satisfy them gave them nothing but trouble. *"And while the flesh was yet between their teeth, ere it was chewed, the wrath of the Lord was kindled against the people, and the Lord smote the people with a very great plague"* (Num. 11:33).

Israel received her heart's desire. But because Israel's heart was not kept, it carried within itself the seeds of selfishness, lust, disappointment, corruption, and death. Israel had to learn by experience that getting what the heart desires is dangerous, unless the heart is sanctified.

Thank goodness, we do not have to learn that by experience, but we can learn that by history. Oh, my friend, we learn from Israel that every time we get out of God's perfect will and into God's permissive will by the gate of lusting, pressing, impatience, and self-interest, we are asking for double trouble.

Let us keep our hearts with all diligence so that all of our heart's desires may be holy. Let us not seek for anything but God's perfect will. If we do so, we shall be saved from quail blessings, quail marriages, quail homes, and quail vacations. Anything with quail in it will lead to disappointment.

The people asked for quail, but God satisfied them with the bread of heaven (Ps. 105:40). Go for the bread!

On Choosing a King

And said unto him, Behold, thou art old,
and thy sons walk not in thy ways: now make
us a king to judge us like all the nations.

—1 Samuel 8:5

Israel wanted a king just as she wanted quail. It was not God's perfect will for Israel to have a king. God wanted to be king over Israel as He had been since the birth of this nation.

Did not God adequately provide for Israel? What earthly king could have opened up the Red Sea and caused the waters from the Jordan River to rise *"up upon an heap"* (Josh. 3:16)? What king could have brought water out of the rock or manna from heaven? What king could have provided for a nation shoes that would not show any wear after forty years? What king could set a pillar of fire amongst his people to warm them by night and a cloud to cool them by day? What king could have brought down the walls of Jericho by a shout? What king could have won the battle against the Philistines by using a clap of thunder from the heavens? What king is there like unto the Lord? Yet, Israel wanted a king *"like all the nations."*

When Israel saw the prophet's sons not following their father's godly example, they became nervous. Did they not remember all that God had done for them, and did they not know that God could raise up another prophet like Samuel? Did they not know that the prophetic office never comes by heredity? No, they wanted a king like other nations. So, God gave them their heart's desire, and it was the kings who took them into Babylonian captivity, into prison and shame.

Again, our heart's desire, unless it is sanctified, may not only give us the beaks, feathers, and bones of quail in our diets, but also kings who entomb us in the darkness of our selfish souls.

They Rejected God

*And the Lord said unto Samuel, Hearken unto
the voice of the people in all that they say unto thee: for
they have not rejected thee, but they have rejected
me, that I should not reign over them.*

—1 Samuel 8:7

Samuel was displeased over Israel's choice to have a king, but God's response was to let them have a king. By asking for a king, Israel rejected God.

God took this heart's desire of His people as a rejection of Himself. He said, *"...they have rejected me"*! So, the kings were born out of the rejection of God. How many programs and plans does God allow the church to have that are born out of her rejection of God and His plans and dreams?

God knew that quail was not good for Israel, yet, He gave her quail because she asked for it. God knew that kings would bring trouble for Israel, but He gave her kings because she asked for them. Thus, the long line of accounts of how they did that which was evil in the sight of the Lord continued, and Israel chose evil throughout the history of most of her kings.

Is it any wonder that the only prayer the Lord taught His disciples began with the petition, *"Thy kingdom come. Thy will be done in earth, as it is in heaven"* (Matt. 6:10)? God never wanted any other kingdom but His own. He never wanted any other will but His will followed on earth as it is in heaven.

Yes, let us follow the admonition of Jesus, *"...seek ye first the kingdom of God, and his righteousness"* (Matt. 6:33). In choosing His kingdom each moment of the day, we keep choosing the King of kings to continue ruling over us. And with His rule, we shall never suffer want.

Meat for the Moment

*Jesus saith unto them, My meat
is to do the will of him that sent me,
and to finish his work.*

—John 4:34

We need meat to accomplish God's work. Jesus' "meat" was doing His Father's will, and when we are in God's will, we are able to accomplish God's mission. Yet, sometimes, the church tries to accomplish and to finish God's work without living off of God's "meat."

There is no confusion, nor misunderstanding, when it comes to the mission of the church; such as the saving and sanctification of men, the unification of the body of Christ, and the outpouring of the Holy Spirit. The problem is not in that the church does not know the mission, but it is with her not always knowing how to bring it to pass.

The disciples also knew that Jesus' mission was to preach the kingdom. They entered into it with great zeal, but they kept finding themselves in the wrong places, doing the wrong things, and having the wrong attitudes. When it was time for them to tarry with Jesus at the well, they found themselves in the grocery store in Sychar. In doing so, they missed Jesus' first fruits of the Gentiles, the first soul harvested of His entire ministry.

They knew the mission, as we all do, but they lacked sensitivity when it came to finding the "meat" for the moment. The "meat," God's perfect will for the moment, always puts us in the right place at the right time with the right attitude.

May we all learn about this "divine meat," God's will for the moment, that we will learn not to be in the wrong place when a soul is ready to be harvested at a well.

God's Mercy Is Conditional

*But the mercy of the Lord is from
everlasting to everlasting upon them that fear
him...To such as keep his covenant, and to those
that remember his commandments to do them.*

—Psalm 103:17–18

The mercy of the Lord is conditional. The reason why it is conditional is because, if it were not, it would be a license to sin. So, to the question, *"Shall we continue in sin,"* Paul gives a stern *"God forbid"* (Rom. 6:1–2).

God's mercy demands a certain behavior, a certain attitude and condition of heart before it enters into the life of a man. The mercy of the Lord is conditional in two important respects: first, for those who fear Him and, second, for those who obey Him. It is first for the penitent sinner who has come to the fear of the Lord which is the beginning of wisdom, causing him to say, "Lord, be merciful to me a sinner."

It is secondly for those who obey Him, who keep His commandments, that when they fall, as King David did, they can get back up and resume their course with God.

God's mercy is not cheap. It cost Him His only Son! God's mercy is not undemanding. It demands holiness. It will never be given where there is no intent or desire to forsake sin, to repent of it, or to despise it. God's mercy is never a license to go from sin to sin, but it is for the contrite, the broken, the penitent, seeking purity of heart; and for that heart, it will never fail in its gracious work.

Yes, indeed, *"All the paths of the Lord are mercy and truth unto such as keep his covenant and his testimonies"* (Ps. 25:10).

God's mercy is conditional. His mercy requires a certain heart attitude to cause it to flow from the throne of God. And those who have that attitude will never be found without it.

Remaining Undeceived

And he said, Take heed that ye be not
deceived: for many shall come in my name,
saying, I am Christ; and the time draweth
near: go ye not therefore after them.

—Luke 21:8

Jesus predicted the calamities of the endtimes: wars, commotion, earthquakes, persecution, pestilence, famines, signs in the sky, and worst of all, many shall be deceived. How are we going to escape the deception of the false Christs when *"The heart is deceitful above all things"* (Jer. 17:9)? False apostles, Paul says, will transform *"themselves into the apostles of Christ"* (2 Cor. 11:13). How are we going to escape the greatest deceiver of all ages, knowing the devil is as an angel of light? How can we, in the last days, do better than the Pharisees, scribes, and lawyers of old who did not recognize who Jesus was? How can we be saved from following a wrong apostle at the expense of following a right apostle whom God has sent for our nourishment, protection, and blessing?

Well, are we not glad that God's Word has an answer for everything we need to know? So, here is the answer that will save us from deception: *"But exhort one another daily, while it is called To day; lest any of you be hardened through the deceitfulness of sin"* (Heb. 3:13). Those who exhort one another daily cannot be deceived! Oh, what an eye opener. Oh, how that encourages us to get on the telephone in a hurry to call someone with Scripture and prayer. The ones who exhort one another daily are spared from deception because they are the ones who live lives of self-denial, obedience, prayer, and praise. These spiritual disciplines keep the fire of God burning in their souls and are a strong evidence of a life given to God. Yes, exhorting one another daily was always important, but it is so much more important in these last days.

Jesus' Greatest Weapon

*Evening, and morning, and at
noon, will I pray, and cry aloud:
and he shall hear my voice.*

—Psalm 55:17

To be prayerless is to be powerless, and to be powerless is to be useless. Prayer is the power that moves the arm of God. Some have said that God does nothing but by prayer.

Jesus put prayer above everything else. Even though He was the Son of God, He said, *"I can of mine own self do nothing"* (John 5:30). Often He withdrew Himself for long periods of time to call on the power of His Father to accomplish the Father's work. Paul's words are no less impressive, *"...making mention of you in our prayers"* and *"...praying always for you"* (1 Thess. 1:2; Col. 1:3).

Why do we not know what those wonderful divines knew—that we cannot do without much prayer? When will we learn that revival meetings, missions conferences, Sunday school classes, radio programs, church buses, and gymnasiums can never substitute for prayer? Jesus and Paul, without the aid of these modern methods, still changed the world. In spite of our best efforts, because of prayerlessness, we fail to change the world. Observe, instead, the way the world changes us!

The church machinery in America is bigger than it has ever been before, and yet, we have more crime, more adultery, more fornication, more pornography, more drugs, more broken homes, and more lonely hearts than ever. Though the church continue with her modern day machinery, let us pray every morning, noon, and night, that God might hear our voice and bring change to the world.

Prayer is the greatest force in the universe—use it!

"Howbeit"!

━━◄▒▒▓▌ℯ▐▓▒▒►━━

*David said unto Nathan, I have sinned
against the Lord. And Nathan said unto David,
The Lord also hath put away thy sin; thou shalt not die.
Howbeit, because by this deed thou hast given great
occasion to the enemies of the Lord to blaspheme,
the child also that is born unto
thee shall surely die.*

—2 Samuel 12:13–14

It is wonderful to experience the forgiveness of sin, but with every forgiveness of sin there is a "howbeit."

Using an analogy, sin is as a boy throwing a stone into a calm lake. Once it has been thrown, one ripple will lead to the next, and the next, and the next. An angler may forgive the boy for having thrown the stone and disturbed his fishing, but nothing can be done by the boy or the fisherman to stop the ripples. So it is with God concerning the forgiveness of our sins. God will forgive us, but the ripples will go on and on until they reach the shores of time.

David was forgiven for having committed adultery, but he faced several "howbeits" for this disobedience, *"the sword shall never depart from thine house...I will raise up evil against thee out of thine own house, and I will take thy wives before thine eyes, and give them unto thy neighbor...I will do this thing before all Israel...the child also that is born unto thee shall surely die"* (2 Sam. 12:10–14).

David was forgiven. His sin was put away, removed as far as the east is from the west, but look at the wagon he had to pull for the rest of his life. Look at the thousands of people who died in battle because of David's day of sin. Once we have sinned, things will never be quite the same as they otherwise would have been. Let us despise, and abhor, and hate sin with all our hearts, so we don't have to contend with "howbeits" the rest of our lives.

Receiving God's Messenger

*He that receiveth you receiveth me, and
he that receiveth me receiveth him that sent me.*

—Matthew 10:40

Wherefore I beseech you, be ye followers of me.

—1 Corinthians 4:16

*Obey them that have the rule over you, and
submit yourselves: for they watch for your souls,
as they that must give account.*

—Hebrews 13:17

Many well-meaning Christians pride themselves in following no one except Jesus. You have heard it said, "Never follow a man." Yet, what are we going to do with Scriptures like the above where Jesus and the apostles put following one of His servants on the same level of importance as following Him?

Twelve apostles were sent out on their first mission without Jesus going with them. He told them to take nothing with them except faith in God. Then, He told them that if a home would not receive them, it would be better for Sodom and Gomorrah on Judgment Day than for that home. Yes, *"He that receiveth you receiveth me."*

Friend, to receive a man of God, to receive his message, to receive him into your home, to give him a cup of cold water, is a much greater deed than you can possibly imagine. Conversely, to reject a servant's message, to refuse to hear and follow him as he follows Christ, to refuse to provide comfort and encouragement for him in this great battle against evil, is very serious indeed (Matt. 10:15).

Oh, let us get rid of this attitude: "I shall serve and follow no man except Jesus." For this attitude deeply grieves the Lord. No, we cannot separate the servant from his Master, nor can we separate the Master from his servant. That is the testimony of Matthew, chapter 10. Let us never forget it. Christ and His messengers are one.

Warm Hearts

-⋘⟪⟫⟫⋙-

And are built upon the foundation of the
apostles and prophets, Jesus Christ himself
being the chief corner stone.

—Ephesians 2:20

This text tells us what Jesus builds His church upon. He does not build His church upon doctrine but upon men who know and teach His doctrines.

To God, men have always been more important than doctrines. Jesus did not come to die for doctrines but for men. That is not to say that doctrines are not important. Doctrines are very important. The church needs them, and Jesus taught them. But doctrines are letter, and men are spirit. We need both letter and spirit, but letter must never triumph over spirit.

The Pharisees were men of the letter, and they disregarded the "spirit" and "souls" of men. To them, doctrine was more important than men; therefore, they despised tax collectors, publicans, Romans, and, in plain language, "sinners." Under their leadership, the people became like sheep without a shepherd, and when they saw sin, as with the woman caught in adultery, they were quick to apply and to honor their doctrine. To them, saving the doctrine was more important than saving the woman.

But Jesus saw the woman as being more important than the law, and by adding grace to law, He saved her. No doubt, because of these truths, the apostle Paul said that *"the letter killeth, but the spirit giveth life"* (2 Cor. 3:6). Since Pentecost, how many Christians have been killed by the letter of the church? No one knows.

Oh, how wonderful that Jesus would build His church on men of compassion, men of holiness, men of wisdom, and men of truth. May we reflect His spirit. Yes, the foundation of His church is not cold letters, but warm hearts.

One Lord, One Faith, One Body

⟶≪≫⟵

There is one body, and one Spirit, even
as ye are called in one hope of your calling;
One Lord, one faith, one baptism.

—Ephesians 4:4–5

It looks like there is only one church, one body, one faith, one Lord, and one baptism in God's eyes, doesn't it? Denominations were not God's idea. Indeed, they were only born after the Holy Spirit lost His grip on the various local assemblies.

Denominations began when the letter became more important than the spirit. They began when the inflexible doctrines of pharisaical mindsets entered the minds and the hearts of God's blood-washed ones. Denominations began when men forgot where they came from and for what reason they are here. Indeed, the seeds of doctrinal division were already in clear evidence in Paul's letters to the Corinthians, for he writes, *"...that every one of you saith, I am of Paul; and I of Apollos; and I of Cephas; and I of Christ"* (1 Cor. 1:12).

If there is division, then where is Christ? If there is strife, then what happens to the parts that Jesus attempts to fitly frame together? If there is division, strife, and competition amongst church members, then where will you find the holy temple of God? Following Christ and ever keeping before themselves the cross of self-denial is what kept the disciples together and finally ushered in the day of Pentecost.

Let us take down all man-made barriers between us. Let us forsake the pharisaical spirit of division and surrender ourselves anew to Him, for this is our only hope for the Great Awakening prophesied by the prophet Joel. Worldwide revival will only come through a united body of believers under the lordship of Jesus Christ that has returned to the simplicity of one Lord, one faith, and one baptism.

The Carpenter

━━◅⊶⊷▻━━

And I say also unto thee, That thou art Peter,
and upon this rock I will build my church; and the
gates of hell shall not prevail against it.

—Matthew 16:18

"I will build my church." Here, we see the physical Carpenter turning into a spiritual Carpenter. Here, we see the Creator becoming a Maker. Yes, with this text, we have half of all Christ's teaching on the church. So let us take heed of it. You can go through all of the Gospels and never see Jesus building anything except for this, *"I will build my church."*

No one was more qualified to build than Jesus. He was the Carpenter of all carpenters. This building of the church would be the crowning work of all His carpentry. The building of this church would be a greater work than that of Noah building the ark or of Solomon building the temple. For this work of Jesus was to bring about the building and construction of His own body, that would last beyond time into eternity. Indeed, its structure would be so strong that the gates of hell could not prevail against it.

"I will build my church." Here, Jesus tells us that the building of the church is no one's business but His. If He builds the church, it will be His church, He will indwell it, He will lead it, He will sustain it, He will protect it, and He will perfect it.

If He does not build it, He will not indwell it, nor sustain it, nor protect it. Let us not compete with Christ's church-building business, but let us rather allow Him to build us into His glorious body which is His church. Yes, what this Carpenter puts together will outshine the creation of the universe to be the crowning work of all He has ever done.

Jesus' Teaching on the Church

And if he shall neglect to hear them, tell it unto the church:
but if he neglect to hear the church, let him be unto
thee as an heathen man and a publican.

—Matthew 18:17

When you read Jesus' words, *"I will build my church"* (Matt. 16:18), you read one-half of all of His teachings on the church. Here is the second half of Christ's teachings on the church, and it relates to the need of unity in the body of Christ.

As we mentioned yesterday, Christ's building of the church does not, of course, refer to the building of a physical structure needed to house God's people in inclement weather, but to the building of a holy temple, of an *ekklesia*, of a group of people called out of the world to be all for God. So, Christ's part, in reference to the church, is the building of the spiritual body, and our part is to create and preserve unity in that body. This means we must deal with the problems in our midst that cause division and strife.

Therefore, Jesus said in our text that if there is anything between any two persons that not He but we are to take care of it. Jesus' word is that when a brother trespasses against a brother, let there be three attempts to solve the problem. First, let there be a one-to-one attempt. Secondly, two or more persons should attempt to resolve the conflict; and, finally, let the whole church deal, if necessary, with the matter of a brother's sin. If the transgressor does not listen to the church, he is to be viewed as an unbeliever.

Oh, how Jesus cherishes unity, for it is at the heart of even His high priestly prayer, *"That they all may be one...even as we are one"* (John 17:21–22).

Let us strive for unity, and let us work on it Jesus' way, and, more importantly, in Jesus' spirit.

The Boldest Prayer

*For this cause I bow my knees unto the Father...that
ye might be filled with all the fulness of God.*
—Ephesians 3:14, 19

The boldest prayer of Abraham was when he interceded for Sodom. The boldest prayer of Moses was when he asked God to spare Israel after the incident of the golden calf. The boldest prayer of Jesus was when He prayed to His Father *"That they all may be one...even as we are one"* (John 17:21–22).

The boldest prayer of Paul was for the fullness of God within every believer's heart which is the foundation for oneness.

Let me ask you: what is your boldest prayer? How much do you think God can do in your life? What are God's limits for your personal, spiritual growth?

Let us first notice that Paul's bold prayer for the fullness of God was based on the unsearchable riches and glory of God (Eph. 3:8, 19). If we were to look at our weaknesses, the fullness of God within us is an impossibility. But when we look at the unlimited reservoir of God's riches and glory, provided for us to draw from, yes, we can and shall *"be filled with all the fulness of God."*

Second, notice why we can have this fullness. We can have it because Paul tells us that in Christ Jesus dwelt all the fullness of God bodily (Col. 2:9).

So then, if we give ourselves to Jesus unreservedly as the Master of our lives, the fullness of God in Him will dwell with Him in our earthly bodies, just as it dwelt in Christ's mortal body while He was on earth. No, this does not give us a halo. Jesus did not have a halo because of God's fullness within Him. No, it will not make men recognize that divine fullness within us, but it will be there, nonetheless, and God will see it and be pleased with it.

Hear His Voice!

But as it is written, Eye hath not seen, nor ear heard, neither have entered into the heart of man, the things which God hath prepared for them that love him.

—1 Corinthians 2:9

We observe here that God has marvelous things prepared for all of His children. These are blessings of things beyond our wildest dreams and fondest hopes. But how do we get to those things already prepared for us? The answer is: by the voice of God.

Man was created to live by the voice of God. Whenever man lived by that voice, he was happy and safe. Everything that God ever started was by His voice. The stars in the heavens, the flowers in the field, the fish in the streams, and the birds in the air are all the result of the voice of God.

The nation of Israel was created by God speaking to Abraham. Her deliverance out of Egypt was by God speaking to Moses. The temple was built by God speaking to David and to Solomon. Jesus, the Savior, lived by the voice of God. He was called the Word, and He taught His disciples to live by the same voice. It was by God's voice that Peter ministered to the Jews and Paul went to the Gentiles.

Indeed, what distinguishes a living church from a dead church is that a living church is led by His voice, and a dead church is led by man's thoughts. And so, it is by our hearing His voice that we can be guided into the precious things that God has prepared for us. Jesus said, *"My sheep hear my voice, and I know them, and they follow me"* (John 10:27).

Oh, my friend, learn to live by this voice, and all that was destined to be yours from the foundation of the world shall indeed become yours.

Raise the Standard

And Jabez was more honourable than his brethren...
And Jabez called on the God of Israel...and God
granted him that which he requested.
—1 Chronicles 4:9–10

If we want God to grant us what we request, we must also be a Jabez: more honorable than our brethren. Notice the text does not say that Jabez was honorable, which many people are indeed, but the Scripture says, *"more honourable."*

This more honorable status of Jabez can also be said of John the apostle, who declares, *"And whatsoever we ask, we receive of him, because we keep his commandments* (which is honorable)*, and do those things that are pleasing in his sight* (which is the more honorable part)*"* (1 John 3:22, comments added).

In case you have pondered the question as to why many of your prayers have not been answered, begin with this query: Am I living an honorable life? Is my life without spots, wrinkles, blemishes or such things? Do I live righteously, obeying all the commandments of the Lord? That, my friend, is living honorably.

But now, once you are there, once you keep His commandments, there is yet a step above that: it is that you consistently begin to search out and do those things which are pleasing in His sight. If you do so, you also will be a *more honourable* person like Jabez and John. When you pray, heaven will hear and will be faithful and delighted to respond. If you do so, you will be a standard-setter for the Christian community and a bright beacon of light in this world of sin and woe.

Praise Must Not Be Despised

*And it came to pass, as the ark of the covenant of the
Lord came to the city of David, that Michal the daughter
of Saul looking out at a window saw king David dancing
and playing: and she despised him in her heart.*

—1 Chronicles 15:29

David and the elders, with joy and praise, brought the ark
to the City of David. *"Thus all Israel brought up the ark of
the covenant of the Lord with shouting, and with sound of
the cornet, and with trumpets, and with cymbals, making a
noise with psalteries and harps"* (1 Chron. 15:28). There was
a great praise session before the Lord!

But Michal despised David in her heart. Michal is a
symbol of the reprobate, praiseless church. Michal came out
of Saul, who rejected God's supremacy, and she had a form
of religion that was devoid of God's Spirit. Michal did not
praise the Lord, and, because of this spirit, she was barren.

David, a symbol of the true church, took a good look at
the ark. He could see mercy, fruit, and bread, and thus he
shouted praises and danced before the Lord. My friend, if
you would ever get a really close look at what God has for
you, you would also praise and shout before the Lord.

David's psalms are filled with praise. Paul admonishes
us to rejoice evermore. We must not despise praise as Michal
did, for heaven is full of it. And the time to begin praise is in
the here and now. The power and the glory of God works
through a heart which praises the Lord!

Faultless before His Presence

Now unto him that is able to keep you from falling, and to present you faultless before the presence of his glory with exceeding joy.

—Jude 24

How is Jesus possibly able to present us perfect before God? First, let us know that the only way anyone can appear before God's throne and live is in perfection. No sin can stand in God's brilliant light. Secondly, notice that no one will get into the presence of that great throne of God without the help of Jesus. The only One that is able to keep us is also the only One who is able to present us. Thirdly, we know that there are two vital elements essential for Jesus to present us perfect to the throne of God: we must walk in the light which we have, and we need constant cleansing by the blood of Jesus. John says, *"But if we walk in the light, as he is in the light, we have fellowship one with another, and the blood of Jesus Christ his Son cleanseth us from all sin"* (1 John 1:7). As we walk in the light of God, even in whatever way we come short in doing so, we have the blood of the Lamb to take care of the rest of our need in order to make us perfect before Him.

So, as blood-washed saints of light, our fellowship with Christ begins here and will come to its fulness when we shall see Him there, for *"when he shall appear, we shall be like him"* (1 John 3:2), ready to stand before His throne. *"O give thanks unto the Lord; for he is good: for his mercy endureth for ever"* (Ps. 136:1).

Having Been with Jesus

*For this cause we also, since the day we
heard it,...desire that ye might be filled with
the knowledge of his will in all wisdom
and spiritual understanding.*

—Colossians 1:9

There are several ways by which we can come to the knowledge of God's will. First, there is the written Word in the Bible by which God revealed very much of His will to us humankind. Second, we can know God's will by revelation through the Holy Spirit. Paul said, *"And I went up by revelation"* (Gal. 2:2). Third, we can know God's will through intimacy with His Son. The more we are with a friend or a spouse, the more we know what they prefer or dislike. A man who has been married a few years knows many of the deepest desires, dreams, and aspirations of his wife.

As we spend much time with Jesus and partake of His Spirit, we often know instantly what He thinks about a television program, a sports event, a conversation, a vacation plan, or many other matters. We take on the mind of Christ so that what is in His mind will also be in our minds.

Godly people are God-like people, and what God likes, they like, what grieves God, grieves them, and what God despises, they despise. Oh, the godly often cannot give a clear-cut explanation about their likes and dislikes other than to say, "I have been with Jesus."

180° Repentance

*Now I rejoice, not that ye were made
sorry, but that ye sorrowed to repentance.*

—2 Corinthians 7:9

Repentance can best be described as a turning away from
our Self-life to a God-centered life. We can compare that to
a 180° turn.

Unfortunately, too many of our turns are less than 180°.
All too often, we are sorry for our sins but not sorry enough
to make a full 180. We end up with a 140 or 160 or 170° turn
and miss the mark of genuine repentance. We neglect to
ask for forgiveness from a certain brother, or we keep holding on to some god under our saddle (Gen. 31:34).

There is no joy in heaven over sorrow about sin that falls
short of the complete repentance of a 180° turn. Paul
rejoiced in that the Corinthians *"were made sorry...[unto]
repentance"* (2 Cor. 7:9) after living in a godless manner.
For God, all sins are a turning away from God. To Him, there
are no greater or lesser sins. Every sin separates from God.
Not the wages of some sin, but the wages of all sin is death.
"...the soul that sinneth, it shall die" (Ezek. 18:4).

Adam and Eve's sin of eating the wrong fruit was sin unto
death. So was David's lusting after Bathsheba and his numbering of the troops. So was Saul's in sparing Agag the king.
So also was the sin of Achan in hiding the Babylonian treasures under his tent. No sin can stand before God as an
acceptable sin. No repentance less than 180° will restore
unto us the joy of our salvation.

Yes, let us be sorry when we sin; indeed, not just sorry,
but sorry enough to repent fully, to get us back on the track
of God's perfect will.

Doubting Is Faithlessness

*Except I shall see in his hands the
print of the nails, and put my finger into the
print of the nails, and thrust my hand
into his side, I will not believe.*

—John 20:25

There is far too much joking about doubting Thomas. There are too many on our church boards and committees who pride themselves in being "doubting Thomases." The pride of being a doubting Thomas and of insisting on feeling and seeing before believing is a serious problem to the church and to the kingdom of God. The doubting Thomas attitude is not of the Holy Spirit.

It is this doubting spirit that caused Israel to balk at the Red Sea, and it is also this spirit that kept Israel out of Canaan at Kadesh. This same attitude caused Israel to rise up against Moses, and it led eventually to the tragic death of many on the wrong side of Jordan.

Because it fell short of the stuff that makes for genuine discipleship, Jesus had no compliments for this faithless, doubting, hollow belief. In His opinion, Thomas was not a man who had little faith or weak faith, but rather, no faith. Hence, Jesus' response to Thomas was, *"Reach hither thy finger, and behold my hands...and be not faithless, but believing"* (John 20:27). Yes, "faithlessness" was Jesus' definition of Thomas' spirit of doubting.

Yet, thank God, when Thomas drew near to Jesus, faithlessness ended and faithfulness began. Let us also draw near to our Savior that we may doubt our doubts and believe.

Are We Looking for Signs?

---

*Then certain of the scribes and of the Pharisees
answered, saying, Master, we would see a sign from thee.
But he answered and said unto them, An evil and
adulterous generation seeketh after a sign.*
—Matthew 12:38–39

Biblical literature abounds in signs and wonders. Our God is a miracle-working God. That which is natural to Him is supernatural to us. Yet, signs must never be the ultimate reason for our belief, for, if our faith is built on signs, we shall cease to believe when signs come to an end. Our faith must find deeper springs than visible phenomena. This is why Jesus said to Thomas (after he insisted on seeing the wounds of our Lord), *"blessed are they that have not seen, and yet have believed"* (John 20:29).

Jesus also said, *"An evil and adulterous generation seeketh after a sign."* Where does that put all those church folk who gather around the miracle workers? What does that tell us about their hearts? What does an adulterous generation mean in this context but that it is people loving the miracles more than the Savior who does them!

Yes, thank God for the signs; but so much the better for us if we come to faith by the Word, rather than by signs. Indeed, *"How beautiful are the feet of them that preach the gospel of peace, and bring glad tidings of good things"* (Rom. 10:15).

Signs are aids to believers whose faith is weak. They can help to turn "doubting Thomases" into faithful disciples. But signs will never give us spiritual life—only the Word will. And it is the Word that *"is a lamp unto* [our] *feet, and a light unto* [our] *path"* (Ps. 119:105).

Abiding Faith

*Now faith is the substance of things
hoped for, the evidence of things not seen.*

—Hebrews 11:1

Faith means being sure of the things we hope for and knowing that something is real even if we cannot behold it with the natural eye. There is nothing like the examples of faith that follow this verse in Hebrews 11, which we call the Westminster Abbey of the Bible. You see, as England buried her heroes at Westminster, so we have this glorious cemetery in Hebrews 11 of many of God's best.

All of these heroes of Hebrews 11 believed without seeing, without seeing the signs for which the Scribes and Pharisees sought. All of them knew that a faith based on the visible would perish with the visible, but faith based upon the invisible God who never perishes would be a faith abiding forever. Crossing all rivers; tearing down all strongholds; and enduring all the assaults of the world, the flesh, and the devil is faith abiding forever. Ah, how mighty is that faith based not on what is seen but on the revelation of God's Word to the heart.

Yes, such was the faith of Peter who knew Jesus as the Messiah—not by His miracles. Even false prophets do miracles, but Peter knew by the Holy Spirit revealing to him that Jesus was the Savior, the Son of the living God. So, after Peter's revelation, Jesus then responded, *"Blessed art thou, Simon Barjona: for flesh and blood hath not revealed it unto thee, but my Father which is in heaven"* (Matt. 16:17).

So, my friend, faith based entirely on God's Word is faith that will help us to be faithful even in the darkest hours of the soul.

Praise the Lord!

*And to stand every morning to thank
and praise the Lord, and likewise at even.*
—1 Chronicles 23:30

We must lift our hearts in praise to God. God inhabits the praises of His people (Ps. 22:3). David knew this truth. So when the ark of God was brought back to the city of David and placed into the center of the tent that David had pitched for it, he immediately ordered praise. He called on certain Levites to *"thank and praise"* the Lord. He appointed others to play their trumpets continually before the ark of God (1 Chron. 15:24). David realized the need for praise at the beginning of his reign, and even more so at the end. Prior to making Solomon king, he appointed four thousand men to praise the Lord continually (1 Chron. 23:5–6).

If the saints of God will couple their faith with praise, there will be victory after victory. Do you want victory? Begin to praise God! Do you want victory for the church? Get a few saints to praise God together, and many a wall will be broken down, and souls will be saved, sanctified, and lifted. Bodies will be healed, and the devils will flee. God inhabits the praises of His people.

Begin every morning with praise, and continue with praise throughout the day and into the evening. Build praise around your petitions. Build praise around your family and the people of God. Yes, *"Let every thing that hath breath praise the Lord. Praise ye the Lord"* (Ps. 150:6).

Diversity

*Now there are diversities of
gifts...differences of administrations
...diversities of operations...*

—1 Corinthians 12:4–6

We learn from this Corinthian letter that diversity is the rule when it comes to the work of the Holy Spirit. We also learn this from Jesus when He said to Nicodemus, *"The wind bloweth where it listeth, and thou hearest the sound thereof, but canst not tell whence it cometh, and whither it goeth: so is every one that is born of the Spirit"* (John 3:8).

Our message today is that the inner leading of the Holy Spirit is unpredictable. God leads His dear children along, but seldom does He give them more direction than one step at a time. The children of Israel did not know from one day to the next where the cloud and the fiery pillar would lead them through the wilderness. Jesus did not know in the morning where He would be at night.

Yes, the Holy Spirit is like the wind. Concerning the saints, there is a great degree of unpredictability outside of their earthly duties, yet, there is perfect predictability that they will always do the will of God.

When the Holy Spirit is permitted to lead in the church, no two church services will ever be the same, and the monotony in religious services will end. The Holy Spirit will begin to lead the service with such pinpoint precision that every need of every parishioner will be met. For example, there will be times when there will be no hymns or a few, no preaching and much prayer.

Therefore, when you think about the Holy Spirit, diversity is the key word: diversity of gifts, diversity of administrations, and diversity of operations. Yes, God will work through each individual person and church in His beautiful, unique, creative, refreshing, and life-giving way, if we will only let Him.

We Beheld His Glory

꧁꧂

*And the Word was made flesh, and
dwelt among us, (and we beheld his glory,
the glory as of the only begotten of the
Father,) full of grace and truth.*

—John 1:14

Through the incarnation, the Word, which had been hidden in the shadows of the Old Testament revealed itself to mankind. Now, for the first time in history, we find the Word saying, "If you know me, you know the Father. If you see me, you have seen the Father. If you touch me, you touch the Father." What a revelation! What a revolutionary change from the hidden to the revealed! What a gift of God!

But then it says, *"we beheld his glory."* Well, who is "we"? "We," first of all, is John who wrote this, and, secondly, it is the other apostles, Peter and James, who were with John on the Mount of Transfiguration. Yet, in a broader sense, "we" is also the inner circle, including Mary Magdalene, Joanna, and Lazarus. They did not see Christ's glory in His heavenly robe but in His earthly divinity. Judas was also in the inner circle, but only physically—not spiritually. That is one reason why he betrayed our Lord.

Oh, may we step into the inner circle of our Lord, not just physically but spiritually, in order that we, too, might behold the glory hidden to all those who only follow the Master for the loaves and fishes. Yes, we may behold His glory, howbeit, now through a glass, darkly. But soon, we shall see it in its fulness, and then we shall be like Him.

LOVE: the Standard of Our Devotion

———————

*Thou shalt love the Lord thy God with all thy
heart, and with all thy soul, and with all thy mind.
This is the first and great commandment.*

—Matthew 22:37–38

Since the commandment to love is the greatest of all commandments, it follows that the withholding of love is the source of all sins. There is no sin except that it comes out of the withholding of love to God and to man.

This is true of the sins of the flesh: murder, theft, or adultery. They all come out of the sin of withholding love to our God and to our fellow man. And so it is also with the sins of the spirit: criticism, envy, jealousy, lust, pride, self-pity, and blasphemy. All are born out of our not loving God with all of our heart.

He who withholds no love that is due God and man fulfills all the law and the prophets. He who loves entirely is entirely happy, and his soul is delighted beyond reason. The soul that loves is so thrilled, that poor circumstances and poor treatment cannot dim the bliss of loving the only object the angels have chosen to praise forever. We conclude that the heart which does not, or will not, love God is miserable, spiritually depraved, desperately wicked, and idolatrous.

The church of Ephesus had wonderfully religious works, labor, patience, and courage, but she had left her first love (Rev. 2:4). The sin of the church of Ephesus was the sin of withholding love. Yes, she had left her first love. So, she was admonished to repent of that sin lest she lose the light of the Holy Spirit. May we no longer withhold love, either to God or to man, for lovelessness is the root of all sin.

The Queen of Theologies

━━◆◆◆◆◆◆◆━━

And they continued steadfastly in
the apostles' doctrine and fellowship...
—Acts 2:42, 46

It is interesting to note that the first activity of the first Christians was not the reading of the Bible (that is, the Old Testament). Something more significant became the focus of their attention: *"the apostles' doctrine."*

So, in a moment's time, in a single day, apostolic theology became the queen of all theologies. This theology is by revelation and not by reason. As the apostle Paul says, *"How that by revelation he made known unto me the mystery...Which in other ages was not made known unto the sons of men, as it is now revealed unto his holy apostles and prophets by the Spirit"* (Eph. 3:3–5).

Therefore, from Pentecost onward, all Scripture must be viewed through a new set of eyes, the eyes of the early apostles! Through them alone do we have the proper understanding of Adam's fall. Through them alone we now see clearly the scarlet thread running all the way through the Bible. Through them alone can we now see God's divine plan for the ages to come.

"...they continued stedfastly in the apostles' doctrine." All theology—the theology of the law, of the historical books, of the wisdom literature, of the prophets, and of the Gospels—is now to be viewed as the Holy Spirit gave revelation to the apostles. Beware of those who, to their own lusts, degrade any of the teachings of the apostles, especially those of Paul. By direction of the Holy Spirit, Paul became the architect of Christian theology. If you meddle with him, you meddle with God. People who have trouble getting under the authority of Pauline teachings generally have trouble getting under the authority of any true servant of God. So, let us do as the early Christians and wholeheartedly accept and continue in the apostles' doctrine.

Apostolic Doctrine

---✦✦✦---

*And they continued
stedfastly in the apostles' doctrine.*

—Acts 2:42

Today, let us go on a historic journey of the apostles. Apostles are not found in the Old Testament. The apostolic office was instituted by Jesus after a full night of prayer (Luke 6:12–13). Mark tells us that the apostles were called to be with Jesus and that they were sent forth to preach, to heal, and to cast out devils (Mark 3:14). From this passage some deduce that the apostolic calling is primarily a missionary calling. However, as we continue on our journey, we see that the apostolic calling is greater than this.

Paul tells us that the church is built on the foundation of the apostles and prophets, with Jesus Christ as the chief cornerstone (Eph. 2:20). Hence, it is to them that God revealed the foundational doctrines of the church and the great mystery which was hidden throughout all the ages, *"which is Christ in you, the hope of glory"* (Col. 1:27). What was once inconceivable to man—that God would make man His dwelling-place—is now both conceivable and real in all true sons of God. Oh, what tremendous revelation the apostles have given!

As God spoke to Moses to give us the Old Testament covenant, so He spoke to the apostles to give us the New Testament covenant.

Further, the apostles were ordained for the *"perfecting of the saints, for the work of the ministry, for the edifying of the body of Christ"* (Eph. 4:11–13). As long as the body of Christ needs edifying and perfecting, I believe God will continue to send apostles. As the church age began with apostles, so I believe God will use apostles in a special way in the end time to prepare the church for the great wedding: the Marriage Feast of the Lamb.

Hate One's Family?

*If any man come to me, and hate not
his father, and mother, and wife, and children,
and brethren, and sisters, yea, and his own
life also, he cannot be my disciple.*

—Luke 14:26

This is strong talk, and many scholars have been tempted to change the word "hate" into something softer. Yet the best and most literal translation from the Greek of this word "hate" is "to regard with ill will, to detest, to abhor." Of course, if you consider a contextual translation drawing from the sum of all biblical truth, you can say that what Jesus means is that in comparison, our love to our blood family should be much smaller than our love to God. For unless this is so, our family will keep pulling us away from the will of God.

It is for this reason that Abraham, the father of faith, had to leave his kindred way behind before God could do anything with him. God had to send him far enough away that it would be impossible and impractical for him to attend a single family reunion, wedding party, or funeral.

The fact that Jesus has asked only a few of us today to put such vast geographic distance between us and our kin should not necessarily be misinterpreted that we should have more liberties than Abraham. Our contact with our families, or anything else, should be in the Holy Spirit and for no other reason.

So, we must understand that everything of the Christian's life must be placed under the good umbrella of "Thy kingdom come, Thy will be done." Anything less than that will only bear the fruits of eventual disappointment, decay, and death. Readjust your family relationship to bring it into God's perfect will. That's what Jesus did, and, eventually, as far as we know, all of His family were saved.

The Great Commission

———

Go ye therefore, and teach all nations,
baptizing them in the name of the Father,
and of the Son, and of the Holy Ghost.

—Matthew 28:19

This Scripture has been called the "Great Commission" by many people. It might be better if we called this "one of the many great commissions" of our Lord. Perhaps, we should just redefine what many call *the* Great Commission so as to give it a more universal and biblical meaning. Therefore, let us say that the Great Commission is whatever God wills for the moment. This is what Jesus did, for He said, *"My meat is to do the will of him that sent me, and to finish his work"* (John 4:34).

Doing God's will for the moment is something we all can get in on: the secretary, the factory worker, the lawyer, the nurse, the homemaker, the gardener, and the shoeshine boy. If we limit the Great Commission to only the foreign field, we who are not going shall all have to settle for mediocrity and second place in the Christian walk. In fact, if we accept the common perception of the Great Commission, then Jesus never fulfilled it. He insisted that He was just called to the house of Israel, never to set foot on foreign soil.

Oh, how thankful we are that Jesus made *"Thy kingdom come. Thy will be done"* the first and foremost goal of life. That, my friend, we can do. It is herein that we can find our happiness, peace, and fulfillment each moment.

So let us remember that capturing *each moment* entirely for God is the greatest commission we can ever fulfill.

By Every Word

*But he answered and said, It is written, Man
shall not live by bread alone, but by every word
that proceedeth out of the mouth of God.*

—Matthew 4:4

There are many believers trying to live on part of the Word of God. Some say that all we need is John 3:16, *"For God so loved the world, that he gave his only begotten Son, that whosoever believeth in him should not perish, but have everlasting life."* Some say that we need only the four gospels. Others say that we can do away with the Old Testament which was written by the Jews and for the Jews. But Jesus said that we must live *"...by every word that proceedeth out of the mouth of God."*

That "every word" includes Genesis, Exodus, and Leviticus. It includes all the words that God spoke in the wisdom literature, in the prophets, in the Gospels, in the Acts, the Epistles, and the Revelation. It includes whatever God tells us through the inner voice, for He said, *"My sheep hear my voice"* (John 10:27). Yes, we are to live by every word of God. Every word God ever spoke is for our nourishment, sustenance, and life.

When Jesus answered Satan in today's verse (Matt. 4:4), He quoted the Old Testament, the New Testament not yet having been written. To each satanic attack, Jesus responded with *"It is written."* When He was twelve, He knew the Old Testament so well that he confounded the scholars at Jerusalem.

Yes, to believe in the Lord Jesus means to believe all that He taught and all that He believed, not only to believe who He is. *"All scripture is given by inspiration of God"* (2 Tim. 3:16), and must be believed and lived by. Yes, let us also live by every word that has ever proceeded from the mouth of God. May we let none of His words fall to the ground.

The Purpose of the Word

———◆◆———

*All scripture is given by inspiration of God, and is
profitable for doctrine, for reproof, for correction, for
instruction in righteousness: That the man of God may
be perfect, throughly furnished unto all good works.*
—2 Timothy 3:16–17

The ultimate end of Bible study is twofold: spiritual perfection and ministry; *"That the man of God may be perfect...."* This means that we must first let the Word of God speak to our hearts to do its correcting, chastening, cleansing, reforming, nurturing, healing, reviving, and perfecting unto holiness. We can study the Scriptures, and we can get our doctorate of theology as the Pharisees did, but unless our hearts are in the process of being made perfect, we are falling far short of Christ's redemptive expectations.

If there was only one good thing a seminary was to accomplish in the life of its young students, it would be for those students to graduate with a new heart, one like Christ's: a pure heart; kind, patient, long-suffering, full of mercy, humble, meek, and sensitive to the precious Holy Spirit's prompting and guidance. Truly, that is the ultimate purpose of all Scripture for all men: having a heart like unto God's heart, furnished unto all good works.

Studying the Scripture just to perpetuate doctrinal division and pride in scholarship is one of the greatest abominations of the day. But to allow its cleansing and sanctifying work to be done in our hearts, in order to equip us to bring in God's harvest, is surely the ultimate intent revealed in our precious Bible.

In One Accord

---

*And by the hands of the apostles were many signs
and wonders wrought among the people; (and they
were all with one accord in Solomon's porch.*

—Acts 5:12

"*And by the hands of the apostles were many signs and
wonders wrought among the people.*" Here we see ordinary
men, fishermen and tax collectors, doing extraordinary
things. Yes, "*And with great power gave the apostles witness of the resurrection of the Lord Jesus*" (Acts 4:33). Where
did all this power suddenly come from? The answer is
simple: it came through their being in "*one accord*" (Acts
2:1). Peter, who was afraid to witness to the servants in
Caiaphas' courtyard, now had the courage to preach a
strange and revolutionary message to thousands because
of Jesus' followers having come to one accord, giving them
all an anointing of boldness.

Being in one accord equals power. It is a law of New Testament physics. Being in one accord brought three thousand,
then five thousand more new Christians into the kingdom
of God until there were multitudes surrendering their lives
to the lordship of Christ (Acts 5). The first chapters of Acts
teach us this valuable lesson that the more "one-accordness"
in the pews, the more power of God in the pulpit.

Jesus could do no mighty works in Nazareth because of
their unbelief. Most churches do not need a new minister
every three years, but they do need the spirit of "one-
accordness." It is then when God's power will come to the
pulpit, and the minister will move from the natural to the
supernatural. So, all things being equal, power through
oneness in the pews will bring to the pulpit the power to
save, sanctify, and heal.

Out of This World

───◀▦◍▦▶───

And believers were the more added to the Lord,
multitudes both of men and women.

—Acts 5:14

Isn't this a pastor's dream? On the first day of the church, we saw three thousand saved; but what are we going to say about the multitudes who were being added in a matter of days? It was now no longer possible to count the converts. Oh, what a harvest. Here in Acts 5, we see Pentecost being "out-Pentecosted." Then, add to that the acts of healing, *"and they were healed every one"* (v. 16). Indeed, in this chapter of Acts, we see Pentecost reaching its maximum in saving, healing, and sanctifying power. It could not get any better than this, only in that it would continue until the end of time.

They brought the sick from everywhere, from Jerusalem, and the adjacent cities. Hospitals were emptied. Men were seen carrying stretchers with the sick along the highways and byways as they traveled to where the apostles were. Others, more able—the blind, the lepers, the limping, the deaf, the dumb—moved on donkeys and on foot toward the miracle site, and they were all healed. Oh, my friend, what are we going to observe once the world sees the church as one, when all believers are once again joined together in holy love?

So, coming to one accord is not an impossible dream. It is history that needs repeating, and the results will be out of this world.

There Is a Chariot for You

Then the Spirit said unto Philip, Go near,
and join thyself to this chariot.

—Acts 8:29

There is a chariot for you to ride today and every day. It is the chariot of God's will.

One day, Philip found himself as a spiritual leader in a great revival in Samaria. The next day, he found himself in the Gaza strip in a chariot preaching to only one man. The day after that, he found himself in Azotus preaching his way through many cities on his way to Caesarea. Each day of Philip's life was different. Each day was filled with new exploits on the highways of God's marvelous kingdom. In this splendid domain, Philip joyfully preached to one person as much as he did to thousands.

To what and to whom do we attribute all of this beautiful life? We might say, the key of his life is found in these words, *"the Spirit said unto Philip, Go."* He, the Holy Spirit, is the One who filled this early deacon, and He, the Holy Spirit, is the One who led him each day. Would to God we would confess all our sins; would to God we would give up all our personal preferences and plans; would to God we would humble ourselves before Him, and we, too, would hear the Spirit's guidance.

Yes, God has a chariot for every one of us, and if we will be all we can be for God, our chariot will never miss a divine appointment.

Not for the World

---◀︎◁◦▷▶︎---

I pray for them: I pray not for the world, but for
them which thou hast given me; for they are thine.

—John 17:9

"I pray for them: I pray not for the world." These, indeed, are surprising words of our Lord. One would think that the world has boundless needs to be prayed over, such as the hungry, the sick, the displaced, the poor, the lonely, the mentally ill, the prisoners, the refugees, the ones who have been treated unjustly, etc. Yet, Jesus said, *"I pray not for the world."* God gave His only begotten Son that the world through Him may be saved, yet He says, *"I pray not for the world, but for them which thou hast given me; for they are thine."*

Jesus' prayers are for His people, for His body, the church. This tells us that the problem is not so much with the world as it is with the church. Jesus said in Samaria that the fields are already white for harvest, telling us that the world is more ready to be saved than the church is ready to save her. The best of religious observers and the best of theologians of that day saw nothing in Samaria; in fact, they had crossed off Samaria on their plan of evangelism. But Jesus saw fields ripe for harvest there. And the proof that He was right about this is in Acts 8:6, *"...the people [in Samaria] with one accord gave heed unto those things which Philip spake."*

Yes, my friend, as far as world evangelism is concerned, the world is ready, but the church is not yet ready. For she has not come to oneness that the power of God might fall. Therefore, Jesus prayed not for the world, but for the church that she *"may be one; as thou, Father, art in me, and I in thee, that they also may be one in us: that the world may believe that thou has sent me"* (John 17:21). Jesus prayed for the church that she might become the salt of the earth to save the world.

The Apostolic Burden

*I exhort therefore, that, first of all,
supplications, prayers, intercessions, and
giving of thanks, be made for all men; For
kings, and for all that are in authority.*

—1 Timothy 2:1–2

One of the most amazing things about Paul's prayer ministry is that, although he exhorts us through Timothy to pray for everyone on the face of the earth, there is not one single Scripture passage to be found in all the writings of Paul where we see him actually praying for the world.

Paul's phrase of Colossians 1:3, *"praying always for you,"* marks the spirit and the reality of his prayer life as seen in all of his thirteen epistles. So, since he *always* prayed for God's people day and night, sometimes with tears and sometimes with joy, there was no praying on his part for the unbelievers. This is the apostolic burden, and it does not differ from Jesus' prayer we considered yesterday, *"I pray not for the world, but for them which thou hast given me; for they are thine"* (John 17:9). Further, we learn by the words of Hebrews 7:25 that, even now, Jesus continues His prayer life for the faithful, *"...he ever liveth to make intercession for them."*

What does all this tell us? Certainly, that it is much more important to pray for the saints than for the world. It is the saints who are under the attacks of the wicked one, for the devil already has the world. And it is the saints alone who hold the keys to the salvation of the world. Pray for kings, yes, but so much the more, pray for God's people.

The Latter Rain

—◦⊸⫘∫⫘⊸◦—

*That they all may be one; as thou, Father, art in me,
and I in thee, that they also may be one in us: that
the world may believe that thou hast sent me.*

—John 17:21

$\mathbf{H}$ere is the heart of the high priestly prayer of Jesus. Here we see the deepest into the heart of our Lord. Here we see the substance of what He is still praying for at the right hand of the Father. He *"ever liveth to make intercession for them"* (Heb. 7:25). The program and the prayer vigil that Jesus began while on earth is still the same: *"That they all may be one."* Since that was at the heart of Jesus' prayer life then, and since it is so now, why shouldn't it also be at the heart of our prayer life?

Furthermore, as we saw yesterday, this prayer was also in the hearts of the early apostles. We read in 1 Corinthians 1:10, *"Now I beseech you, brethren, by the name of our Lord Jesus Christ, that ye all speak the same thing, and...that ye be perfectly joined together in the same mind and in the same judgment."* Or, listen to the dream of Paul in Philippians 2:2, *"Fulfil ye my joy, that ye be likeminded, having the same love, being of one accord, of one mind."*

Now, is such oneness really possible? As we learned earlier, biblical history says yes, for it says, *"And the multitude of them that believed were of one heart and of one soul"* (Acts 4:32). Being in one accord was the key for the *"early rain,"* and it will also usher in the *"latter rain"* (Joel 2:23–24; Acts 2:16–21).

Yes, someday, Jesus' prayer for oneness will be answered through a torrential outpouring of the Spirit such as the world has never seen before.

Early Influences

And the child grew, and she brought him unto Pharaoh's daughter, and he became her son.

—Exodus 2:10

Many scholars believe that Jochebed, the mother of Moses, kept her son for about three to six years before Pharaoh's daughter took over his care. It is marvelous that Jochebed was able to put something about the fear of God, the love of the law of God and His people, into the heart of this little boy, Moses. All the paganism, all the wise men of Egypt, all the influences of an immoral court, and all the wealth of the king's palace could not take out of Moses' heart what Jochebed put into it in those first formative years. The upbringing of Moses in those few early years was so God-centered that Moses never forgot who his real brethren were and who his real God was. Thus, it says in Exodus 2:11, *"And it came to pass in those days, when Moses was grown, that he went out unto his brethren, and looked on their burdens."*

The first five years of a child's life are so impressionable that, generally, what is placed into his life in those years will stay with him forever. This is why some Roman Catholics have said all along, "Give us your child for the first few years of life, and he will be a Catholic forever."

In a home where the values of eternity are neglected or pursued inconsistently, and where the influences of the world are allowed to seep into the child's mind, the child is likely to lose out on that divine purpose for which he was born into the world. But a praying, God-fearing mother and father thoroughly addicted to the things of God will never fail to leave an indelible impression on the heart and soul of their child.

Habit without Heart

—⟨⟨⟨⟨⟨⟨⟩⟩⟩⟩⟩⟩—

*Having a form of godliness, but denying the
power thereof: from such turn away.*

—2 Timothy 3:5

Having a form of godliness without having the power of
godliness is a result of developing habits without developing the heart. Man's preoccupation with habits at the neglect
of the heart is an age-old problem. The God of the Hebrews
lamented this when He cried out to ritualistic, religious
Israel by saying, *"Oh that there were such an heart in them,
that they would fear me, and keep all my commandments
always, that it might be well with them, and with their
children for ever!"* (Deut. 5:29).

Samuel expressed a similar disappointment to Saul when
he said, *"to obey is better than sacrifice"* (1 Sam. 15:22). The
church world of all ages has never been lacking in religious
habits, or the cultivation and preservation of religious ritu-
als and forms, but oh, how she has always been lacking in
power, in seeking God and loving God with all her heart,
soul, mind, and strength.

God's search has always been for a heart like His: a holy
heart, a loving heart, a righteous heart, a gracious heart,
and an obedient heart. Man is impressed and intrigued by
religious art and pomp, but God looks for hearts sanctified
and ready to receive His power.

Yes, there has never been a shortage of habits and forms,
of marvelous Christian art and architecture. As good as that
can be, it is always form without spiritual power that
troubles God. No wonder the cry of Joel is still with us,
*"...rend your heart, and not your garments, and turn unto
the Lord your God: for he is gracious and merciful, slow to
anger, and of great kindness"* (Joel 2:13).

If we can have both form and power, let's go for both. But
if we have to choose between them, let's go for the power!

Knowing Where You Belong

*Having a form of godliness, but denying the
power thereof: from such turn away.*
—2 Timothy 3:5

"...from such turn away." There are many things from which
a true saint must turn away. The most beloved devotional
book, the Psalms, begins with the admonition to turn away
from the council of the ungodly, the way of the sinner, and
the seat of the scornful.

Our minds must be guarded as much as possible from
the evil influences of irreligion. But, neither should our
hearts be exposed to false religion, a religion full of good
doctrine but empty of divine power. Oh, how important this
all makes the admonition of *"Not forsaking the assembling
of ourselves together"* (Heb. 10:25).

Friend, it is in the fellowship with the blood-washed
saints where we belong. The godly must fellowship with
the godly. The godly must pray, sing, worship, and praise
with the godly. They must *"exhort one another daily, while
it is called To day; lest any of you be hardened through the
deceitfulness of sin"* (Heb. 3:13). Yes, how sweet and how
precious, how invigorating and cleansing is the fellowship
of the saints. Indeed, *"if we walk in the light...we have
fellowship one with another, and the blood of Jesus Christ
his Son cleanseth us from all sin"* (1 John 1:7).

Where there is obedience, there is light, and where there
is light, there is the cleansing blood of the Lamb and the
fellowship of the Holy Ghost. All those who lack fellowship
with the Holy Spirit only have a form of godliness. Yes, from
such turn away, unless, of course, you have a sure word of
prophecy to snatch them from the eternal fires of hell.

Loving Pleasure More than God

*This know also, that in the last days perilous
times shall come. For men shall be lovers of their
own selves, covetous, boasters, proud, blasphemers,
disobedient to parents, unthankful, unholy, Without
natural affection, trucebreakers, false accusers,
incontinent, fierce, despisers of those that are
good, Traitors, heady, highminded, lovers
of pleasures more than lovers of God.*

—2 Timothy 3:1–4

The problem of the last days will not be atheism, nor irreligion, but incomplete religion. The problem will not be that men will not love God, but that they will not love God enough. So, notice the subtle truth of our text in these words: *"...lovers of pleasures more than lovers of God."* It is not the absence of love, but the shortage of love that will be the problem. Nor will the problem be the absence of prayer, of morality, of devotion, or of church attendance and programs, but the lack of wholehearted devotion in all of these areas.

Men will love God, but they will love pleasures more than God. All of the evils that Paul mentions here in Timothy will be committed by those who love God, but love pleasures more than God.

So, as the day approaches, let us not worry about atheism or agnosticism, but let us concern ourselves with the spread of evangelical lukewarmness. Rightly did Jesus ask Peter just before His ascension, *"Simon, son of Jonas, lovest thou me more than these?"* (John 21:15). And more rightly does Jesus ask all of us this question today: Lovest thou me more than all the pleasures of the world?

One Penalty

*For the wages of sin is death; but
the gift of God is eternal life through
Jesus Christ our Lord.*

—Romans 6:23

"For the wages of sin is death." Yes, there was only one punishment under Moses for all deliberate sin, and that was death.

Man's books of law abound with a myriad of punishments for a myriad of sins and transgressions. There is a one-year, a ten-year, and a lifelong prison sentence. There is a complicated system of parole. Then, there are the appeals courts. And, in addition to that, we have minimum and maximum security prisons.

God's system of jurisprudence is much simpler. One punishment fits all crimes of willful transgression. There is death for adultery, death for rebellious children, death for those cursing father and mother, death for breaking the Sabbath day, death for blasphemy, etc. No sin can stand before God. To Him, there are no light or heavy sins. The wages of all sins is death.

God, through Moses, told us what sin is when He gave us the Ten Commandments. Jesus came many years later and made sin bigger yet when He said that sin is not only in killing a brother but in hating a brother. Adultery is not only in sleeping with another man's wife, but in just lusting after her.

But as Jesus made sin bigger, He also made grace bigger. He also made the atonement bigger and better. As He made the punishment for sin simple, so did He also make the cure for sin simple: the blood of Jesus! Yes, *"the wages of sin is death; but the gift of God is eternal life through Jesus Christ our Lord"* (Rom. 6:23). Aren't you glad?

Christic Delivers

...the soul that sinneth, it shall die.

—Ezekiel 18:4

God never ordered the building of prisons, but He did make allowance for the building of cemeteries or burial places. For the wages of sin is death. Jesus said *"That except your righteousness shall exceed the righteousness of the scribes and Pharisees, ye shall in no case enter into the kingdom of heaven"* (Matt. 5:20).

Oh, how strict and how demanding are the laws of God. Do not ever say that Christ is more tolerant than Moses. Do not ever say that grace requires less than law. No! A thousand times, No! Grace requires more than the righteousness of the scribes and the Pharisees. It requires more than keeping the laws. It requires more than prayers and fasting and tithing, more than proselytizing and going to church. Grace requires all that plus the keeping of the heart without covetousness, adultery, pride, selfishness, and resentment.

Oh, how much stricter Jesus is than Moses. And because of the demands of grace, God sent His Son, Jesus, through whom we are not only forgiven, cleansed, and reconciled to God, but we are delivered daily from the scourge of sin as we follow Him in humble faith, submission, and power.

The Murderous Spirit Is Never Far from Man

━━◄▧◊▧►━━

*That the blood of all the prophets, which
was shed from the foundation of the world,
may be required of this generation.*

—Luke 11:50

Here, in Luke 11, Jesus delivers the most scorching address of His career to the Pharisees, scribes, and lawyers. As you may have observed, Jesus treated the harlots, tax collectors, and publicans with greater kindness than the religious leaders.

To the sinning masses, to those keenly conscious of their sins and shortcomings, Jesus was the gentle Shepherd. Matthew records, *"But when he saw the multitudes, he was moved with compassion on them, because they fainted, and were scattered abroad, as sheep having no shepherd"* (Matt. 9:36).

But there was no compassion with our Lord for most of the leaders. The fainting, scattered condition of the church is generally a reflection of the absence of true Christ-likeness in many of her ministers. It is to them that Jesus said, *"That the blood of all the prophets, which was shed from the foundation of the world, may be required of this generation"* (Luke 11:50). What an indictment!

The reason Jesus held these Pharisees responsible for the death of every prophet martyred since the Creation is that, had these same leaders been alive in the days of Abel, Samuel, Moses, and Jeremiah, they would have killed these prophets, too. The spirit of criticism, resentment, judgment, and murder was lodged ever so deeply in their hearts.

Yes, my friends, at all cost, let us resist this spirit in our own lives, and let us pray that our leaders may be undeserving of this strong condemnation.

Called to Be Saints

To all that be in Rome, beloved
of God, called to be saints...

—Romans 1:7

What are some of the characteristics of saints? Saints follow Jesus and not the world. They realize that the highest accomplishment on the earth is doing the will of God and doing it consistently, even as Jesus always did the will of His Father. For doing the will of God is the ultimate in Christlikeness.

Saints are those who are cheerful when it is difficult to be cheerful. Paul and Silas were cast into the inner prison. Their backs were bleeding, and their feet were in the stocks, but at midnight they prayed and sang praises to God, and the prisoners heard them. When others are overcome by gloom and hopelessness, the saints continue to rejoice. The saints are not thermometers reflecting the temperature but thermostats setting the temperature.

Saints are those who have control of their tongue. Saints are those who have the love of God shed abroad in their hearts by the Holy Spirit who is given to them. Saints are the ones who forbear and forgive one another even as Christ has also forgiven them. Saints are those who go by revelation rather than by reason. They trust the Lord with all their heart and lean not to their own understanding, in all their ways acknowledging Him (Prov. 3:5–6). And the list goes on.

My friend, come along and become a beloved of God, a saint, a jewel in the Master's crown. Yes, all of us are called to be saints.

God Is Angry at the Transgressor

━━━━

*God judgeth the righteous, and God is
angry with the wicked every day.*

—Psalm 7:11

We are overloaded with the doctrine of love and mercy, and "under-loaded" with the doctrine of fearing the anger of the Lord. It is not preached that God is angry with the wicked every day. In fact, popular opinion has it that God is not angry at the sinner but at his sin only.

When your child shoots a hole in your neighbor's window, are you angry at the gun or are you angry at the child? Do you punish the gun or the child? Was God angry at the golden calf or at the ones who made it? Was God angry at the lie that Ananias and Sapphira told, or was He angry at the liars? Was God angry at the adultery or at David for having committed it?

If God is only angry at sin and not the sinner, He would have to send only sin to hell and not the sinner. But our Bible teaches us that *"God is angry with the wicked every day."* And His anger in most all of the instances in the Bible is directed at His own, disobedient children.

Unless we think that it is only in the Old Testament that God becomes angry, let us consider these words of Jesus: *"He that obeyeth not the son of God shall not see life, but the wrath of God abideth upon him"* (John 3:36 ASV). Paul chimes in with a similar saying, *"For the wrath of God is revealed from heaven against all ungodliness and unrighteousness of men, who hold the truth in unrighteousness"* (Rom. 1:18). The Old Testament God is also the New Testament God.

Yes, it is a fearful thing to fall into the hands of an angry God, who shall cast the wicked into an everlasting fire prepared for the devil and his angels.

September 4

The Power of Restraint

*In those days came John the Baptist,
preaching in the wilderness of Judea.*

—Matthew 3:1

Except for Jesus, is there any one in history of whom more has been promised than John? The angel of God said, *"For he shall be great in the sight of the Lord...and he shall be filled with the Holy Ghost, even from his mother's womb. And many of the children of Israel shall he turn to the Lord their God"* (Luke 1:15–16).

In all the Bible, how many can you find who were Spirit-baptized at birth? Indeed, a Spirit-filled baby confounds the brightest minds in systematic theology. Is there any wonder that Jesus called John the greatest man born of woman?

But now, what did John do with this Spirit power? Did he at an early age decide to become a child evangelist and a miracle worker? No! Did he go to Jerusalem to get a good theological education to complement the divine presence resting within his soul? No! As far as the record is concerned, John did nothing with his gift, his power, his potential, and his influence for thirty years.

We think that once we have the power, a gift, or influence, we can walk through open doors. And so we do. But, we learn from John that the godly obey. They use the power of restraint and move only in God's perfect time.

We read that when God's perfect time came for John, all of Jerusalem and Judea came to the wilderness to repent and to be baptized by him. And because John waited and refused all the open doors for thirty years, he thus was honored to prepare the masses for the ministry of his Master as no one else. God is the God of restraint, and so are all those who have His presence. Because of his waiting, John did not have to go to the people. Instead, God brought the people to him.

250

Pray

*Continue in prayer, and watch in
the same with thanksgiving.*

—Colossians 4:2

Let us consider some of the wonderful aspects of prayer. Prayer is the holiest exercise of the believer. Prayer is solace in the midst of trouble. Prayer is the solver of our doubts and the remover of our perplexities. Prayer is safety in the midst of danger. Prayer is an unfailing resource in adversity. Prayer is balance in prosperity. Prayer is a weapon in every conflict. It is the key which opens the door to heavenly treasures. *"Continue in prayer..."*

Oh, what rich blessings there are in prayer. Can you see why it is the holiest and most noble exercise in the world, and readily accessible to the poor, the rich, the unlearned, the educated, from the youngest of children to the oldest of saints?

And not only is prayer wonderful in its effect on the one praying but also on that for which he prays. For prayer can cross the widest oceans and the highest mountains. It can penetrate every prison wall, reaching into every hospital and palace in the world. Prayer can stop armies, still storms, and soothe the hurt of a little girl who lost her doll.

Oh, do we know the value of prayer as Jesus and Paul did? They tell us to pray without ceasing.

Yes, you all have started in prayer, but, perhaps, some of you have left your prayer closet. The message today is *"Continue in prayer..."*

Israel Was Weary of God

He spread a cloud for a covering;
and fire to give light in the night.

—Psalm 105:39

Man tires easily of the things of God. Practically nothing was a greater proof that God was with Israel in the wilderness than the cloud by day and the fire by night.

Oh, what fire that was, for it required no fuel, no wood, no oil, and no coal. Each night, at the setting of the sun, it was there. It required no match to start it. What a fire! It kept those camped near it at the same temperature as those camped at the edge of the grounds. It left no ashes, and it required no help from man to shut it down. It provided enough light to find one's way at night, but not so much as to prevent sleep. It was the perfect light and heat for the night as the cloud was perfect for cooling during the day.

In that wilderness, temperatures easily get to freezing at night and to one-hundred degrees Fahrenheit or more in the afternoons. God provided a divinely, thermostatically, comfort-controlled environment. The cloud just rested over the camp each day and at no other place. It came there regardless of wind conditions, dew points, and relative humidity percentages.

Yet, the record says that despite all this that they would not believe in Him. They murmured, and were destroyed in the wilderness for their unbelief. May we never become weary of the presence of God in our midst, even in our hearts, and of the greatness of His forgiving love.

The Devil Is Ever Near

And he brought him to Jerusalem,
and set him on a pinnacle of the temple...

—Luke 4:9

There is no proof from this text that the devil was actually in the temple, but he was definitely on the temple. We know that where God's people are, or where they gather, the devil is likely to be very near.

Satan has no greater interest but to ever be near the Christian's side to accuse, to confuse, to buffet, to remind them of old sins, and to tempt them. So the devil was with Jesus at the temple and he was right there with him also in the wilderness of temptation. The devil attended the first communion service Jesus ever held. For the Scriptures say, *"And after the sop Satan entered into him* [Judas]*"* (John 13:27). Yes, Satan made his entrance into Judas right there in the Upper Room.

The devil hindered the apostle Paul from making a journey to Thessalonica (1 Thess. 2:18). The devil was there in that perfect garden of Paradise to take the first couple into sin, and he was surrounding the perfect man, Job, in order to strip him of his health, wealth, and family.

Yes, my friend, he was cast out of heaven and has been the accuser of the brethren ever since. *"And the great dragon was cast out, that old serpent, called the Devil, and Satan, which deceiveth the whole world...Woe to the inhabiters of the earth and of the sea! for the devil is come down unto you"* (Rev. 12:9, 12).

Therefore, let us be bold and courageous, knowing that wherever the Lord is, there the devil is also.

God Says, "Forget!"
The Devil Says, "Remember!"

———⚕———

For I acknowledge my transgressions:
and my sin is ever before me.

—Psalm 51:3

In this statement, the Psalmist not only expresses his personal dilemma, but he expresses the dilemma of all saints universal.

God through Christ will forgive us our sins. He will bury them in the sea of forgetfulness. He will remove them as far as east is from west. He will blot them out. Yes, says the Word, *"though your sins be as scarlet, they shall be as white as snow"* (Isa. 1:18). That is God's action and attitude toward our sins.

But the devil has a different program for our past sins. God's program is to forgive and forget our sins. The devil's program is to remember and accuse us of our past, forgiven sins. The devil's program is not a cleansing program but a program of putting the filth of the past back into the present.

"Yes, my sins are ever before me," states David. Paul also acknowledges this when he called himself the chief of sinners because he had persecuted the church.

Indeed, we cannot prevent the devil from bringing back the sins of the past, but we can and shall refuse to take the guilt of those sins back upon us. That guilt has been done away with by Christ once and for all. Let us believe that, stand on it, and proclaim it. For *"If we confess our sins, he is faithful and just to forgive us our sins, and to cleanse us from all unrighteousness"* (1 John 1:9).

The Cleansing of Faith

—◦ⅉⅉ◦—

And the Lord said unto Moses, Make
thee a fiery serpent, and set it upon a pole:
and it shall come to pass, that every one that
is bitten, when he looketh upon it, shall live.
—Numbers 21:8

God's ways are always in the supernatural. They are always beyond the natural, beyond the comprehensible, and beyond man's fondest imaginations and highest dreams.

Which medical society would ever come up with a serpent of brass for a cure for snake bites? Or which doctor would suggest clay and spittle as a cure for blindness? Or which psychiatrist would suggest that the cure for most emotional problems is the confession of sins? *"Make thee a fiery serpent, and set it upon a pole."*

Now, who was to make a serpent, and who was to set it up, and who was to tell the people to look at it? It was Moses. God has to have a man who believes in the supernatural, and who will trust Him with all his heart and lean not to his own understanding to expedite a supernatural cure. Moses was such a believer. Had Moses leaned upon his own understanding, this cure would never have happened.

So, miracles tend to congregate where there is faith—pure, unspoiled faith. In fact, it is this kind of faith only, as demonstrated by Moses, that draws miracles from the skies. But when faith ceases to draw miracles, it is time for it to have a thorough, spiritual cleansing.

Be a Moses, holy and wholly committed to God, so that like him, you cease to be a problem but rather become a solution to the ills and sins of men. The world still needs men and women who raise fiery serpents when the snakes come out of their holes.

Tarrying for Transformation

———◆———

...tarry ye in the city of Jerusalem, until ye
be endued with power from on high.

—Luke 24:49

Unfortunately, scholars have stuck the words "Great Commission" to the "go ye" into all the world rather than the "tarry ye" in Jerusalem. Had the "tarry" been included in the "go ye" as part of the Great Commission, church history would have been written quite differently.

The eleven disciples that Jesus commissioned to "tarry" thought they were ready to go. When Jesus was still with them, they had tasted the power of God in preaching, casting out devils, and in healing the sick. But, after their initial experience, these disciples quickly fell back into their regular self-seeking routines, wanting to know who among them was the greatest. The seventy who were sent out with like power, having had similar success, left Jesus altogether.

Jesus' words to them was "tarry ye" this time before you go out again. So, "tarry ye" this time before you go out, in order that there will be no retreat to failure, no self-seeking, nor self-glory. So, "tarry ye." But tarry how long?

The disciples were told exactly how long to tarry. They were to tarry until they were endued with power, whether it would take ten hours, ten days, ten months, or ten years. They were told to tarry until they could corporately be trusted with the power that would give birth to the church to equip her for worldwide evangelism.

So, "tarry" they did, until they came to oneness. When that occurred, the world began to be turned right-side-up. May we all learn to "tarry," individually and corporately.

His Yoke Is Easy

Take my yoke upon you, and learn of me;
for I am meek and lowly in heart: and ye
shall find rest unto your souls. For my
yoke is easy, and my burden is light.
—Matthew 11:29–30

First, let us notice whose yoke we must take upon ourselves. It is the yoke of Jesus. No man born into the world is ever to take upon himself any yoke but Christ's. The whole purpose of any man's life is wrapped up in Christ's yoke, for our own yokes only get us into trouble. They are heavy, cumbersome, depressing, suppressive, and oppressive.

It is impossible to do God's will without His yoke. It is impossible to be sanctified without His yoke. It is impossible to go to heaven without His yoke. To be yoked up with Him means to become one with Him.

Secondly, notice that this yoke must be taken up voluntarily. Jesus never presses us into His yoke. He only pleads with us to *"Take my yoke upon you."*

Thirdly, notice the relationship between you and the Lord in this yoke. You are the apprentice, and He is the Master. He sets the direction, and you follow along. He sets the pace, and you get into step. He determines the load, and you help pull it, and He will see to it that it will never become cumbersome. Remember, He is always on the other side of it.

Now then, what is His yoke? Simply speaking: His yoke is His will. So Jesus says, "Follower, learn of me as you are yoked with me." Only those who are yoked with Him will learn of Him.

Oh, what a marvelous way to travel! Don't you want to start your journey with Him today?

Meekness Is Power

---◆◆◆---

...for I am meek and lowly in heart:
and ye shall find rest unto your souls.

—Matthew 11:29

The reason why we need to be yoked with Him is not only by virtue of His power, but by virtue of His spirit, *"...for I am meek and lowly."* Power without meekness is dangerous. We learned that from all great leaders who failed miserably in the end, like King Saul, Napoleon, and Hitler, to mention just a few.

Meekness leads to the right use of power. The wise use of power leads to the restrained use of power. This is why the first beatitude is *"Blessed are the poor in spirit: for their's is the kingdom of heaven"* (Matt. 5:3). The kingdom of heaven and the Spirit of God come in power only to the meek and lowly of heart.

Moses was the most powerful man in his generation because he was also the meekest man of his generation. So was David in his time, because he had a broken and a contrite heart which made him a meek man after God's own heart. Now let us consider the rest of this verse: *"...and ye shall find rest unto your souls."*

Rest! What a pleasant word and what a soothing word it is. This is not an outer rest but an inner rest, as promised in Christ's yoke. Jesus always had this rest, and it was with Him when he heard of the plot of the Pharisees to kill Him. He had this rest when He was in the midst of the raging sea of Galilee. And it was there with Him when all the disciples forsook Him.

Oh, what a beautiful pearl is this meekness and rest. Wherever you find the one, you will always find the other.

Christ's Cross and Our Cross

*And he that taketh not his cross,
and followeth after me, is not worthy of me.*

—Matthew 10:38

The process of redemption unto discipleship requires two crosses. First, we need Christ's cross and the Christ of the cross. It is through Him and His cross that we are reconciled to God. The other cross is our cross, the cross we must carry daily.

His cross on which He purchased our redemption was physical and historical, but ours is spiritual and ever applicable in the present. His cross was universal—ours is personal. His cross gets us on the divine road, but our cross keeps us on the road called "Narrow." It is impossible to follow Jesus without our cross. *"And he that taketh not his cross...is not worthy of me."*

Now, what is this cross for? The cross is an instrument of death upon which every plan and program of our Self-life must be crucified. Yes, indeed, Self must be put to death, because in our Self-life we will never submit to Jesus. The Self within us has its own agenda and its own kingdom. It must be crucified. So, for Jesus' kingdom to come and for His will to be done, the Self and its kingdom have to perish, because they are contrary to the will of God.

Although Jesus' death on the cross for us was once and for all, the death to Self must be a continuous process for us to experience the continuous resurrection power of the Lord Jesus Christ. Self must be denied moment by moment through self-crucifixion so that we may be able to obey and follow God. So, except a man deny himself and take up his cross daily, he cannot be Christ's disciple (Luke 9:23).

A Call to Be Strong

Be strong and of a good courage.

—Joshua 1:6

Two of the most important decisions each of us must make in life are to let Christ be our Lord and then to choose to be strong.

Before Joshua could be trusted with leading the Israelites into the Promised Land, he had to make a conscious decision to be strong. Four times God commands Joshua to be strong in his charge to take Canaan.

Dear one, get it into your heart that if you have received Christ, you must also make a conscious decision to be strong. Nowhere in the Bible does God admonish anyone to be weak. No, we don't have to work at becoming weak—we are weak, every one of us. Yet, this gives us no excuse for not pulling ourselves together to love God with all our heart, soul, mind, and strength.

Canaan is for the strong. The kingdom is for the strong, for Jesus said, *"the kingdom of heaven suffereth violence, and the violent taketh it by force"* (Matt. 11:12). The church needs strong leaders and strong soldiers—strong in faith, strong in obedience, strong in love, patience, and prayer, and in utter dependence upon the Lord. The church needs people who will put their body and its passions under subjection, who will put on the garment of discipline and never take it off again.

So, to be strong is not an elective but a requirement for a victorious Christian life. Therefore, let us close with these words of Paul: *"...quit you like men, be strong"* (1 Cor. 16:13); *"Finally, my brethren, be strong in the Lord, and in the power of his might"* (Eph. 6:10); and *"Wherefore lift up the hands which hang down, and the feeble knees; And make straight paths for your feet"* (Heb. 12:12–13).

THE LAW: the Sinner's Enemy

━━◐◖§◗◑━━

Wherefore the law was our schoolmaster
to bring us unto Christ, that we
might be justified by faith.

—Galatians 3:24

The moral law is like a mirror that reflects the awesome radiance and holiness of God. The purpose of the law is to show us the righteousness of God and the weakness and sinfulness of man. The law wants to bring the sinner to such a point of frustration and condemnation that he cries out, *"O wretched man that I am! who shall deliver me from the body of this death?"* (Rom. 7:24).

Therefore, Paul says in Galatians that the law is our schoolmaster. This schoolmaster is to teach us that the heart of man *"is deceitful above all things, and desperately wicked"* (Jer. 17:9). The law helps the sinner to recognize that he cannot be righteous on his own merits, and that he needs a Savior, for *"all our righteousnesses are as filthy rags"* (Isa. 64:6). Truly, outside of Christ, *"There is none righteous, no, not one,"* and *"For all have sinned, and come short of the glory of God"* (Rom. 3:10, 23).

That is what the law tells the unregenerate man, that he must be reproved, regenerated, refined. The law tells man that he cannot reform, train, and educate himself to meet the demands of God. Man just has to be made over. He has to receive a new heart and a new spirit. He must be converted and become a man of faith. He must be justified by faith to have peace with God through our Lord Jesus Christ.

Let us not despise God's schoolmaster. Let us allow its full work in our lives that we might come to the end of ourselves and accept Christ, Who is *"the end of the law for righteousness"* (Rom. 10:4).

THE LAW: Fulfilled in Us

*That the righteousness of the law
might be fulfilled in us, who walk not
after the flesh, but after the spirit.*

—Romans 8:4

The apostle Paul tells us that the flesh could not keep the law. No flesh shall glory before God. *"For all have sinned, and come short of the glory of God"* (Rom. 3:23). This is Pauline theology on the negative side of salvation.

But on the positive side of salvation, we are born of God, *"That the righteousness of the law might be fulfilled in us, who walk not after the flesh, but after the spirit."* Christ by His indwelling Spirit takes us from the negative to the positive; from the "I can't" to the "I can." Through Christ, we are brought from despair to hope, from condemnation to acceptance, from weakness to strength, from fear to faith, and from insufficiency to sufficiency. Oh, what a Savior!

"God sending his own Son in the likeness of sinful flesh, and for sin, condemned sin in the flesh: That the righteousness of the law might be fulfilled in us, who walk not after the flesh, but after the Spirit" (Rom. 8:3–4). Again, through Christ in us, we can keep the law. Through Christ in us, we do not covet, we do not commit adultery, and we do not steal. Through Christ in us, we walk after the Spirit, and the law is fulfilled in us. Let us not be antinomians, enemies of the law, for the law convicts the sinner and protects the saint.

As Jesus fulfilled the law in His flesh, He now fulfills His law in our flesh. Oh, what a gift is this Christ! He is Savior, sanctifier, and enabler!

THE LAW: the Spirit Is Greater

...except your righteousness shall exceed the righteousness of the scribes and Pharisees, ye shall in no case enter into the kingdom of heaven.

—Matthew 5:20

Jesus did not discard nor belittle the righteousness of the law. He never looked at the law as His enemy but always as His friend. And so, we, too, must have this attitude toward the law as brought out by these words of Jesus: *"whosoever shall do and teach them* [these commandments], *the same shall be called great in the kingdom of heaven"* (Matt. 5:19).

As our verse today says, our righteousness should exceed the righteousness of the Pharisees. The doing and teaching of this righteousness demanded a strict observance of the tithe; *"for ye pay tithe of mint and anise and cummin..."* (Matt. 23:23). It included much prayer, regular periods of fasting, and strict observance of the holy days. It encompassed a jealousy for God, and obedience to all that God revealed.

Jesus did not condemn this kind of righteousness. He said it was good, but not good enough. We need to go beyond it, and we need to add to it the beautiful elements of the Beatitudes and the rest of the Sermon on the Mount. These elements would include: brokenness, humility, flexibility, love, purity of heart, compassion, generosity, trust, and meekness. For the letter of the law without the spirit kills, and the spirit without the letter is as a body without a skeleton. Yes, we need both: letter and spirit.

Yet, the standard of the Spirit is higher than the standard of the letter, and this is why Jesus said that our righteousness must exceed that of the Pharisees.

Christ's Troubled Soul

Now is my soul troubled; and what shall I say?
Father, save me from this hour: but for
this cause came I unto this hour.

—John 12:27

It is not unusual for man to be troubled. Job 5:7 tells us that *"man is born unto trouble, as the sparks fly upward."*

The question, however, I would try to bring before you today is, "What are you troubled about?" Are you troubled about finances, about the economy, about the future, about your children, about the weather, about your health, about the state of the nation, about your job or your marriage, or about a lost opportunity?

It is natural to be troubled about many things, but my next question is, "Are you troubled about what troubled Jesus?" He said, *"Now is my soul troubled..."* Jesus was troubled about the fact that by the end of the week, He, the most holy One of Israel, the spotless Lamb of God, would become the worst sinner who ever lived on the face of the earth as He would take upon Himself the sin of the whole world, bearing it upon the cross. It is the prospect of sin touching Him, His divine soul, that was His greatest trouble, to the point that it took Him to the ground in Gethsemane, where in agony over this, His sweat became as drops of blood falling to the ground. *"Now is my soul troubled..."*

My friend, how much does the prospect of some spot of sin, of some blemish of evil, or of some wrinkle of disobedience falling upon your soul by evening trouble you? Are you as troubled over sin in your life as Jesus was? Tell me how much you are troubled when you discover a stain of sin in your heart, and I will tell you how much you love Jesus and how much you are like unto Him.

Oh, may the Lord have mercy on us that all our other troubles become like nothing compared to the thought of sin in our blood-washed souls.

The Driving Force of Discontentment

But godliness with contentment is great gain.
—1 Timothy 6:6

The first woman, Eve, was discontented when she reached for the forbidden fruit. The advertising industry has made a fortune off discontentment ever since.

Discontentment is a great money maker in today's society. Television, radio ads, shop windows, and magazines all display merchandise which are aimed at making us discontented with what we have. In fact, generating discontentment with what we have is the first priority of every salesman. The salesman is eager to help us to buy something better, promising us more happiness, and in the process, filling his pocket with our money.

With the rapid advance of science and technology, the things we have today are quickly considered outmoded, out of taste, out of style, and inefficient by tomorrow. Add to that easy credit, and we are encouraged to borrow, which adds to our debt to man, and only decreases our credit with God.

Yet, the only reason why we often fall into this tragic trap of the devil is because within our hearts is the root of discontentment with God Himself. When we are truly God's, our abiding in Christ will give us such joy and contentment with Him that we would rather spend our money for His kingdom than on many a new thing that is entirely unnecessary. When we are truly Christ's, we are more interested in building up treasures in heaven *"where neither moth nor rust doth corrupt, and where thieves do not break through nor steal"* (Matt. 6:20).

So, the cure for discontentment with what we have is simply our getting more of Christ. The more we have of Him, the less we need of this world.

Do We Need All This?

...and be content with such things as ye have.

—Hebrews 13:5

Not only are most individuals under financial stress, but many churches are as well. How often do we hear from pastors speaking of their churches, "We are financially stressed to the limit. We cannot borrow any more, and if we lose ten more members, we cannot make our mortgage payments."

Why all of this? Is this the will of God? Do we need church buses to boost our Sunday school attendance? Do we need a church gymnasium to keep our young people and to reach others? Do we need the best sound system? Do we need the finest of instruments to sing for the glory of God?

Since God could make His presence known to His children of the early church, even without church buildings, why do we think we need so much more? Since God is happy with our making a joyful noise, why do we have to become debtors to banks to procure expensive instruments? Since the youth under Moses in the wilderness were saved and kept by the power of God through the fires burning in Moses, Joshua, and Caleb's hearts, what makes us think we need gymnasiums to do it today?

Oh, let us be content, and only buy and borrow when the Holy Spirit really leads. When He leads it will be wonderful, and the Shekinah glory will stay with us, but if we buy and borrow without His direction, we will have temples without glory and hearts without Christ.

The Good of Giving

Verily I say unto you, That this poor widow hath cast more in, than all they which have cast into the treasury: For all they did cast in of their abundance; but she of her want did cast in all that she had, even all her living.

—Mark 12:43–44

One day, Jesus sat by the treasury and He watched how people cast money into that treasury. Notice that Jesus has an intense interest in our tithes and offerings. He is watching our giving.

In reference to that, it is not as important to whom or to what we give, as that we give, and that we do it with a right spirit. The widow gave to a temple from which the Shekinah glory had long departed. The fact that this money was apparently wasted on a dead, condemned institution ready to be abolished did not bother Jesus at all. For Him, that she gave, and how she gave, was more important than to what she gave.

So, let us not be overly concerned with what religious institutions do with our tithe. That is their problem, not ours. Let us give as generously and cheerfully as this woman, and God will honor us.

Second, we learn from this example that covetousness is the deepest sin of our Self-life, and it is best conquered by giving rather than by receiving. It is better for us to give even to the least noble cause than to keep the money for ourselves. This will help us to keep covetous roots from springing up within our hearts. *"For the love of money is the root of all evil"* (1 Tim. 6:10).

So, Jesus' attention is more on the giving end than the receiving end. Let it be so with us, also.

267

No Darkness in God

This then is the message which we have heard of him, and declare unto you, that God is light, and in him is no darkness at all.

—1 John 1:5

John the apostle makes about twenty-four references in his gospel to light. In fact, he begins with a reference to light and darkness (John 1:4–5). Hence, John's gospel can rightly be called the "Gospel of Light." And no other gospel writer connects more firmly to the first truth of all Christian theology, namely that God is light and God is a separator of light from darkness. *"Let there be light"* was God's first word; God's dividing of the light from the darkness was His first act (Gen. 1:3–4). There is nothing more important for us to know than that. The doctrine of salvation, sanctification, the church, and practical Christian living must all be built on that principle. This great truth is also reiterated in the beginning of John's epistle where he says that *"God is light, and in him is no darkness at all"* (1 John 1:5).

Pity those corrupters of theology who portray Jesus as the great compromiser, as the great peace-maker, as the great mixer of light and darkness to bring us all to oneness in some great, gray fog. Pity those who call upon the holy to become a little less holy and the unholy a little more holy to bring us all to the same table. Pity those who fear division more than holiness, and light more than darkness. No, light was separated from darkness at the very beginning, and no doctrine is worth a cent that does not recognize that the children of light and the children of darkness are two different species. They will never be friends but are destined to be mortal enemies forever.

A Place to Be Radical

And if thy right hand offend thee,
cut it off, and cast it from thee.

—Matthew 5:30

I told someone years ago that if he kept excusing himself from prayer each morning, he should do the following: "Knock out a window every time you make an excuse for not keeping the morning prayer vigil. It will soon become too expensive to make excuses."

This is the principle in the Sermon on the Mount which says, *"And if thy right hand offend thee, cut it off."* That is to say, if you cannot discipline yourself, get radical so that, by all means, you might make it to the Great Supper. Nothing must ever take preeminence over the will of God. Nothing!

In many areas of life, we are called to balance and to moderation. But, when it comes to seeking first His kingdom, radical measures are not out of the question. Having considered this principle of the Sermon on the Mount, let us view the following radical teachings of our Lord: *"If any man come to me, and hate not his father, and mother, and wife...he cannot be my disciple"* (Luke 14:26); *"whosoever he be...that forsaketh not all that he hath, he cannot be my disciple"* (14:33); *"Follow me; and let the dead bury their dead"* (Matt. 8:22); *"If a man abide not in me, he is cast forth...and...burned"* (John 15:6).

My friend, there is a place for radicalism in Christianity, and let's never forget it. God used radical means to save us, and it will take radical means for us to get to heaven.

Being Offended

Yet hath he not root in himself, but
dureth for a while: for when tribulation
or persecution ariseth because of the
word, by and by he is offended.

—Matthew 13:21

The Scriptures predict that in the last days many shall be offended (Matt. 24:10). The fruit of an offense is generally resentment, disappointment, and hard feelings. Since we are at the end of the age, ungodly and lukewarm Christians will be more easily offended by the godly than at any time in history.

It is impossible to prevent offenses. In fact, whenever divinity meets up with carnality, there is an offense.

Jesus Himself was called the *"rock of offence"* (Isa. 8:14). He offended many people, and most likely more people were offended by Him than by any person in previous history. The Gospels confirm this in passages such as, *"And they were offended in him"* (Matt. 13:57) and *"Then saith Jesus unto them, All ye shall be offended because of me"* (Matt. 26:31). And Matthew 15:12 tells us that the Pharisees were offended at Jesus.

Well, what is the cause of an offense? In our opening text, we find one of the reasons: no roots! Many have received the Word with joy, but have refused thereafter to put their roots into the soil of self-denial and obedience and, hence, they are easily offended. They have become weathervane Christians, always more influenced by momentary impressions than by a deep relationship with Jesus Christ.

Put your roots down, crucify the old nature, and you will be able to say with David, *"Great peace have they which love thy law: and nothing shall offend them"* (Ps 119:165).

Christ Does Not Coddle His Babies

And when Jesus knew it, he saith unto
them, Why reason ye, because ye have no bread?
perceive ye not yet, neither understand?
have ye your heart yet hardened?

—Mark 8:17

The book of Hebrews tells us, *"For whom the Lord loveth he chasteneth, and scourgeth every son whom he receiveth"* (12:6). Yes, He disciplines every son whom He receives, and it might as well say, "...every son as soon as he is received."

The new convert must quickly learn to endure hardship, and to be a good soldier of Jesus Christ (2 Tim. 2:3). God does not pamper nor coddle his babies. As soon as they are born, they are in a war which requires the full armor of God. The devil is no respecter of youth. He will attack the newborn babe in Christ long before his first day is over.

So, in Christianity, the training and disciplining of the new convert not only precedes the battle, but it is often concurrent with it. Hence, Jesus had strong, but loving, interactions with His new and young disciples, calling them "hard of heart."

Thus Jesus said to Peter, *"Get thee behind me, Satan"* (Mark 8:33), before the roots of Peter's faith were firmly in the ground. Hence, Jesus called the Syrophenician woman a dog at His first encounter with her (Mark 7:26–30). Yes, Jesus scourges every son whom He receives when He receives him.

Beloved, do not despise the chastening of the Lord. It means He loves you, and because He loves you, He prepares you for warfare and conquest immediately. Christ does not coddle His babies.

271

Receiving Rebuke

But Jesus said unto her, Let the children first
be filled: for it is not meet to take the children's
bread, and to cast it unto the dogs.

—Mark 7:27

Not too many people would stay in church if their pastor would compare them to dogs. Nor would many appreciate it if their minister would identify them with Satan, as Jesus did with Peter when He said to him, *"Get thee behind me, Satan: thou art an offence unto me: for thou savourest not the things that be of God, but those that be of men"* (Mat. 16:23).

Most of us do not take rebuke too well, do we? Many of us are rather easily offended and would leave the fellowship of the church under much less rebuke than Peter and the Syrophenician woman experienced.

So then, what caused these hardy souls to stay with our Lord, totally ignoring the verbal pounding of the Son of Man? The answer is simple: faith, love, and vision. If these are in poor supply, our feathers are easily ruffled, even at the slightest breeze.

It is shallowness of faith, love, and vision that caused King Saul to lose his kingdom, Judas to betray Jesus, many disciples to forsake Him, and Demas to leave Paul. It is the lack of faith, love, and vision that has caused millions to leave their pastors over straight talk, that has caused other millions to leave their spouses over offenses that should have been ignored.

Peter took the strong rebuke, and that is one of the reasons why he became the chief apostle. The Syrophenician woman took the strong rebuke, and that is one of the reasons why her daughter was delivered from a devil. What is it that you have missed because you have allowed yourself to be offended?

Two Halves

These words spake Jesus, and lifted up his eyes to heaven, and said, Father, the hour is come; glorify thy Son, that thy Son also may glorify thee.

—John 17:1

John 17 has Jesus' longest recorded discourse with His Father. One of the remarkable revelations of this high priestly prayer is how Jesus really felt about His disciples.

Throughout the Gospels, we find our Lord at times chiding His disciples for their little faith and hardened hearts. But in this great prayer, Jesus says to His Father, *"they have kept thy word...And all mine are thine, and thine are mine; and I am glorified in them"* (John 17:6, 10). Oh, what a difference there is between what Jesus says to His disciples and what He tells His Father!

Now, is this a contradiction? The answer is no. What we have here is merely two pieces of a whole—two halves. Jesus did not want His disciples to know how happy He was with them, how overjoyed, how grateful, despite their weaknesses. He knows all too well that pride cometh before destruction, and for Him to tell His disciples what He told His Father, no doubt, would have inflated their little heads beyond the level of spiritual sanity.

Jesus, and His Father, have never, and will never, pamper His people. But how deep and precious is the love of the Lord to those who have forsaken all to follow Him! How pleased He is with every effort you make to be more like Him! How thrilled He is when He sees you being kind, thoughtful, and compassionate!

Yes, as we grope about in our spiritual inadequacies and moral fumbling, our Savior says to His Father, *"I am glorified in them."*

The Holy Spirit Will Guide You

Howbeit when he, the Spirit of truth, is come,
he will guide you into all truth.

—John 16:13

It is impossible for any one of us to know much of the will of God without the indwelling of the Holy Spirit. The Holy Spirit opens our spiritual ears. Hence, a person without the Holy Spirit is like a home without a telephone receiver or like a man without ears—he can speak, but he cannot hear. A man without the Holy Spirit is like a deaf man! He can sing, he can pray, he can serve, he can worship, he can go to the mission field, he can preach, and he can read the Word of God, but he cannot hear. Unless we have the Holy Spirit living within us and guiding us, we will be on a mission disconnected from the Master; we will guess, we will assume, we will reason as to what we think the Lord would have us do, but we will not hear from Him.

The precious Holy Spirit was given to convict us, to sanctify us, and to guide us. What Jesus did for the disciples in giving them daily instruction by His word as to where they were to go, when they were to leave, and what they were to say; so the Holy Spirit was promised to do for every believer, once Jesus sent Him to the church on Pentecost. Every day that Jesus was with the twelve, they were at the right place, at the right time, with the right mission. So it is with everyone that is filled with the Holy Spirit.

My friend, how do we get there? The same way the disciples got to that marvelous place: by forsaking all, taking up the cross, and following Him. Oh, the wonder, the blessing, and the fullness of these words: *"he will guide you."*

Israel Favored Aaron

And the people murmured against Moses,
saying, What shall we drink?

—Exodus 15:24

Israel had a lot more trouble with Moses than with Aaron. The more time that transpired in these forty years in the desert, the more people favored Aaron over Moses. Let us look at some reasons why this was so.

1. Aaron spent most of his time with the people—Moses, with God. People like it when a spiritual leader has time for them. God likes it when a leader has time for Him.

2. Aaron was a better communicator and a politician. Aaron had explanations for everything. Moses never explained anything, but only said the words, *"Thus saith the Lord..."* This hardly ever satisfies people, and it raised suspicion in the hearts of the multitude of murmurers.

3. Aaron was much more like the people. They still had a lot of Egypt in their hearts and so did Aaron.

Even so it is today. People can identify much more with the man on the platform of the church who has a piece of the golden calf in his heart than the one who has heaven's purity in his soul. The purity of a man of God is always a great threat to hearts who still long for the leeks and the garlic of the old world.

Pure men like Moses, who get provoked at sin, appear radical to the church. They appear "unbalanced," "unrealistic," and "out of touch." Consequently, many people will continue to murmur against the Moseses and favor the Aarons.

What Do You Owe?

*Owe no man any thing, but to love
one another: for he that loveth another
hath fulfilled the law.*

—Romans 13:8

How much do you owe, and to whom do you owe it? You really only own what you have paid for entirely. So then, what do you really own?

A man living in a shack and riding a bicycle all paid for is richer than the man who lives in a twenty-room house with three lovely cars in the garage not paid for. The man in the shack is richer because: (1) he has found contentment with such things as he has; (2) he has exercised discipline, a notable requirement for discipleship; (3) he is not a slave to any financial institution; and (4) he is free from the love of the world.

How grieved is the Holy Spirit at our lack of contentment and our constant reaching for things beyond our financial means? Too many believers have become slaves to the banks rather than to Christ. So, when the Holy Spirit leads for them to go visit a mission station in Africa, or to help a needy saint, they sanctimoniously say, "I would sure like to, but I can't."

Oh, why can't you, my dear friend? It is often because the devil has tricked you and bound you with financial debt that comes out of a heart that needs to be cleansed from the love of the things of the world.

Yes, may we be cleansed of the love of the world and owe only to Jesus and His lofty cause all we are and have.

Paradise Restored
The First Church Problem

*But a certain man named Ananias, with
Sapphira his wife, sold a possession, And
kept back part of the price.*

—Acts 5:1–2

Here, we have the first problem in the life of the church.
Did Peter hear what Jesus told him in Matthew 18? Indeed,
he did (*see* Matt. 18:15–17).

The church was pure and in one accord. Yes, they not
only had oneness of mind and judgment, but also oneness of
heart and soul (Acts 4:32). Because of the power of God
working through the church, there were wonderful miracles
of healing of all manner of sicknesses, and the saving and
sanctifying of souls went on unabated. In Acts 2, we see that
the power of God will work in any one congregation in relationship to her oneness. This was also true when oneness
was restored in Acts 5:12, for the power of God was present
to heal all people (v. 16).

Now, in this early chapter of Acts, God has His second
Eden, His second Paradise on earth. This was a pure, a holy,
a precious garden of God's presence like the first. But here,
too, the devil chose to enter in and to deceive a couple. The
new Adam and Eve of the garden were now Ananias and
Sapphira.

So, what did Peter do? Did he ignore the problem? Did
he just pray for the cancer to go away? No! Peter had been
with Jesus, and he confronted the problem with the help of
the Holy Spirit, as Jesus gave instructions in Matthew 18.

May those of us who are in authority do likewise, however, remembering to never do it without much love and
the help and guidance of our precious Lord.

277

October 2

Unequal Distribution
The Second Church Problem

And in those days,...there arose a murmuring
of the Grecians against the Hebrews, because their
widows were neglected in the daily ministration.

—Acts 6:1

Peter addressed the first church problem without delay. The cancer created by Ananias and Sapphira was removed, unity was restored, and God did even greater miracles now, *"Insomuch that they brought forth the sick into the streets, and laid them on beds and couches, that at the least the shadow of Peter passing by might overshadow some of them"* (Acts 5:15). This would have never happened had Peter ignored the problem of Ananias and Sapphira.

In today's passage, Peter addressed the second problem in the church: the care of the widows. What all has the church missed because of her habit of circumventing problems for the fear of man? How many millions have not been healed and saved because church leaders lack the closeness of Jesus, the obedience, and the fortitude to address the cancers in the body of Christ?

So, in the neglect of the widows, we have problem number two. It was resolved by the twelve calling all the disciples together. Deacons were appointed, harmony was restored, the power of the Holy Spirit moved back into the body of Christ, and now even a great number of priests were obedient to the faith (Acts 6:7).

Yes, the early church, the Spirit-filled church, had a problem-solving attitude because she worshipped a problem-solving God. She removed every stain from her garment as soon as it appeared before she continued her journey with Christ. Let us also draw closer to our Savior for wisdom and for boldness, and to hear His voice whenever His body becomes stained.

278

Strong on Truth, Weak on Love
The Third Church Problem

—⟪⟫⟪⟫—

*And certain men...said, Except ye be circumcised
after the manner of Moses, ye cannot be saved. When
therefore Paul and Barnabas had no small dissension and
disputation with them, they determined that Paul
and Barnabas...should go up to Jerusalem.*

—Acts 15:1–2

Today, we look at the third problem of disunity in the history of the church. When the question of circumcision came up, a council was convened in Jerusalem which decided that the Gentile believers did not have to be circumcised or keep the Law of Moses in order to be saved.

The first problem was a deep, inner, spiritual problem in the life of Ananias and Sapphira. The second was a physical problem of unequal distribution among the widows. The third was a problem of doctrinal disunity amongst church leaders. All of these problems were stains on the new bride of Christ, and each had its own peculiar nature. It's wonderful that the apostles addressed these various problems, because most of our problems are somewhat related to those found in the book of Acts: dishonesty, murmuring, and doctrinal disagreement. Let us learn that doctrinal problems, if unsolved, generally lead to church splits and the formation of new denominations or religious movements.

Seldom do religious leaders have more love than they have truth. Would to God that leaders would be just as passionate lovers of the brotherhood as they are champions of their doctrines. Wherever truth is upheld at the expense of love amongst brethren, splits occur. Because God's love in the brotherhood was as strong here as love for the truth, a church split was avoided. May we also speak the truth in love that we *"may grow up into him in all things, which is the head, even Christ"* (Eph. 4:15).

Solitude Is as Holy as Work

—◄▰▮▮ ◗▮▮▮◄—

*And in the morning, rising up a great
while before day, he went out, and departed
into a solitary place, and there prayed.*

—Mark 1:35

Our Lord's greatest entertainment was solitude. His rest between missions was not in, "Let's do something," but rather in withdrawing Himself. When do we listen to the One who wants to give us our mission? If we spend hours talking, do we not also need hours for listening? There is no greater, no cheaper, and no better entertainment than solitude.

The man who goes from mission to mission without solitude will eventually cease to have a mission. Misdirected zeal often leads to misdirected ministries, and deserves no admiration or commendation. Working ourselves to death for the cause of Christ without Christ working through us may give us a feeling of satisfaction, but it puts no smile on the Savior's face.

Jesus said we will always have the poor with us; so also the lost, the sick, and the lonely. We must never let human need and misery overwhelm us and destroy us. We, as Jesus, must stay in control of our spiritual, mental, and physical strength, and that means frequent times of withdrawal.

As Jesus took time to pray, so must we. As Jesus took time to rest, so must we. As Jesus took time to feast, so must we. As He was entertained by solitude, so must we be. Yes, the multitudes needed Jesus, but so did He need His Father and the Father Him. Should it be any different for us?

A Man of Humble Modesty

And he charged him to tell no man...

—Luke 5:14

In this verse, Jesus charges a completely healed leper to tell no one what had just happened to him. Why? Because Jesus sought no honor for the miracles He performed.

Jesus was the divine Son, yet He used extreme caution in His declarations about His office. Most of the time, He was silent about His Sonship; and when He identified Himself with it, He did it in such a humble way that it always glorified the Father and never the Son.

Jesus seldom used His office as a platform of authority, but rather He let His character and the truth He proclaimed stake out their own claims. Jesus relished presenting Himself as a servant, and His actions revealed that the servant spirit was in His heart.

Jesus never rose to a level where the simple, mundane things ceased to be part of His life. It was never beyond His dignity to associate with the undesirables of society, but rather, His dignity consisted in seeking the friendship of the needy, the lowly, and the humble at heart.

Jesus never made exaggerated or hopeful claims as are often made today, such as, "We are going to have a great meeting," "The Holy Ghost is going to do great things," "Revival is just around the corner," or "God is going to heal and sanctify many in this meeting," etc.

Jesus never broadcast a meeting ahead of time, He never used human methods to draw crowds, and He never bragged about a meeting before it started or when it was over. Yes, Jesus was a man of humble modesty.

A Ministry without Statistics

For whoever shall do the will of my Father
which is in heaven, the same is my
brother, and sister, and mother.

—Matthew 12:50

To Jesus, success was not big rallies. When the multitudes came, He taught them, but He made no human effort to have them come.

People came by the thousands because they saw hope, love, and wisdom in Him, and not because they were told to be there. Those who came to Him and followed Him did so without coercion.

To Him, success was not in numbers. He never counted how many were saved, or healed, or in attendance. Others did, but not Jesus. Jesus refused the numbers business lest He would make it a measure of success, for success to Him was nothing other than doing *"the will of my Father"* from morning until night, and then through the night.

If we go after numbers, we miss God's will: we become competitive, prejudiced, judgmental, envious, jealous, hard-driving, demanding, coercive, conceited, and proud. We become depressed with the downs and prideful with the ups. We become governed by statistics and miss the blind Bartimaeuses on the waysides of life.

Had Jesus gone by the numbers, He would have had every reason to be more and more depressed. He first lost the multitude, then the seventy, and then, for a moment at the cross, He lost the twelve.

When Jesus died, He had nothing left but a bloody body and the satisfaction of having done the will of God every second of His life. And all those who likewise do the will of the Father are His brothers, sisters, and mothers.

Don't Belittle What You Have

⎯⫟⫷⫸⫟⎯

*Philip answered him, Two hundred pennyworth
of bread is not sufficient for them, that
every one of them may take a little.*

—John 6:7

Two hundred pennyworth ($30) of bread would have bought by far more bread than the little boy had to offer! Jesus' first plan was to accomplish the miracle of the feeding of the 5,000 through Philip, buying bread with what was in the treasury, for He said to Philip, *"Whence shall we buy bread...?"* (v. 5). The question Philip was to answer was "Where is the nearest bakery," not "How much do we have?" for Jesus *"himself knew what he would do"* (v. 6). Jesus had a plan for this miracle. All He needed was a man to give a little, however little he had, and Jesus would do the rest. But Philip belittled what he had, and so he missed being a channel of that miracle.

My friend, are you belittling what you have? My offering is too little—I might as well not give. Our prayer meeting is too small—I might as well not go. My faith is too weak—I might as well not expect anything. My witness is too inadequate—I might as well keep quiet. Don't belittle what you have.

Moses had one stick, and he defeated the whole Egyptian army. Elisha had a bowl of salt, and he healed the bitter spring at Jericho. Dorcas had a needle and thread, and she made garments for many of the saints. Jesus proved (tested) Philip, but Philip flunked the test. Now, don't you flunk it. Give the Lord what little you have—by faith—and He will do the rest, by making you a channel of miracle after miracle.

Faith Leads to Understanding ·

—⟨⟨⟨⟨⟨ ⟩⟩⟩⟩⟩—

And I John...fell down to worship
before the feet of the angel which
shewed me these things.

—Revelation 22:8

Few books have led to as many controversies, speculations, and bizarre doctrinal positions as the Revelation. Man is as confused about the end of the Bible as he is about the beginning of it.

To solve the problem, we must remember that both Genesis and the Revelation are first of all to be believed. In the world, understanding precedes faith; but in the kingdom, understanding follows faith. *"Through faith we understand that the worlds were framed by the word of God"* (Heb. 11:3). Therefore, also, the first words of the Apostles' Creed are "I Believe..." So then, believe what you read in the Revelation without forcing yourself to understand. In God's time, understanding will follow your faith.

And, if you rightly believe, the first thing you will learn to understand about the Revelation is that you must fall down and worship the Lord. It is only from that position that further understanding will come to your heart.

So, as faith is the first door to understanding, worship is the second. Worship will then lead to obedience, and obedience to the knowledge of the holy. In this manner, as you approach the Revelation, God will reveal to you every part of it that you need to know as your heart is prepared to receive it.

In the realm of divine truth, understanding will never lead to faith, but faith will always lead to the understanding of the secrets of the kingdom of God. Therefore, Solomon said, *"Trust in the Lord with all thine heart; and lean not unto thine own understanding"* (Prov. 3:5).

The Last Fact of History

Even so, come, Lord Jesus.

—Revelation 22:20

The last fact of history concerning humankind is the prayer of the righteous, *"Even so, come, Lord Jesus."* Jesus will come when the church has made herself ready and is praying for His coming.

In the kingdom of God, the Bridegroom comes at the invitation of the bride and not at His own choosing. He then takes her to His Marriage Supper where all things will then be ready.

So, you have the picture of man in control in both the first and last chapters of the Bible. In Genesis 1, you hear God saying to Adam, "Take dominion." In the last chapter, man is to pray, *"Even so, come, Lord Jesus."* God gave this control to man. Of course, it is not absolute. It is always relative, finite, delegated, and limited. God remains the absolute monarch over the earth, and He continues to ride upon the wings of the wind, and still gives His food to the beasts and to the young ravens which cry (Ps. 18:10; Job 38:39–41).

Yet, the overall picture is that after the creation of the universe, God stepped back to allow us to have dominion. And so it is with the church, that after Jesus laid the foundation of the church, He stepped back and gave the keys of the church to His followers. From then on, it has not been His doing as much as ours in the binding and the loosing. Therefore, Jesus said, *"Whatsoever ye shall bind on earth shall be bound in heaven; and whatsoever ye shall loose on earth shall be loosed in heaven"* (Matt. 18:18).

So our Lord says to His bride, "You are in control. Make yourself ready. Pray, *'Even so, come, Lord Jesus.'"*

The Holy Spirit Is Like the Wind

*The wind bloweth where it
listeth, and thou hearest the sound
thereof, but canst not tell whence it cometh,
and whither it goeth: so is every one
that is born of the Spirit.*

—John 3:8

"*...So is everyone that is born of the Spirit.*" The born-again are unpredictable, yet not irresponsible. But their responsibility is entirely shifted to the Holy Spirit.

Where do we go to see this best illustrated, but in the life of Jesus as portrayed in the Gospels. Has there ever been a life that has been so absolutely free of human plans and designs? Was there ever a day when Jesus told His disciples, "Tomorrow, we are going to such and such a place"?

Jesus only moved when the Spirit bade Him move, and although His divine mission was predictable, the particulars leading to the fulfillment of that mission were only revealed to our Lord moment by moment. And, then, those who followed Him daily had no choice but to fit into His ways in order to stay with Him.

Now, has that changed any? Or do we also have to live as His first followers, ever fitting into the Master's unpredictable, exciting plans? Indeed, as the text tells us, the Holy Spirit is still like the wind, and those who are born of Him will continue to live like the first disciples.

The Biblical Heart

Keep thy heart with all diligence;
for out of it are the issues of life.

—Proverbs 4:23

The "biblical heart" circulates and supplies the whole spiritual man with its life-giving fluid. What is in the heart will get into every fiber of a person's being. The heart, then, can be the seat of wickedness or of purity, of deceit or of righteousness, of hate or of love, of foolishness or of sobriety. Whatever is in the heart will settle into the fiber of the whole spiritual man, affecting and dominating all human behavior.

The unregenerate heart is desperately wicked. Out of it *"proceed evil thoughts, murders, adulteries, fornications, thefts, false witness, blasphemies"* (Matt. 15:19). Disobedience, criticism, resentment, and Self-will create the calcification or the hardening of the "biblical heart" and its spiritual arteries. This hardening of our heart will render us unfit to hear the voice of Jesus and to follow His guidance. But God is able to give us a new heart, a clean and an obedient heart (Ezek. 36:26). And once a new heart is received, it is only through self-denial and childlike trust, moment by moment, that our heart can be kept, the Lord helping us.

Indeed, the heart of man must become part of our Christian anthropology in the understanding of man. Truly, any minister or layman who devotes his entire life to the transformation, the nurture, and the keeping of the heart will be a wise person. So let us all join Charles Wesley in this beautiful hymn:

O for a heart to praise my God,
A heart from sin set free,
A heart that always feels Thy blood,
So freely spilt for me![8]

The First Treasurer Was a Thief

This he said, not that he cared for the poor;
but because he was a thief, and had the bag,
and bare what was put therein.

—John 12:6

If we can call this little band of twelve disciples the first church in the making, then I think we will have to come to grips with the fact that her treasurer was a thief.

Job qualifications for church treasurers have always called for persons with impeccable character and integrity. Indeed, no one should have any problems with such qualifications, yet each one of us knows that Jesus was a lot less particular.

Most certainly, He appointed Judas to such a "high" office of trust, knowing his disqualifications. In addition to that, Jesus never complained about the lack of money, nor did He ever reveal Judas' sin to the rest of His disciples.

Judas was an apostle and a thief. What a combination! Yet he was never fired or condemned for his thievery. Instead, he was loved by Jesus like all the rest.

Oh, how many ministries would sink if their money flow were stopped or were diverted! But Jesus' ship of Zion could not be sunk by the shortage of money, for the Master was able to pull as many coins as were needed out of the Sea of Galilee at any time. The first treasurer of a church was a thief appointed by Jesus.

Oh, what a story to teach us to be less concerned about money and more concerned about having the faith, the spirit, and the heart of our Lord Jesus. If you were forced to make a choice between a loveless church with a perfect treasurer, or a loving church with a dishonest treasurer, what would be your choice? Where would Jesus go? Let us be more concerned with godliness than financial matters.

Kingdom Rules Are Different

Jesus answered,
My kingdom is not of this world.

—John 18:36

Let us continue our talk about money. First, we learned that giving was designed to save us from covetousness and stinginess, and to help us to see that the whole nature of God is a giving nature, a God who causes the rain to fall on the just and on the unjust alike. The habit of giving generously will save us from *"the love of money"* which is *"the root of all evil: which while some coveted after, they have erred from the faith"* (1 Tim. 6:10).

This means that for our soul's sake, and for our salvation's sake, it is better for us to throw our tithe and offerings into a ditch than to not give at all. For the love of money is worse than a dollar in the mud. Of course, fortunately, there are better places for us to give our money than to ditches, but I give you this illustration so that you will get the principle.

Further we learned that Jesus' ministry could not be sunk by financial scandals or shortages. Neither the abundance of money in His treasury nor the lack of it had any influence upon His ministry whatsoever.

Clearly, Jesus was not in it for the money, and He could not be forced out of it for the lack of it. His kingdom was *"not of this world."* For whatever He could not get from man, He got from His Father, because He practiced what He preached: *"But seek ye first the kingdom of God, and his righteousness; and all these things shall be added unto you"* (Matt. 6:33).

We have strayed in our ministries from the beautiful example of utter dependence upon God, to the weekly fretting and sweating about tithes and offerings. Let our dependence on man become less and our trust in God and His unlimited resources greater. He wants it so.

Why Bother?

This he said, not that he cared for the poor;
but because he was a thief, and had the bag,
and bare what was put therein.

—John 12:6

I would like for you to think for a few moments about all the things that bother you. Now, consider this: Do the things that bother you, bother God? And if the things that bother you don't bother God, why bother? Many Christians die, having spent much of their lives bothering and fretting about things that never bothered God.

It would have bothered the disciples and the financial contributors to Jesus' ministry had they known that their money seldom reached the intended need, but this did not bother Jesus. It bothered Aaron and Miriam immensely that Moses had married an Ethiopian. But what bothered God was not the Ethiopian woman but the criticism and the seeds of rebellion that He saw in the hearts of the accusers. The disciples were bothered because they found a man casting out devils but not following Jesus. They said, *"we forbade him, because he followeth not us"* (Mark 9:38). These signs of competition and apparent lack of loyalty really troubled them, but Jesus was not bothered by the renegade exorcist but rather by the critical spirit of his inner circle, and so He said, *"Forbid him not"* (v. 39).

How many concerns and burdens do we carry, and how many things do we fret over that are no real concern to God at all? If it does not bother God, then why should it bother us? So, let us not be bothered, except by the things that bother God. And God is only bothered by a disobedient heart and an un-Christlike spirit.

Touch Not God's Anointed

━━━━⟨⟩━━━━

*And they gathered themselves together
against Moses and against Aaron, and said unto
them, Ye take too much upon you, seeing all the
congregation are holy, every one of them, and the
Lord is among them: wherefore then lift ye up
yourselves above the congregation of the Lord?*

—Numbers 16:3

Moses did not lift himself above the congregation. For in the next verse, it says, *"And when Moses heard it, he fell upon his face"* (v. 4). It is the congregation that did not know how to fall upon her face. So, the weakness she thought she saw in Moses was really in herself. Unless we stay on our faces, spiritually speaking, in brokenness, in humility, and in nothingness, we will become collaborators in the plans of the discontented.

How many churches have been destroyed by unbroken, self-seeking sheep, rising up against the shepherd? They do not seem to know that the beam in their own eye is of much greater concern to God than the mote that is in the shepherd's eye. Let us not touch God's anointed one (1 Sam. 26:11)!

Rising up against a man of God was not even right in the case of King Saul when this anointed one was more interested in promoting his own glory than the glory of God (*see* 1 Sam. 26:9–10). Yes, it is never right to usurp human authority over divinely appointed authority.

So, God opened up the earth and swallowed the opposition to Moses, a very clear proof that the congregation was not *"holy, every one of them,"* as the 250 princes claimed. History tells us that it is wiser for us to work on our own faults than on the faults of others.

Beware of the Dogs

—⊸⊸⊸⊸⊸—

*And Ahab spake unto Naboth, saying, Give me thy
vineyard...And Naboth said to Ahab, The Lord forbid it...
And it came to pass, when Jezebel heard that Naboth was
stoned, and was dead, that Jezebel said to Ahab, Arise,
take possession of the vineyard of Naboth.*

—1 Kings 21:2–3, 15

We must know others' "property rights." God is very sensitive about that. We must know when we step on the spiritual property of an apostle, or a prophet, or a pastor, or an evangelist, or a teacher, or, for that matter, on any of the least of God's servants.

No passage in the Bible more clearly illustrates God's opinion about property rights than this passage in 1 Kings. Naboth lived when Ahab was king of Israel, but Ahab's idolatrous wife, Jezebel, ran the kingdom. It says that *"Jezebel cut off the prophets of the Lord"* (1 Kings 18:4). She put high places with foreign gods all over the country.

One would think that God would strike her dead for all of that. But, no, what caused God's judgment to come upon her, to the extent that God had her cast out of a high building and consumed by dogs, was that she violated the property rights of a humble man of God and had him killed.

Jezebel showed no respect for the property rights of Naboth. Do not dig in the garden of God's anointed ones, nor take away from them what is rightfully theirs. Do not exploit the widows, the orphans, the weak, and the feeble. Do not withhold your tithes from the servants of the Lord and His ministry, for it may, someday, also bring your life to the dogs.

Revolution Rejected

⤙◆⤙◆⤚

Let every soul be subject unto the higher powers.
For there is no power but of God: the powers
that be are ordained of God.

—Romans 13:1

This was written when over half of the population of Rome was in slavery. And, although not all slaves were treated poorly, all were denied certain freedoms, and many were treated brutally. Under the Roman system, Christians, too, were soon denied their religious freedom, so that they were driven into the catacombs to worship. Jews were commanded to leave the country.

Yet, Paul did nothing politically to emancipate the slaves from the yoke of Rome. Nor did he do anything to press Rome for religious freedom. Paul knew that Christ had not come to bring social revolution, but spiritual transformation. He knew that our liberty in Christ, by not serving the flesh, was great enough to afford us all the treasures of heaven in any circumstance of life.

Short of the evangelization of the Roman Empire, Paul's words to slaves were, *"Servants, be obedient to them that are your masters...as unto Christ...With good will doing service, as to the Lord"* (Eph. 6:5, 7). He wanted the slaves to remember that their masters also had a Master in heaven.

Although others try to change our perishing world by social, political, and military means, the apostles' approach was the opposite: change the world by transforming individual hearts into an attitude of Christ-like service in spite of society's ills.

Recognize that the earth's worst enemy is anarchy and rebellion. God's worst enemy is sin. God does not tell us to change the kingdoms of earth, but to possess His kingdom, for it says, *"Blessed are the poor in spirit: for their's is the kingdom of heaven"* (Matt. 5:3).

The Strategy of Separation

*And the devil said unto him, If thou
be the Son of God, command this stone
that it be made bread.*

—Luke 4:3

We see here that the devil's first strategy at the beginning of Christ's public ministry was to separate Him from the Father. It has always been the strategy of Satan to separate the lesser from the greater in authority, in order to disrupt the unity of the church of God.

This is not to say that Christ is a lesser person in the Trinity, but rather, we must notice that Jesus left His place of equality. On leaving heaven, He emptied Himself of Himself, that is, of His glory, to become a servant to all (Phil. 2:6–7). He had to become the least to serve us all. So, in reference to His earthly ministry, He became the lesser, and Satan tried to separate Him from the Father, the greater. Satan tried to make Jesus independent of His Father.

Satan tempted Him to use His power to make bread out of stone without consulting the Father! But Jesus resisted this temptation. Praise the Lord! How subtle and preposterous was Satan to so tempt Jesus at the beginning of His ministry.

Had Jesus given in to this temptation, it would have been the end of His anointing—it would have canceled Calvary! Both the second and third temptations Jesus suffered were also designed to separate the Son from the Father.

Oh, the devil knows the power of unity. As he tried to separate the Son from the Father, he now tries to separate every follower from his ordained leader. Beware, saint of God!

John and Jesus

——◦‹‹‹‹◦›››◦——

*Now when John had heard in the prison the works of
Christ, he sent two of his disciples, And said unto him, Art
thou he that should come, or do we look for another?*
—Matthew 11:2–3

By Jesus' admission, John the Baptist was the greatest
man born of woman (v. 11), greater than Enoch, Abraham,
Moses, and Elijah. Yet, in this Scripture, we see John's heart
in doubt. This is amazing. After all, John was the one who
said, *"Behold the Lamb of God, which taketh away the sin of
the world"* (John 1:29), and *"He must increase, but I must
decrease"* (3:30). Besides Jesus, John was the only man who
was full of the Holy Spirit from his mother's womb, and it is
that which made him, next to Christ, the most perfect man
since Adam.

John also was the only one of Jesus' early acquaintances
who saw Jesus as a universal Savior coming to take away
the sin of the world. Then, as John baptized Jesus, he saw
the Spirit descending upon Jesus as a heavenly dove. Next,
John turned some of his disciples over to Jesus, yet, he himself did not enter with these disciples into the inner circle
of our Lord. Hence, John became an admirer but not a
follower. The greatest man born of woman!

How hard is it to follow when you are great? How easy is
it to lose a vision? Surely, it is easier to get a vision than to
keep one. And, it is far easier to have a vision than to live
up to its consequential demands.

Separation of the lesser from the greater, of the servant
from the master, will always bring tragedy, darkness, suffering, and death. The greatest man born of woman, with
the greatest vision, died the most humiliating and lonely
death, somewhat separated from the man he admired the
most.

My friend, strive to stay united with the one God has
chosen for you to follow.

The Bridge of Anointing

⊸━◦◖◗◦━⊷

For Demas hath forsaken me,
having loved this present world.

—2 Timothy 4:10

Consider more passages on the subject of separation. Paul also says in this same epistle, *"...all they which are in Asia be turned away from me"* (1 Tim. 1:15). What suffering Paul went through because so many separated themselves from him, and what burdens he had to bear that should have been carried by his followers. What souls missed hearing the Gospel because so many went their own way?

Consistent followers were, and are, hard to find. One starts, then quits. Another starts, and then he quits also. One was offended over Paul's length of preaching, another over his handling of finance, and another may have been wearied by his frequent journeys, etc. Finally, Paul found Timothy, a believer who never quit! Oh, what power, what nourishment, and what help these two men received from one another.

Timothy's bridge for his anointing was his connection with Paul. Demas broke the bridge to his anointing when he left Paul. Had he stayed with Paul, oh, could we possibly also have had First and Second Demas, as we have First and Second Timothy in our Bibles?

John the Baptist's anointing came out of his bridge with Jesus. Jesus' anointing came out of His bridge with His Father. Your anointing may well come out of your bridge with God's ordained minister for you. Do not allow the devil to separate you from God's anointed ones.

Consider the anointing that was lost through the children of Israel separating from Moses; Absalom from David; the fifty prophets from Elijah; John from Jesus, as well as the seventy; and Demas from Paul. Oh, the cost of all these separations to the work of God. Indeed, seldom does what God put together stay together.

Pass Over and Go On

*And thus shall ye eat it; with your
loins girded, your shoes on your feet, and
your staff in your hand; and ye shall eat
it in haste: it is the Lord's passover.*

—Exodus 12:11

In this Old Testament passage, we see the doctrine of the rebirth in typology. The Passover speaks of conversion or salvation. It is a passing over from the old life to the new. Israel had only one night of the blood coverage to get out of Egypt. One night! After the children of Israel had painted the blood of the lamb on the door posts and lintel, they were told to eat the Passover lamb in haste, because it was the Lord's Passover.

Dear ones, once a man is born again, he had better get on the move for the Promised Land; he had better get on the road of obedience. Any Hebrew who stayed one more night in Egypt would have been slain by Pharaoh's men. The blood of the lamb covered Israel for one night only in the region of Goshen in Egypt. If they wanted further protection, it would be theirs only as they walked in obedience toward the Promised Land.

So, our religion is not a sit-down religion, nor a sleep-in-late religion, nor a sit-it-out religion, but a pass over and move on, dynamic life of faith. Friend, have you passed over, or are you sitting in Goshen living under the illusion that since you were safe there yesterday, you will be safe there tomorrow? Pass over and pass on! Your safety now is under the cloud by day and the pillar of fire by night. The blood-covering now is only near the ark of the covenant, and nowhere else. Yes, my friend, the blood is where the cross is. Gird up your loins, put on your shoes, grasp your staff, and begin to walk with God.

The Supreme Temptation

*And he went a little further, and fell on his
face, and prayed, saying, O my Father, if it be
possible, let this cup pass from me.*

—Matthew 26:39

A temptation is a desire to have something that we ought
not to have. So, temptation is desire. We find the most dras-
tic New Testament temptation in Jesus' battle in the Garden
of Gethsemane. It is there where He almost died of sorrow
before He even reached the cross. He needed prayer, and
He asked for prayer, for the battle was severe.

Jesus was at the point of fatal collapse under the sever-
ity of the temptation to let the cup pass from Him, for it
says that he *"fell on His face."* Then, Jesus prayed, *"O my
Father, if it be possible, let this cup pass from me."*

Jesus wanted to avoid the cup that held all the sins of all
mankind for, I believe, these strong reasons: (1) because sin
was so despicable to Him that He could hardly bear to take
it upon Himself; (2) with sin on Him, He would be separated from His Father; and (3) humanity always naturally
draws back from suffering and death.

Jesus' cross, His suffering, was in taking sin. Ours is in
rejecting sin. In fact, all temptation is either about receiving or rejecting the cross. And Jesus' struggle was so strong
that it took Him to the ground, causing Him to sweat drops
of blood (Luke 22:44).

And His words, *"if it be possible, let this cup pass from
me,"* were the expression of a body that was sanctified, and
yet tempted severely to find another way. Jesus had
desires just like you and I, so we learn that it is not a sin to
say *"let this cup pass from me,"* if we also add this prayer,
"not my will, but thine, be done" (Luke 22:42).

Yes, Jesus understands you and your temptations. And,
therefore, He will give you grace to overcome them.

Holiness Is a Choice

*And when the woman saw that the tree was good
for food, and that it was pleasant to the eyes, and a
tree to be desired to make one wise, she took of the
fruit thereof, and did eat, and gave also unto
her husband with her; and he did eat.*

—Genesis 3:6

Adam and Eve were not created holy. They were created innocent. God placed two trees in the garden that Adam and Eve were not to eat of. God created man a moral free agent—a person who had the capacity to make moral choices toward good or evil. Now, this implies that God had to give man the two elements to make moral choices: (1) a desire to sin, and (2) the will not to give in to that desire.

Then, God allowed Satan to bring man to his first moral choice. Eve, having been created innocent, now, for the first time, had the choice whether she wanted to be holy or unholy. Holiness is a choice. The temptation was presented—the desire to do wrong was there—but so was the power of the will and the grace of God not to.

Eve allowed "the desire to" to reign. She gave in to the temptation of the flesh rather than being willing to obey God. Eve chose not to be holy!

Every time we don't resist temptation, we choose to be unholy. Our every "desire to" toward evil must be overcome by "the will not to," by the grace of God. As Jesus overcame, so can we, for He is within us. Yes, truly, truly, *"God is faithful, who will not suffer you to be tempted above that ye are able; but will with the temptation also make a way to escape, that ye may be able to bear it"* (1 Cor. 10:13).

This is God's promise that the Christian never, ever has to sin again. For He *"is able to keep you from falling, and to present you faultless before the presence of his glory with exceeding joy"* (Jude 24). Holiness is a choice, and he who consistently makes holy choices is a holy man.

299

PRAISE: Loud and Clear

---◄▩▩◖▢◗▩▩►---

By him therefore let us offer the sacrifice of
praise to God continually, that is, the fruit
of our lips, giving thanks to his name.

—Hebrews 13:15

There are well over seventy-five admonitions in the Bible encouraging us to praise the Lord. I remind you, however, that these calls to praise are not requests for thoughts of praise or for whispered or mumbled expressions of gratitude. Rather, they are calls for hearty, verbal expressions of thanksgiving toward Him who made us, who saved us, and who keeps us.

Indeed, verbal praise, *"the fruit of our lips,"* is what the writer of Hebrews had in mind when he wrote this verse that we read today. Now, if the church would pay as much attention to the seventy-five plus calls to praise as to the one clear passage on spiritual rebirth, what kind of a church would we have?

All of creation is in praise to God. God said to Job, *"Where wast thou when I laid the foundations of the earth...When the morning stars sang together, and all the sons of God shouted for joy?"* (Job 38:4, 7). So, praise preceded time, and praise will outlast time, as the Revelation so clearly tells us.

Yes, all of creation is praising God—except for most of humankind. How many theologians, Christian scholars, ministers, deacons, and church members do you know who fulfill their daily sacrifice of making praise *"the fruit of* [their] *lips,"* and who teach others to do likewise?

Since praise was built into creation, and you are one of His redeemed creatures, doesn't it seem right that you should chime in with a daily sacrifice of praise that rises like sweet incense to the throne of God?

The Holy Spirit Convicts the World of Sin

*And he, when he is come, will convict the world in
respect of sin, and of righteousness, and of judgment:
of sin, because they believe not on me.*

—John 16:8–9 ASV

There are three stages in the history of conviction. The
first period is from Adam to Moses, where man was convicted by his conscience. The law had not yet been given,
nor had the Holy Spirit come. Hence, the only vehicle of
conviction at that time was man's conscience. The conscience
is the moral compass in the soul of every man which corre-
sponds to the moral values in the mind of God, either
accusing us or excusing us (Romans 2:15). Every time this
moral compass is overridden by the will of man, it loses
some of its sensitivity until, eventually, a man's conscience
can become so insensitive that he can do all kinds of evil
things without feeling any guilt about it at all (1 Tim. 4:2).

In the first period of the history of conviction, man consistently overruled this message of the conscience, causing
his wickedness to become so great that God had to destroy
mankind in a great flood. Only righteous Noah and his
family escaped.

The second period in the history of conviction began
when the Law of God was given at Mount Sinai. God gave
the Law to further restrain man from evil.

When Jesus left, He sent the Holy Spirit, and we are now
in the last stage of the history of conviction. Presently, we
are convicted by our conscience, by the moral laws of God,
and by the Holy Spirit. We see that throughout history, God
has consistently tightened the seatbelt of conviction. He has
worked at deepening and broadening conviction so that no
hidden sin will remain undealt with, in order that He might
fill us with Himself, which is the promise of our salvation.

The Holy Spirit Convicts the World of Righteousness

And he, when he is come, will convict the world in respect of sin, and of righteousness, and of judgment:... of righteousness, because I go to the Father, and ye behold me no more.

—John 16:8, 10 ASV

The Holy Spirit convicts and convinces the world of righteousness. This means that the Holy Spirit will show the world what righteousness is all about. Comparatively, if the righteousness of God in the Old Testament appeared to us as a star, that same righteousness revealed through Christ is like the sun, shining so much the brighter. In fact, Jesus is called the *"Sun of righteousness"* (Mal. 4:2).

This righteousness of God in Christ was hidden to man until the Holy Spirit came. The Pharisees could not see it at all, the masses saw an occasional glimpse of it, Nicodemus saw its shadow, and the disciples saw it in veiled images. But since the Holy Spirit has come, the righteousness of God in Christ is revealed as the brightness of the sun.

In practical terms, what does this mean? The Holy Spirit will convict the world of righteousness by the right way Jesus lived among us and by the right way He lives within us. He never looked at a woman to lust after her—that is righteousness. When hit on one cheek, He offered the other—that is righteousness. When reviled, He reviled not again—that is righteousness. When asked to go one mile, He offered to go the second also—that is righteousness. He loved His enemies, and He always did the will of His Father in heaven—that also is righteousness.

The Holy Spirit does convict the world of righteousness, of the right way of living and thinking, through the work and example of our Lord Jesus Christ. As He lived rightly in this world, let us now do likewise.

The Holy Spirit Convicts the World of Judgment

━━◁◆▷━━

And he, when he is come, will convict the world in respect
of sin, and of righteousness, and of judgment:...of judgment,
because the prince of this world hath been judged.
—John 16:8, 11 ASV

Since the prince of the world, the devil, has now been defeated through Christ, the Holy Spirit is sent to put the world on notice that a universal Judgment Day is at hand. As has been said, "Payday, someday!" The day will come when *"we shall all stand before the judgment seat of Christ"* (Rom. 14:10), and every knee shall bow and every man, woman, and child from all time shall confess Jesus as Lord.

In the dispensation of Law, there was no knowledge of such a grand day. But the Holy Spirit has now placed such knowledge of the judgment clearly into all human hearts. The story is told of a learned atheist who went from college to college to convince students that there was no God and that the Bible was a hoax. But when this professor lay on his deathbed, an acquaintance came to visit and said, "Friend, I suppose I'll never see you again," to which the atheist replied, "I will see you in hell." Then after the acquaintance left, the dying unbeliever called for a Roman Catholic priest to give the last rites (communion) and prayer for the dying.

The Holy Spirit convicts the world of sin, righteousness, and of judgment. It says, *"the world,"* and that means everyone from every culture, race, nation, religion, or philosophical orientation that exists. *"The fool hath said in his heart, There is no God"* (Ps. 14:1). Since the advent of the Holy Spirit, particularly, no man can honestly deny his innate knowledge of the fact that someday he will have to give an account of himself before an invisible God. My friend, prepare to meet thy God—He will be there waiting for you.

Some Things Are Not to Be Told

*And Ham, the father of Canaan, saw the
nakedness of his father, and told his two brethren
without. And Shem and Japheth took a garment,
and laid it upon both their shoulders, and went
backward, and covered the nakedness of their
father; and their faces were backward, and
they saw not their father's nakedness.*

—Genesis 9:22–23

What do you cover, and what do you leave uncovered? What do you tell your brethren, and what do you keep to your heart?

Noah walked with God. He was not an alcoholic, nor was he a man who lacked self-control; but, he was simply a man inexperienced with grapes having aged. Consequently, we can call this unfortunate drunkenness an incident of innocence or carelessness, for God says nothing about it in Hebrews 11 when He speaks of the life of Noah. There, in fact, God calls Noah an heir of righteousness.

Ham saw his father's nakedness and gossiped about it to his brothers. Oh, my friend, how are you dealing with the sins and weaknesses of your spouse, your parents, your children, your brothers, your friends, your pastor, and even your enemies? What is the depth and extent of your compassion? How quick are you to judge, to pass sentence, and to tell? Is there anything you have told someone about someone else that should never have been told, marring that someone's reputation?

Oh, perhaps this is the time to make some confession and to ask forgiveness, for Jesus said, *"And as ye would that men should do to you, do ye also to them likewise"* (Luke. 6:31). As you want your reputation guarded, so do likewise for others.

Ham told what he saw. Shem and Japheth covered what they knew. Are you a coverer or are you a teller?

A Drunken Man Awakes as a Prophet

*And Noah awoke from his wine, and knew
what his younger son had done unto him. And he said,
Cursed be Canaan; a servant of servants shall he be unto his brethren. And he said, Blessed be the Lord God
of Shem; and Canaan shall be his servant. God shall
enlarge Japheth, and he shall dwell in the tents
of Shem; and Canaan shall be his servant.*

—Genesis 9:24–27

Noah awoke, not as a man weakened, but simply as a man wiser, knowing that if you drink wine that has been standing, it will do you in. No, Noah did not wake up as a condemned sinner, but as a prophet of God.

Noah prophetically curses Ham's son Canaan (this is the origin of the Canaanites), because a son of a man of God did not do all he could to guard the reputation of that man of God. And the curse was not for telling a lie but for telling truth that was not to be told. Indeed, it can be just as devastating to tell the truth as a lie, when it is told out of place, out of spirit, and out of time.

Observe the prophecy concerning Japheth: *"God shall enlarge Japheth."* This means that all Asia, Europe, and the Americas would come out of Japheth. Finally, consider the blessing to Shem. Shem is the forefather of Abraham, of Israel, and of our Savior. If we guard the reputation of God's servants and, for that matter, the reputation of all of God's people, if we cover their weaknesses and faults, then God will enlarge our tents.

 Let us conclude with verse 19: *"These are the three sons of Noah: and of them was the whole earth overspead."* Spiritually speaking, of which spirit of these three sons are you? Are you a Ham, a Shem, or a Japheth? Again, are you a coverer or an exposer? And finally, aren't you glad that Jesus has covered your sins and that He does not talk to anyone about them—period?!

Let Your Eye Be Single

---◀▥▥◉▥▥▶---

*The light of the body is the eye: if therefore thine eye
be single, thy whole body shall be full of light.*

—Matthew 6:22

When we don't first seek the kingdom of God always, our eye is not single. That means our vision, being distracted, causes things to come into our spiritual body that bring dimness, darkness, and confusion to our soul. In fact, we will become deceived.

We learn from this passage in the Sermon on the Mount that it takes only one bit of the lust of the flesh, the love of the world, and the pride of life to cast our whole spiritual body into darkness. One look over the wall, as in the case of David, ended the spiritual life of the great illuminator—who gave us so many beautiful psalms—until he repented. One grasp for a Babylonian garment brought similar darkness to Achan (Josh. 7:16). One bite of the forbidden fruit plunged Eve and the whole human race into depravity. It took only one attachment to one thing of the earth to blind the rich young ruler to what God had for him. Oh, my friend, notice how one sin, one look, one bite, one disobedience, can deceive us and bring the whole body into darkness.

No wonder Jesus says, *"No man can serve two masters: for either he will hate the one, and love the other; or else he will hold to the one, and despise the other. Ye cannot serve God and mammon"* (Matt. 6:24). It's not that one should not serve both God and mammon, but that it is impossible to serve those two particular masters at the same time.

As one fly in a glass of milk causes us to declare the whole drink unfit, as one spot on a dress makes us call it unclean, so one sin, any one sin not repented of, has enough deception in it to get us off the narrow road.

No Other Name

*The heart is deceitful above all things, and
desperately wicked: who can know it?*

—Jeremiah 17:9

One only needs to look within oneself to find the most deceitful thing in the world: the heart. One sin of Eve brought deception to every human heart, and so King David lamented, *"in sin did my mother conceive me"* (Ps. 51:5). Because sin got into the spiritual bloodstream of man, it is perpetuated from generation to generation. Hence, Paul's words, *"For all have sinned, and come short of the glory of God"* (Rom. 3:23) and *"There is none righteous, no, not one"* (3:10).

This is the sad dilemma of the human race: born in sin, deceived by sin, blinded by sin, and held in chains by sin. But, thank God, Jesus came to save us from our sins, to cleanse our spiritual bloodstream with His own precious blood, and to present us faultless before the throne of God.

His blood removes the sin and, therewith, the deception, the blindness, and the shame so that the chains of iniquity are broken. On top of that glorious salvation, Christ keeps removing our sin as we walk in the light as He is in the light. That walk with Jesus brings us into sweet fellowship with one another, and into a continual cleansing through His precious blood.

Is there anybody like Jesus in Buddhism, in Islam, in Hinduism, in Confucianism, in any "ism"? Indeed, Jesus Christ came into the world to save sinners, and *"there is none other name under heaven given among men, whereby we must be saved"* (Acts 4:12).

November 1

Covetousness

—◦◦◦◦◦◦—

*I had not known sin...except the law
had said, Thou shalt not covet.*

—Romans 7:7

To covet means to have a desire for something that is not ours to have.

Paul claimed to have kept the law as the Pharisees did concerning zeal, as in Philippians 3:6, *"Concerning zeal,...touching the righteousness which is in the law, blameless."* But when it came to the tenth commandment, he found himself a sinner, for he said, *"I had not known sin...except the law had said, Thou shalt not covet."*

The rich young ruler boasted of having kept the law. Jesus said, *"Thou knowest the commandments, Do not commit adultery, Do not kill, Do not steal."* But when Jesus placed the tenth commandment over this rich young ruler's heart and real estate, the young man found himself in sin (Mark 10:19–23).

We can easily break the sin of covetousness up into three parts. The first part is to desire, or to lust after something that is not ours. The second is to fall in love with what we have, and to treat that which we have as if it were our own. Let us remember that, *"Every good gift and every perfect gift is from above"* (James 1:17). Do not be deceived—all we have is God's, and we are only His stewards to take care of His gifts. A third part of covetousness is the end product of the others, which is our unwillingness to give up what God has given us. This shows the depth of the root system of covetousness, and it shows that our love of things has become greater than our love of God, which is idolatry.

Again, the three stages of covetousness are: first, desire; second, deception; and third, idolatry.

Thinking Rightly about God

For as he thinketh in his heart, so is he.

—Proverbs 23:7

How a man perceives God in his heart, so will he act and interact with God. If he thinks God to be a judge, he will live in constant fear of violating a divine law. If he thinks God to be a Santa Claus, he will keep giving God his wish list. If he thinks about God as a fireman, he will only call upon Him in times of crisis. If he thinks about God being transcendent (supernatural) without being imminent, he will hardly ever bother to pray. If he thinks of God as a next-door neighbor, he will live without the fear of the Lord which is the beginning of wisdom.

We must think rightly about God. If we think wrongly about God, we will be off in our moral responses, choices, actions, and reactions, and in many other areas of our theology and interactions with God.

King Saul thought wrongly about God, and so he took the best of the sheep and the oxen. Israel thought wrongly about God, so she thought she could worship Ashtoreth also. James and John thought wrongly about God, so they wanted fire to come down from heaven to destroy the Samaritans.

Yes, my friend, our attitudes, thoughts, and actions reveal how we think about God.

November 3

Man's Wisdom Blocks Faith

━━◆◆◆━━

*I will destroy the wisdom of the wise, and will bring
to nothing the understanding of the prudent.*
—1 Corinthians 1:19

The most beautiful illustration of this text is Moses. Moses had the wisdom of the wise. He had learned all the wisdom of Egypt, studying biology, philosophy, political science, mathematics, geometry, and world history. Yet, what did God need of all that wisdom to make Moses a deliverer? The answer is: none of it!

God had to put Moses into a forty year reeducation program in the very wilderness where he was later to lead the nation of Israel. God had to teach Moses the wisdom of the Lord; lessons of utter dependence upon Him and of not leaning upon his own understanding.

When it was time for Moses to lead Israel into the wilderness, he had to forget what he knew about the land's desolate agricultural state. He had to forget about its impossible climate of scorching heat during the day and sometimes freezing temperatures at night. He had to forget about the lack of lakes and rivers. He had to forget about protesting to God, "This will not work! I have been there!" Moses' faith enabled him to take Israel into a wilderness that, barring quick and powerful miracles, could cause them to perish within a week's time.

Moses had to exchange the wisdom of the wise with the wisdom of God to make his faith work. So, God sent a cloud to cool His people by day and a pillar of fire to warm them by night. He sent bread from the sky and water from the rocks. He made for Israel a place of life in an otherwise uninhabitable wilderness. But God could not do that until He had a man whose earthly wisdom could be laid aside in order to favor the wisdom of God. So, whose wisdom are you operating on: the wisdom of man or the wisdom of God?

310

Starting and Finishing Are Not the Same

—◄══◖◗══►—

*Then said one unto him, Lord, are there few that
be saved? And he said unto them, Strive to enter
in at the strait gate: for many, I say unto you,
will seek to enter in, and shall not be able.*

—Luke 13:23–24

Salvation is a gift, but it is a gift that must be kept through striving. Without the striving or the agonizing (as the Greek really puts it), we will lose what we gain.

In the Parable of the Ten Virgins, Jesus attempts to make no other point but that five virgins had ceased striving. They lost what they had gained. They were foolish, because they were sitting on their gift of salvation. They did not strive to get extra oil. Rather, they employed their time by spending it in personal pleasures. However, the wise virgins spent all their energies by building upon what God had given them. They, as Paul would say, pressed *"toward the mark for the prize of the high calling of God in Christ Jesus"* without vacation or variation (Phil. 3:14).

All of these virgins started, but only half of them finished. Salvation has to be worked out. Paul admonishes us to work out our salvation with fear and trembling (Phil. 2:12). Salvation has to be cultivated and watered. Whatever is not cared for and tended to will die. So the five foolish virgins had as good a start as the wise, but the gates of heaven were closed when they wanted to enter in (Matt. 25:11–12).

Heaven will frown on those who, after they have received this great salvation, refuse to become sincere followers of Jesus. Yes, my friend, you have begun. Are you now stretching to be among the finishers? Jesus said that *"he that endureth to the end shall be saved"* (Matt. 10:22).

Persevering Prayer

---∾ⅢⅢ)ʃⅢⅢ∾---

But the angel said unto him, Fear not, Zacharias:
for thy prayer is heard; and thy wife Elisabeth shall bear
thee a son, and thou shalt call his name John.

—Luke 1:13

After four hundred years of silence in the temple, the first message heard from God was, *"thy prayer is heard."* Hallelujah! Oh, the reward for the endurance of a common priest bearing his reproach of childlessness, but keeping on and on. If there is any chapter that could be written on perseverance, Zacharias should be included.

Think of the obstacles. First, the daily burden of that reproach. Second, the spiritual dryness of the temple worship from whose premises the S3hekinah glory of the Lord had disappeared. Third, the long journey each time to get to the temple. Fourth, the ongoing barrenness of Elizabeth into old age when all women become barren. Yet, none of these things could hinder Zacharias and Elisabeth in persevering prayer.

While praying, it was unknown to them that they were marching ever closer to becoming the parents of the greatest man born of woman, the preparer of the way, full of the Holy Ghost from his mother's womb.

Yes, my friend, there are the most pleasant and gratifying fruits in that large, dark room called the "future," waiting to be revealed to all those who persevere against the plenitude of negatives coming to them from all sides day by day. Let us take courage, praying and not fainting, and we shall yet get to sing our finest song of triumph embodied in these beautiful four words, *"thy prayer is heard."*

The Theology of Permissiveness

*And the Lord God commanded the man,
saying, Of every tree of the garden thou mayest freely
eat: But of the tree of the knowledge of good and evil,
thou shalt not eat of it: for in the day that thou
eatest thereof thou shalt surely die.*
—Genesis 2:16–17

God, first and foremost, is holy, and He expects us to be holy by obeying His commands. This is brought out beautifully in God's first encounter with man in his natural environment. God did not present Himself to Adam as a God of systematic theology, saying, "Here I am. I am omnipotent, omnipresent, omniscient, and awesome." No! God came on the scene as a holy God, saying, "You can eat of all these trees, but you cannot eat of that tree. And if you disobey, you are out."

Immediately after God's first encounter with Adam and Eve, the devil, commenting on this moral theology, made his first encounter with man by saying to Eve, "If you eat of that tree, you are not out," and holy men have battled the devil's permissive theology ever since.

So, both divine (moral) and devilish (permissive) theology were born in the garden. The former keeps us in the garden, the latter takes us out of it. Theology without a holiness-morality is of the devil, and it makes us more like the devil. Yes, this is exactly what much of the theology of the past seventy years has done. It has made man more selfish, more permissive, more sensual, more daring in his sins and transgressions, and less and less like God. Indeed, permissive theology has clearly moved us from a self-denying ethic to a self-fulfilling ethic.

What Is Best for You?

———⊶🙜🙟⊷———

*For ye were sometimes darkness, but now
are ye light in the Lord: walk as children of light:
(For the fruit of the Spirit is in all goodness
and righteousness and truth).*

—Ephesians 5:8–9

We just learned from Genesis that Satan did not destroy God's theology, but he twisted it, he amended it. And with that, Satan turned the lights out for both Adam and Eve. Instantly, they ceased to be children of light, and they became children of darkness. Satan replaced their "God-interest" with "self-interest." "What is best for God?" now became, "What is best for us?"

It is not so much that the devil put God down, but that he put man up by saying to Eve: If you eat this fruit *"ye shall be as gods"* (Gen. 3:5). The devil's theology never shuts God out. He knows we would vigorously reject such propositions. No, the devil simply gives God a secondary place, giving us, ever so subtly, the primary place, without our being aware of it. He did not bother Eve with a "there is no God," but with a *"Ye shall not surely die"* (v. 4).

So, the devil is ever tempting us even as he did with Jesus, not so much as an opposer of the brethren (though such he is), but as a deceiver of the brethren. Therefore, the devil used the Word of God with Jesus in the wilderness even as he did with Eve in the garden, by putting another twist to it. Take the Word of God as it is, and your light will never go out.

What Jesus Preached

━━◆◆◆━━

*Again, the kingdom of heaven is like unto a
merchant man, seeking goodly pearls: Who, when
he had found one pearl of great price, went
and sold all that he had, and bought it.*
—Matthew 13:45–46

Consider some of the other things that Jesus compared the kingdom of heaven to. The kingdom of heaven is like a man that sowed, like a grain of mustard seed, like leaven, like virgins, like a treasure, and like a net. Jesus went everywhere preaching the gospel of the kingdom. He came to earth to establish His kingdom. He began His Beatitudes by saying, *"Blessed are the poor in spirit: for their's is the kingdom of heaven"* (Matt. 5:3). He taught His disciples to pray, *"Thy kingdom come"* (Matt. 6:10). He commissioned them to preach the kingdom, and He said, *"the kingdom of God is within you"* (Luke 17:21). Jesus' message was the kingdom.

He taught that we are born again to see and enter into the kingdom by saying to Nicodemus, *"Except a man be born again, he cannot see the kingdom of God"* (John 3:3). The new life of the Spirit can only be sustained and perpetuated in His kingdom. Therefore, Jesus said that *"the kingdom of heaven suffereth violence, and the violent take it by force"* (Matt. 11:12). And Paul also took upon himself to preach the message of the kingdom, the Acts closing with these words: *"And Paul dwelt...in his own hired house...Preaching the kingdom of God"* (Acts 28:30–31).

The church must return to preaching everywhere the message Jesus preached—the kingdom message—for outside of it, no spiritual life can be sustained.

Dead-end Conversions

*For the kingdom of God is not
meat and drink; but righteousness, and
peace, and joy in the Holy Ghost.*

—Romans 14:17

So, the kingdom of God is not picnics, parties, reunions, fun and games, but righteousness, peace, and joy enjoyed through life in the Holy Spirit. This kingdom brings a new, mostly unexpected, agenda to every one of His saints each day. Unless the kingdom of God is preached and lived everywhere, the newborn in Christ have no kingdom to see or to enter into.

The Gospels employ the word "church" only three times, but the terms, "kingdom of heaven" and "kingdom of God," are used about one hundred times. Without the kingdom of heaven, the church is totally devoid of spirituality, for it is only in the kingdom that there is righteousness, peace, and joy. Without the gospel of the kingdom, we have dead-end conversions, conversions having nowhere to go, conversions without any life-sustaining purpose and hope.

When Jesus came, He brought the kingdom of heaven, a kingdom hitherto unknown to the Jews, a kingdom not of this world—yet in this world—a kingdom that is to be a dwelling place for every man born of God.

Do you have the kingdom of God dwelling within you? If not, you, as a born-again believer, may enter it now by forsaking all and following Jesus in self-denial and obedience. And as you do this, your conversion will turn you into a tree of righteousness, planted by the rivers of living water, that bringeth forth his fruit in his season (Ps. 1:3).

Let Your Hurts Become Pearls

Who, when he was reviled, reviled not again;
when he suffered, he threatened not; but committed
himself to him that judgeth righteously.
—1 Peter 2:23

A pearl is formed when a grain of sand gets into an oyster, irritating its tissue, causing layer upon layer of nacre to form about that grain. When the merchant in the parable was looking for the pearl, he was looking for the Pearl of Great Price. Now the Pearl of Great Price is Jesus, and let us remember that all pearls are created by hurt.

We know that Jesus was hurt. He was mocked. He was ridiculed. He was called the son of the devil, a glutton, a drunkard, an impostor, and a deceiver. He was spat upon, beaten, and nailed to the cross. Yes, Jesus was hurt, but He was not offended (Ps. 119:165). Jesus said upon the cross, *"Father, forgive them; for they know not what they do"* (Luke 23:34). Christ became the Pearl of Great Price through suffering, affliction, abuse, and finally, the hurt of the cross.

My friend, what are we doing with our hurts? Are we letting them fester within us? Are we letting them lead us into the prison house of resentment, criticism, or self-pity? Or, are we letting our hurts turn into pearls? So, let us not cry about our hurts nor blame others for them. Instead, let us thank God for them, for they, more than anything else, will bring us into fellowship with the Lord Jesus Christ.

Wouldn't it be wonderful if all hurt people would become beautiful pearls for Jesus rather than leaving the church in irritation or disappointment? Wouldn't it be wonderful if we would say to our crucifiers, "Father, forgive them." Oh, what a beautiful church, what a glorious church Jesus would have if all the hurts of its members would be turned into pearls!

The Fear of the Lord

...by the fear of the Lord men depart from evil.

—Proverbs 16:6

When evil abounds, we know that the fear of the Lord has left the human heart. Peter and Paul prophesied that in the last days there shall be grievous times and there shall be scoffers walking after their own lusts. Jesus also says that in the last days iniquity shall abound and the love of many shall wax cold. These are sobering words for the end times. Only those who have the fear of the Lord will make it through the moral permissiveness of those last days.

This fear of God is so essential for the integrity of the heart, yet this fear is not a fear of judgment. Rather, it is a fear leading to reverence, respect, and holiness. It is a fear of grieving God, of disappointing our beloved Lord, and of missing His divine plan for our lives.

Because of the lack of the fear of God, children do not obey their parents, students are disrespectful toward their teachers, our prisons are filled to overflowing, our policemen are discouraged and our televisions are full of immorality and violence.

Let us heed again the cry from God's dear heart, *"O that there were such an heart in them, that they would fear me, and keep all my commandments always, that it might be well with them, and with their children for ever!"* (Deut. 5:29). Yes, *"perfect love casteth out fear"* of judgment (1 John 4:18) However, it surely leads to divine soberness, which, in the fear of the Lord, produces holiness of heart.

Love and Fear Are Brothers

*And now, Israel, what doth the Lord thy
God require of thee, but to fear the Lord thy
God, to walk in all his ways, and to love him,
and to serve the Lord thy God with all
thy heart and with all thy soul.*

—Deuteronomy 10:12

In this passage, we have two requirements—not wishes—but requirements of the Lord which we shall ponder today: to love Him and to fear Him. This verse tells us that love for God and the fear of God must coexist in the same heart and soul.

The fear of the Lord prevents us from becoming disrespectful to the Lord. It prevents us from stepping on holy ground without taking off our shoes. The fear of the Lord prevents us from sinning and using the name of the Lord our God in vain. The fear of the Lord helps us prostrate ourselves before Him in awe, wonder, and adoration.

The love of God helps us to draw near Him and to serve Him with joy and singleness of heart. The love of the Lord keeps us from idolatry, from the love of the world and its pitiful and perishable toys. The love of the Lord brings us spiritual and emotional healing and wholeness. Yes, indeed, we were born to receive love and to give it, and in giving our first love to God, we reach the ultimate bliss of the soul on this side of eternity.

Fear and love are brothers. To have only one without the other is dangerous.

The Breeder of Doubts

*But one thing is needful: and Mary hath
chosen that good part, which shall
not be taken away from her.*

—Luke 10:42

I believe most doubt, when it comes to people, is associated with two things: (1) the loss of intimacy with the One once believed in, and (2) exposure to the tales of doubters. The second cause is often nothing but the by-product of the first.

Let us first consider our doubts toward God: toward His love, His forgiveness, His benevolence, His mercy, etc. Loss of intimacy is the main culprit. Simply stated, we are vulnerable to doubt when our daily life of prayer, communion, and praise is reduced to leftover times and greater and greater irregularities. Through that process, the Christian and his God "grow apart." And if we are Christian workers, our head and heart gradually cease to be throne-bound, becoming more and more mission-bound.

So, for many a believer, because of prayerlessness, busyness with the mission of God replaces business with the God of the mission. We become busy for Jesus rather than being busy with Jesus. Mary was busy with Jesus. Martha was busy about Jesus. It was Mary who had chosen the better part.

A man at the feet of Jesus cannot go astray. You have to be busy with your feet to do that. Near to the heart of God, our doubts vanish as the morning mist by the rising of the sun. Away from God, our doubts increase.

Therefore, my friend, draw near to God, and your doubts will vanish. That is the better part Mary chose. And as you draw nigh to Him, He will draw nigh to you (James 4:8).

Let's Stay Together

*Not forsaking the assembling of ourselves
together, as the manner of some...*

—Hebrews 10:25

As implied yesterday concerning doubts towards others—apostles, prophets, evangelists, pastors, and teachers—the culprit, first and foremost, is the loss of intimacy. You make a space between yourself and your pastor, and the devil will find a wedge that will fit that space. Hence, the warmth of intimacy is replaced by a wall of lukewarmness and then coldness. The devil possesses warehouses full of negatives that he can plant into the cracks of your faith toward the servants of Jesus. And not only that, but there are dozens of well-meaning people on your side of the wedge of doubt who will help to reinforce your doubts. Oh, how the fellowship of doubters will receive you gladly.

Therefore, one of the first rules of doubt therapy is: Do not forsake the assembling of yourselves together. Be assured of this: all those who forsake fellowshipping become doubters! And from doubters, they graduate into complainers, critics, and faultfinders. This is a spiritual reality. If you cease to pray for and with the saints of God, in a very little time, you will doubt their love and goodwill toward you.

As in the presence of the fellowship of the saints, your faith is constantly being reaffirmed, so likewise, in the presence of doubters, your doubts are constantly reaffirmed. Once in the company of the doubters, your small doubts will grow into larger doubts, and that will lead to gross misrepresentations and finally to rejection.

Yes, again, if doubt has weakened your faith, go back to where your faith will be strengthened: to the fellowship of the saints of God.

Two Perspectives

And they took him, and cast him into a pit:
and the pit was empty, there was no water in it.

—Genesis 37:24

This early picture of Joseph is not a good one. It is a picture of rejection, of loneliness, of injustice, of want, of hopelessness, and of great suffering. It is a picture invoking pity and compassion. It is a picture causing many to ask: Where is God? or, Why does God allow this? And, indeed, such is the view of man in the face of much suffering of good and godly men.

However, in God's eyes, this was not such a bad picture at all. In fact, this was a wonderful picture to Him. God saw this as a beginning of a mighty work that would prepare Joseph to be the ruler of the greatest empire. Eventually, he would *"bind his princes at his pleasure; and teach his senators wisdom,"* delivering Egypt and Israel from starvation (Ps. 105:17-23). Man looked at Joseph and said, "What a pity." God looked at Joseph and said, "How marvelous!"

God was allowing Joseph to be separated from a life of pleasure and favoritism in order to be placed into a machine that would make a new man out of the old man, a better man out of a good man, and a strong man out of a weak man.

Most men would look at Joseph in the pit and see a picture of sadness, a picture of a man whose luck had run out, and one who had come to a dead end in life. But, to God, Joseph being cast into the pit was part of the fulfillment of the Master's plan for his life. It was the beginning of the fulfillment of Joseph's dreams of the sheaves, the sun, moon, and stars. It was the beginning of deliverance in time of need for both Egypt and Israel.

So, perhaps, too, your calamity in the eyes of man may only be the beginning of a great journey with God.

God Doeth All Things Well

Trust in the Lord with all thine heart;
and lean not unto thine own understanding.
—Proverbs 3:5

Because God's name is I AM, both past and future to Him are rolled into one great present. As God saw it, the moment Joseph sat in the pit was the same moment Joseph sat at the governor's table in Egypt. The moment Joseph was hungry, thirsty, and cold in that pit was to God the same moment Joseph was feasting in luxury in the palace.

To man, the future is like thick darkness, like a wall of heavy fog. Man's vision is just a very short distance into the tomorrow, but God sees all the events from Genesis to Revelation on one great, panoramic canvas. He knows the yesterdays, the todays, and the tomorrows of all of us at all times.

But since our vision and understanding are limited, and since we cannot see beyond our pits of suffering into the throne room ahead of us, we must come to inner rest just as Paul described, *"for I know whom I have believed, and am persuaded that he is able to keep that which I have committed unto him against that day"* (2 Tim. 1:12).

The key to our hope is not in our trying to figure out why we are suffering but in our ceasing to lean on our own understanding, trusting only in the living God.

In all his sufferings, Joseph kept his heart from the poison of resentment, hatred, unbelief, self-pity, and doubt.

Oh, yes, our suffering and waiting in joyful obedience are God's opportunities to take us higher. There are no reasons for pity if we see things in the light of divine history. If we employ our understanding in the time of trouble, we sink. But if we trust, our spiritual branches will spring upwards to embrace what God has prepared for us before the foundation of the world.

Where Is Your Countenance Taking You?

Then there passed by Midianites merchantmen;
and they drew and lifted up Joseph out of the pit,
and sold Joseph to the Ishmeelites for twenty pieces
of silver: and they brought Joseph into Egypt.

—Genesis 37:28

Joseph now leaves the pit to only be sold into slavery. It seems his troubles go from bad to worse. Wouldn't it be wonderful if God would tell us what our sufferings are going to lead us to and what good things they will, in time, bring forth? Wouldn't it have been nice if Joseph had been told that he was on the way to the governorship of Egypt, to the fulfillment of his dreams? No, my friend, it would not have been nice. Knowing takes us out of trusting, and the motto of the righteous is that *"The just shall live by faith"* (Rom. 1:17).

God will never forsake the righteous. Joseph was righteous, and the trust of the righteous produces positive, benevolent attitudes. It is not physical prisons that make us slaves, but it is negative and trustless attitudes that put our souls into chains. Because Joseph never got into the negative, he never became anybody's slave but God's. Nothing can ever take away our choice to serve God, and as long we choose for God, we are freemen everywhere.

Because of all this, nothing had ruined the countenance of godliness on the face of Joseph: not the jealousies of his brothers, nor the empty pit, nor the mercilessly long journey into Egypt, nor the chains in the prisons of that land. In fact, the longer he suffered, the brighter his countenance.

Finally, Joseph's countenance in the midst of suffering took him to the throne. My friend, what is your countenance in the midst of suffering, and where will it take you?

After Melchisedec

—⟨⟩—

For he testifieth, Thou art a priest
for ever after the order of Melchisedec.

—Hebrews 7:17

Jesus was a priest after the order of Melchisedec. What was unique about the priesthood of Melchisedec? First, Melchisedec was the first biblical priest. Secondly, he was both priest and king. No man from Melchisedec to Jesus was allowed to carry both offices. King Saul tried, but it led to disaster (1 Sam. 13:9–14). Thirdly, Melchisedec had a mysterious beginning, and his priesthood would never end.

Now this is all true of Jesus. So, Jesus is a king and a priest after the order of Melchisedec, but this is not all the good news. In Revelation 1:5–6, John tells us that Jesus *"washed us from our sins in his own blood, And hath made us kings and priests unto God and his Father."* Notice, it does not say "will make us," but that He *"hath made us."* The moment we were washed by the blood, we, too, became kings and priests after the order of Melchisedec.

As priests, we are to enter into spiritual warfare, *"For we wrestle not against flesh and blood"* (Eph. 6:12). We are, by prayer, to snatch sinners out of the clutches of the devil and to pray believers into sanctification.

As kings, we are to govern over the nations with a bent knee and a meek spirit. Oh, what a privilege that we, too, are called to be priests after the order of Melchisedec, to a priesthood that will never end.

Aprons Win over Crowns

But it shall not be so among you: but whosoever will be great among you, let him be your minister; And whosoever will be chief among you, let him be your servant.

—Matthew 20:26–27

We learned yesterday that we are both kings and priests like Melchisedec and Jesus. So, how then shall we govern as kings? We shall govern as kings befitting the kingdom of God. And Christ's kingdom is not of this world. Hence, Christ's kings do not rule by earthly principles: by pushing, by pulling, by domineering, and by lording it over others.

Christ's kings govern as Jesus governed: by servanthood, being servants to all. For He said, *"Even as the Son of man came not to be ministered unto, but to minister, and to give his life a ransom for many"* (Matt. 20:28). Paul says in Philippians 2:7 that Jesus took the form of a servant. All of Jesus' kings wear aprons on this earth instead of crowns, which reminds us of another beautiful picture of King Jesus when he put on the apron of humility and washed the disciples' feet.

In Jesus' kingdom, the chief, the greatest man with the most power and authority, who is able "to bind and to loose," is the one who says, "How can I help you?" rather than, "Do such and such unto me." It is the one who washes feet who is greater, rather than the one who says, "Wash my feet." It is the one who has reached the deepest level of brokenness, of poverty of spirit, who best portrays the kingly spirit of our Lord Jesus, and who is most likely to be a candidate to sit either at the left or right side of our Master.

This is the spirit of God's kings, and it is through that spirit that the power of God will even move the hearts of the most wicked of men. Yes, we are kings, but let us never forget that the nature of our kingship is not of this earth.

Dressing Properly

━━◄◉▓◉►━━

*And thou shalt make holy garments for Aaron thy
brother for glory and for beauty...that they may make
Aaron's garments to consecrate him, that he may
minister unto me in the priest's office.*

—Exodus 28:2–3

From this passage onward you have the consistent association of a robe with the priestly office. This robe symbolizes both holiness and mission.

As we look into the Revelation, we see all the saints standing before the throne, wearing robes. Again, their robes also represent holiness through washing by the blood of the Lamb, and mission. So, when you think about this robe in terms of holiness and mission, you visualize character and calling, purity and purpose. Yes, we must have this robe to get to heaven.

To illustrate this, Jesus gave us the Parable of the Wedding Garment (Matthew 22). Here, a man slips by the doorkeeper to attend a wedding without a wedding garment. He slips by the doorkeeper, he slips by the ushers, and he sits at the wedding table, apparently unnoticed by anyone. But when the king came in, he immediately recognized the man without the garment.

This is a spiritual parable. This man represents a believer who got in by making a good profession of his faith. He got into the wedding hall by saying the right things, but Jesus, who is king, saw into his heart, his spiritual life lacking character, calling, purpose, purity, and mission. And so, he cast him out into outer darkness.

Friend, let us be sure that we are dressed properly for our very finest hour, lest we, too, be cast out when and where we least expect it.

The Importance of Prayer

*Ye also, as lively stones, are built up a spiritual
house, an holy priesthood, to offer up spiritual sacrifices,
acceptable to God by Jesus Christ...ye are a
chosen generation, a royal priesthood.*

—1 Peter 2:5, 9

More than anything else, the devil fears and hates Christians praying together. He remembers too well his first defeat against God's congregation at Rephidim. There, Amalek (a type of the devil) was defeated by Moses, Aaron, and Hur praying together. The devil does not care how many soldiers we have in the field, just as long as they don't pray together. The devil fears united prayer!

The devil fights any theology that puts prayer into church services. The devil likes packed sanctuaries for worship and empty ones for prayer. The average church, by putting more emphasis on Sunday morning worship, church picnics, or Bible studies than on prayer, soon convinces the new convert of the unimportance of prayer. Hence, we must realize the devil has the church just about where he wants her to be. We must return to the priesthood of all believers, and that means praise and intercessory prayer.

In the early church, you find nothing much other than prayer and praise. This is what the first generation of Christians were born into. It was only as the church developed and became more organized that she placed less attention on prayer and praise and more and more on preaching, worship, and other programs.

"If my people, which are called by my name, shall humble themselves, and pray..." (2 Chron. 7:14). Those are the first steps to revival. May they get into our hearts so that the glory of the Lord will once again descend upon His people.

Praying Together

...mine house shall be called an house of prayer for all people.
—Isaiah 56:7

When Jesus came to earth, there were some things He did away with, such as the ceremonial law. There were some things He changed, such as those matters recorded in the Sermon on the Mount where He said repeatedly, *"Ye have heard that it was said by them of old time,...But I say unto you..."* (Matt. 5). And there are some things Jesus left unchanged. The latter is the case with the words of God in Isaiah about prayer.

God never called the temple a house of worship because, to God, prayer is the highest form of worship. That is to say, whenever God's people get together, God's primary desire for them is to pray.

The physical temple is now destroyed, but the concept of meeting together in Jesus' name remains. Our primary purpose is still prayer. So whatever house we meet in together in Jesus' name is to be a *"house of prayer."*

In God's mind, prayer is always associated with God's people coming together. *"Again I say unto you, That if two of you shall agree on earth as touching any thing that they shall ask, it shall be done for them of my Father which is in heaven. For where two or three are gathered together in my name, there am I in the midst of them"* (Matt. 18:19–20). If we don't pray together, we are stripped of the power available to us for change, for protection, and for advancement.

So, the devil does not mind us building up the attendance of our Sunday morning services, Christian concerts, missions conferences, and Bible studies as long as he can prevent us from praying together.

When Jesus was in Jerusalem He drove the moneychangers out of the temple to make it again a house of prayer. What would He have to drive out of our churches to make room for prayer amongst us again?

Not for Heaven's Sake

*Yea doubtless, and I count all things
but loss for the excellency of the knowledge
of Christ Jesus my Lord.*

—Philippians 3:8

This is a testimony of a true disciple. This is a testimony that Jesus can build His church on. No, our Savior cannot and will not build His church on those who follow Him for the loaves, fishes, miracles, and blessings. Nor can Jesus build His church upon those who follow Him for heaven's sake rather than for His sake. For too many, going to heaven has become more enticing than following Jesus and living in daily fellowship with Him.

Heaven has been presented as an escape from the sufferings of hell. It has become the centerpiece of much of popular evangelical theology. Heaven is the motivation. Heaven is the prize. Heaven is the exceeding great reward, and Jesus is just a steppingstone to get there.

But, thank God for Job. He, like Paul, was in his faith for God's sake and not for blessing's sake. He lost all: his livestock, his barns, his servants, his children, and his health. Yet, he fell to the ground and worshipped God. Would to God that his wife would have done likewise, but, no, she was in religion for blessing's sake. When the blessings stopped she was done with God.

Oh, friend, do we want heaven or God? Can we have the crown without the cross? If we don't get saved for Christ's sake, to live and die for Christ, heaven will not receive us. Let us remember that Jesus must never become a mere steppingstone, but He must always be sought after as the ultimate prize.

Blessings Do Not Make Us Better

*Then Jesus beholding him loved him, and
said unto him, One thing thou lackest: go thy way,
sell whatsoever thou hast, and give to the poor,
and thou shalt have treasure in heaven: and
come, take up the cross, and follow me.*

—Mark 10:21

The rich young ruler did not know he was in his faith for blessing's sake and not for God's sake until Jesus told him to sell all he had in order to give it to the poor. Judas was following Jesus for blessing's sake; so were Demas, Ananias and Sapphira, and Simon the magician.

As you read the story of Paul—his beatings, his persecutions, his imprisonments, his poverty, his hunger, his shipwreck, his lack of clothing, and of all those in Asia forsaking him—you quickly learn that Paul was serving Jesus for Jesus' sake. Jesus was Paul's exceeding great reward every day of his new life.

Heaven, healing, and prosperity are some of the strong messages we hear today. They are the bonuses, the incentives, and the promises that drive the engine of this type of evangelism. But a greedy attitude of wanting blessings and bonuses has led to many people quitting churches when the desired products of those claims are not delivered. Others have become "church-jumpers," to find ever greater blessings somewhere else.

We must realize that blessings and bonuses do nothing to make people better. They do not purify us, they do not mature us, and they do not build character. In fact, in most cases, quitting prayer meeting or ministries because of things we dislike teaches us nothing except that we are spoiled, morally depraved, desperately wicked, and unfit for the kingdom of God.

All Seek Their Own

*For all seek their own, not the
things which are Jesus Christ's.*

—Philippians 2:21

If the *"all seek their own"* in this text means all the people in all the churches of that time, it is quite an indictment on early Christianity, being only about thirty years old.

Chronological studies of when the Pauline church epistles were written support this view. All Pauline church letters were written prior to his prison epistles (Philippians, Colossians, Ephesians, and Philemon). So, indeed, when Paul said *"all seek their own,"* he includes the Thessalonian church, the Galatian church, the Corinthian church, the Roman church, and the Colossian and Ephesian congregations. After Paul's first imprisonment in Rome, he wrote no further church letters but only three personal letters: two to Timothy and one to Titus.

So, when it comes to churches and people, *"all seek their own"* includes a vast number of the worshippers of God. And indeed, human nature and the pull of the flesh and the devil have not lessened since the days of the Old Testament when God cried out, *"O that thou hadst hearkened to my commandments! then had thy peace been as a river, and thy righteousness as the waves of the sea"* (Is. 48:18).

"...all seek their own." Friend, are you part of this "all" or have you died out to the old life to really and fully embrace the new in the Lord Jesus Christ?

The Philippian Blessing

*And you Philippians yourselves well know
that in the early days of the Gospel ministry,
when I left Macedonia, no church (assembly)
entered into partnership with me and opened
up [a debit and credit] account in giving
and receiving except you only.*

—Philippians 4:15 AMPLIFIED

When did Paul leave Macedonia? How did this church in Macedonia—the Philippian church—get started? We get our answers from Acts 16. In a vision, Paul saw a man speaking to him, saying, *"Come over into Macedonia, and help us"* (Acts 16:9).

Paul went to Philippi of Macedonia and found Lydia, an earnest Jewess. She and her household received Jesus. And so did a certain damsel possessed by an evil spirit. When the damsel was converted, Paul and Silas were thrown into prison. That led to the salvation of the jailer and his household. So, when Paul left Philippi, he left a congregation of at least two families and one damsel!

From that day on, that little growing congregation began to set up a partnership to support the man of God with whatever it took. Oh, what a beautiful story.

Yes, Lydia, the first convert of Macedonia, compelled the apostle to abide in her house, and that wonderful spirit of an open door to men of God stayed in Philippi to the very end of Paul's ministry. No wonder the apostle could give a blessing to the Philippians that was denied all other churches, *"But my God shall supply all your need according to his riches in glory by Christ Jesus"* (Phil. 4:19).

It pleases God if we take good care of His messengers, and perhaps only in this context can we also claim the great Philippian blessing.

In the Bowels of Christ

*I thank my God upon every remembrance of you,
Always in every prayer of mine for you all making
request with joy, For your fellowship in the
gospel from the first day until now.*

—Philippians 1:3–5

We learned yesterday that the Philippian church was the only church that was a joy to the apostle Paul. All other churches, although Paul was thankful for what God had begun in them, were apostolic burdens. But Philippi was an apostolic joy, because Philippi did not seek her own.

Because Philippi sacrificially looked after Paul, Paul could say, *"I have you in my heart,"* and also, *"For God is my record, how greatly I long after you all in the bowels of Jesus Christ"* (Phil. 1:7–8). Notice, it does not say, "in my bowels," but *"in the bowels of Jesus Christ."* That is to say, this connection between Paul and Philippi was of Jesus. It was in the Holy Ghost, and that is the way it is supposed to be between any church and her pastor or missionaries.

You can gather from this longing of Paul to be with the Philippians that their church was the only place he had where he could lay his head. Jesus had no place to lay His head. The Pharisees traversed land and sea in their missionary zeal, but they provided no place for Jesus to lay His head. In fact, they doubted Him, found fault with Him, and killed Him. Thus it has been with most true servants of God throughout the centuries.

May there be many more churches that have a pastor-to-flock bond as that which was found between Paul and the Philippians: *"in the bowels of Jesus Christ."*

Engine Room Christians

*And there was one Anna, a prophetess...And
she was a widow of about fourscore and four years,
which departed not from the temple, but served
God with fastings and prayers night and day.*
—Luke 2:36–37

The church can easily be compared to a mighty ocean liner. It consists, first of all, of a vast number of passengers who travel with the greatest of comfort from one harbor to the next. Their cabins are lovely, and their elaborate meals are consumed in dining rooms of the finest décor. Servants attend to their every wish at the flick of a hand. On pleasant days, they sunbathe on deck or play cards in the game room. These people can be likened to "above waterline Christians" who never venture into the belly of the ship below sea level.

On the opposite end of the spectrum are the "below waterline Christians." They live out their whole existence from seashore to seashore in the bottom of the ship. It is there where they eat, sleep, and work, attending to the engines, working faithfully in the sweat of their brows. Unlike the above sea level passengers, they never see where they are going, but faithfully follow the messages of the captain, manning the engine as requested.

Do you get the picture? What has kept the Ship Zion going throughout the centuries is not the above sea level passengers, but the below sea level prayer warriors who get their commands from the captain of their salvation. Often unknown and unappreciated by the others sunbathing on deck, these few, hidden from the world, keep the ship moving toward its predestined, heavenly port.

Now, what kind of Christian are you? Just a passenger going along for a small sacrifice, or are you an engine-room laborer, sweating, working tirelessly, praying on and on as Anna the prophetess for the completion of God's plan for the ages?

Paul's Gospel in Two Words

*There is therefore now no condemnation
to them which are in Christ Jesus, who walk
not after the flesh, but after the Spirit.*

—Romans 8:1

What John 3:16 is to the Gospels, Romans 8 is to the Pauline epistles. Here is your finest, briefest, and clearest definition of Christianity: *in Christ.* *"There is therefore now no condemnation to them which are* in Christ *Jesus."* From Romans 8:1 on throughout the Pauline writings you have an additional seventy-three references to this *in Christ* theology.

So, *in Christ* defines Christianity, and it defines discipleship. Until we understand the *in Christ* theology, we understand nothing much about Christianity. Once we do understand it, we will then comprehend everything else we need to understand about living with and in Christ Jesus.

Where, then, did Paul get his *in Christ* theology? The answer is simply, from Christ Himself. Its source, no doubt, was from Jesus' teaching in John 15, *"I am the vine, ye are the branches: He that abideth in me, and I in him, the same bringeth forth much fruit: for without me ye can do nothing"* (v. 5). Yes, no doubt, passages like this spawned the *in Christ* theology in the heart of Paul.

By abiding in Christ we draw our life from Him. By Him living in us we have no condemnation, and we will walk in the Spirit, not fulfilling the desires of the flesh. Yes, indeed, that was the mystery hidden in all the ages before the days of the apostles, *"Christ in you, the hope of glory"* (Col. 1:27).

The Holy Spirit

*But if the Spirit of him that raised up Jesus from
the dead dwell in you, he that raised up Christ from
the dead shall also quicken your mortal bodies
by his Spirit that dwelleth in you.*

—Romans 8:11

We cannot read Romans 8 without talking about the Holy
Spirit. As you study Romans you will find that the Holy
Spirit is not mentioned in the first seven chapters of this
book. But beginning with Romans 8:1 through to verse 16
you have fourteen references to the Holy Spirit.

Observe that Paul does not begin his introduction of the
Holy Spirit by telling us who the Holy Spirit is, but Paul
tells us what He can do and does do for those walking with
God. It is more important to know the purpose of the Holy
Spirit than to know all about who He is. In fact, we never
really find out on this side of eternity who the Holy Spirit
is in His fullness, anyhow.

So, Paul here introduces to us the Holy Spirit in relationship to Christ and the Christian in order to make his
definition of Christianity complete. You cannot have Jesus
without the Holy Spirit, and you cannot have the Holy Spirit
without Jesus.

All those who would abide in Jesus must first be convicted by the Holy Spirit. And then, they need the power of
the Holy Spirit to mortify the deeds of the flesh, giving Christ
permanence in their lives. Oh, what a gospel in Romans 8,
dwelling in Christ by walking in the Spirit!

COUNTING THE COST: the Principle

*And whosoever doth not bear his cross, and come
after me, cannot be my disciple. For which of you, intending
to build a tower, sitteth not down first, and counteth
the cost, whether he have sufficient to finish it?*

—Luke 14:27–28

"And whosoever doth not bear his cross" tells us that the cross has a cost. Many new converts have not been told about the cross that they must bear to be disciples of Jesus and to possess the kingdom of God. They are told about the cross of Christ that He bore, the cross He suffered on, the cross He died on, but not about their own cross by which their Self-life is to find its continuous death.

"And whosoever doth not bear his cross, and come after me, cannot be my disciple." This cross is a cost to us, but it is also a gain, for Jesus said, *"and whosoever will lose his life for my sake shall find it"* (Matt. 16:25). It cost Jesus His life to purchase our redemption, but we have to die on our cross to keep it. This is why Paul said, *"I am crucified with Christ"* and why he also states, *"I die daily"* (Gal. 2:20; 1 Cor. 15:31).

Yes, counting the cost before starting the journey with Jesus our Savior is good advice. Because many have not counted the cost, many have backslidden. And Peter said concerning them, *"For it had been better for them not to have known the way of righteousness, than, after they have known it, to turn from the holy commandment delivered unto them."* Therefore, *"the latter end is worse with them than the beginning"* (2 Pet. 2:20, 21).

Take up your cross today and become a disciple of Christ Jesus.

COUNTING THE COST: the Reality

―◁▦▥▷―

And it came to pass, that, as they went
in the way, a certain man said unto him, Lord,
I will follow thee whithersoever thou goest.

—Luke 9:57

As this passage unfolds, we see that three persons were engaged in counting the cost of becoming followers of Jesus.

The first one was a volunteer. He said, *"I will follow thee whithersoever thou goest."* What more can you want in a disciple than this? Jesus, however, wanted to be sure that the man's enthusiasm was not just skin-deep, so He said to him, *"The foxes have holes, and birds of the air have nests; but the Son of man hath not where to lay his head"* (Matt. 8:20). Jesus wanted this man to know that following Him requires the surrender of all our security to become utterly dependent on the Father.

Next, we have the story of Jesus asking a man to follow Him. This man first wanted to bury his father, a request Jesus denied him. While in the first case of this passage Jesus challenged a man to give up his security, in the second case, He challenged a man to give up his tradition: that the son be present at the burial of the father.

In the third case, a man also willing to follow requested a delay so that he could first bid farewell to his family. This request Jesus also denied, for Jesus expects us to give up our family attachment for instant obedience to Him.

My friend, the cost of discipleship requires all of this: giving up our securities, our traditions, and our family sentiments. Are you willing to do all that?

How To Say Good-Bye

*And he left the oxen, and ran after Elijah,
and said, Let me, I pray thee, kiss my father and my
mother, and then I will follow thee. And he said unto
him, Go back again: for what have I done to thee?*

—1 Kings 19:20

Looking back while you are plowing is dangerous both physically and spiritually. The third man in yesterday's lesson from Luke 9 was forbidden by Jesus to say farewell to his family. But in 1 Kings, we see that Elisha was permitted to go back to kiss his family good-bye after Elijah called him into discipleship. What is the difference between the man in Luke 9 and the one in 1 Kings 19?

The man in Luke 9 wanted to go back to refresh and strengthen his family memories of the past. The man in 1 Kings was going back to burn up his past, that is, to let it go up in smoke never to be attracted by it again. And so, Elisha *"took a yoke of oxen, and slew them, and boiled their flesh with the instruments of the oxen, and gave unto the people, and they did eat. Then he arose, and went after Elijah, and ministered unto him"* (1 Kings 19:21). Elisha burned up his plow, using it as firewood to turn his oxen into a farewell dinner as a testimony to his family that he was done with old family ties and that he did not want the oxen and the plow to be there to ever call him back again. Ah, shall we say, "Glory to God!"?

So, if Jesus calls you, and you want to go back for your farewell, will you go back to strengthen your ties, to stir up family sentiments, or to let them go up in smoke until your family claims a like vision for God?

From this point on, Elisha ministered unto Elijah; and when it was time to cross the Jordan, Elisha followed Elijah in hot pursuit until he had a double portion of the Spirit. Oh, my friend, it is worth it to forsake all to follow Jesus.

The Gateway to a Reprobate Life

Because that, when they knew God, they
glorified him not as God, neither were thankful;
but became vain in their imaginations, and
their foolish heart was darkened.

—Romans 1:21

Here the apostle Paul brilliantly traces all sins, perversions, and spiritual decay to the neglect of praise, because *"when they knew God, they glorified him not as God, neither were thankful."* Without rejoicing evermore, giving thanks in everything, and letting everything that hath breath praise the Lord, the human heart is utterly defenseless against the onslaughts of evil from the world, the flesh, and the devil.

So then, the lack of praise leads to the perversion of the mind. They became *"vain in their imaginations."* A praiseless heart leads to impairment in the spiritual mind in grasping and articulating divine truth. It leads to a heart that becomes devoid of Christ's abiding, and subject or susceptible to every evil work and deception.

Praiselessness, as Paul continues in this chapter, leads to pride, idol worship, and a reprobate mind. It leads to unrighteousness, fornication, wickedness, covetousness, maliciousness, envy, murder, strife, deceit, whispering, disobedience, and sexual perversion.

Oh, how readily we can now respond to that great refrain given over and over again in Psalm 107, *"Oh that men would praise the Lord for his goodness, and for his wonderful works to the children of men!"*

Beware when praise, the sacrifice of praise, the fruit of your lips, leaves your life. Darkness will settle into your heart and take you from the banquet of heavenly dainties that once were the delight of your soul, into a life of darkness and alienation from God.

341

A Help Meet

---

*And the Lord God said, It is not good that
the man should be alone; I will make
him an help meet for him.*

—Genesis 2:18

In the very beginning, God created the oldest institution of man: the marriage relationship. Every creation of God culminated with the divine words *"...and God saw that it was good"* (Gen. 1:10, 12, 18, 25). That is, except for the creation of man, where He says, *"It is not good..."*

Today's verse states that man without woman is not good. God said, "I will make him a helper." So, this first picture of man is one of incompleteness, and the first picture of the woman is that of a helper. Only together will both reach their full potential. No man can take away the incompleteness of another man, only a woman can do so, and that is why there is no room for homosexuality.

So, God created woman. Man was created out of the dust of the ground, and woman was created out of the side of a man. The Word says that God built her out of Adam's rib (Gen. 2:21–22).

Has there ever been a more careful, thoughtful, wonderful, intimate thing that came out of the hands of God? Woman is custom made, specifically endowed with great gifts to help the man.

So, the first calling of woman will always be as a helper for man. That is what she was created for, just as a fish was created to swim and a bird to fly. And when a woman is in that element of help, she will fulfill her highest calling in life.

However, if a woman belongs to that small group of women whose calling is to be single, she will find her calling fulfilled in serving the church and her anointed leaders, just as Mary and Martha so wonderfully served Jesus when He was on earth.

The World Is Ready, the Church Is Not

Lift up your eyes, and look on the fields;
for they are white already to harvest.

—John 4:35

Here Jesus was in Samaria, a despicable place for a Jew ever to place his foot upon. Yet, it is in this place where Jesus said that the fields are white unto harvest. Spiritually speaking, it means that the general population of Samaria was ripe and ready to be saved, sanctified, and filled with the Holy Spirit.

Since the fields were white for harvest in Samaria in the first century, would they not also be white for harvest today? I believe that all the fields of the world are white for harvest now, as they were then. Oh, who would ever have thought that this very sinful Samaritan woman was only one step away from being a great missionary? For she soon preached to her whole village about Jesus. The seeds which she sowed then began to sprout and grow and bring forth fruit, *"some thirtyfold, some sixty, and some an hundred"* (Mark 4:20), in that great Samaritan revival mentioned in Acts 8.

Yes, the fields are as white for harvest now as ever. What is lacking is the readiness of the church. The church that brought the Samaritan revival was a pure church, a holy church, a Spirit-filled church. And she continued to bring in the harvest until division, strife, jealousy, competition, and carnality put their ugly spots upon her glorious garment. This is the reason why Jesus prayed in John 17:9, *"I pray not for the world, but for them which thou hast given me."* When the church is ready, the harvest will be brought in.

Church Tumors

Hath the Lord indeed spoken only by Moses?
hath he not spoken also by us? And the Lord heard
it...and, behold, Miriam became leprous.

—Numbers 12:2, 10

Here Aaron and Miriam became a tumor in the congregation of the Lord. A tumor is an organism out of harmony with the body, drawing strength from it but returning nothing to it but poison.

Any person discontented with their God-sent spiritual leader is like the beginning of a church tumor. Then, this person finds others of like discontent, and the tumor grows. These people then will draw strength away from the body of Christ, returning only poison to it, gradually incapacitating the body in the fulfillment of its earthly mission.

So, in this story, Aaron and Miriam became the beginning of a tumor and the focal point of a general discontent with the spirit and leadership of Moses. And with Moses' marriage to an Ethiopian woman, they finally had a specific point by which to "justly" vent their feelings, to usurp authority, and to declare themselves equal to their leader.

That God can speak through persons other than spiritual leaders is indeed true, *"For as many as are led by the Spirit of God, they are the sons of God"* (Rom. 8:14). That God could speak, and had often spoken, through Aaron through the Urim and Thummim, is also without question. But spiritual gifts, regardless of what they are, never entitle us to infringe upon the divine authority vested in the office that goes with leadership.

Do not join a church tumor, and remember that spiritual gifts alone give us no license to lord it over others.

Sin Deceives

*For sin, taking occasion by
the commandment, deceived me...*

—Romans 7:11

The problem facing our nation, and our personal security, is sin. Sin is the worst of all evils in society. Sin causes divorces, rebellion, drunkenness, foolishness, murder, theft, and strife, and it will lead in the end to eternal separation from God.

The apostle Paul said that sin deceives. And to be deceived means to assume that which is false to be true and to think of that which is true to be false. The Pharisees harbored sin in their lives, and so they took that which was true about Jesus to be false, and they took that which was false about Jesus to be true. If we have known sin in our lives, we shall do likewise. We shall mistake false prophets for true prophets and true prophets for false prophets. Sin deceives.

Sin causes us to think that God would have us marry that person while God wants us to marry another person. Sin can cause us to think we ought to go into the ministry when we really should be an usher; to think we ought to buy this house while God wants us in that house; to think that we ought to leave the church when we really need to stay with her; and to think we ought to have a Christian school while God may have other plans.

If we harbor known sin in our hearts, we are deceived. Think of it! All theologians, all seminary professors, all Bible college teachers, and all pastors who have known, unconfessed sin in their lives are deceived, and they deceive their followers. Oh, may we reach for the power of God that sin may no longer have dominion over us.

Sin Kills

Behold, all souls are mine; as the soul
of the father, so also the soul of the son is mine:
the soul that sinneth, it shall die.

—Ezekiel 18:4

Sin not only deceives, but it also kills. *"...the soul that sinneth, it shall die."* This is as certain as the law of gravity. Sin always brings death, and that is part of the spiritual physics of the kingdom of God.

"...the soul that sinneth, it shall die." This statement has neither qualifiers nor exceptions. It is a universal truth applicable to every man in every age. It is no respecter of a person's past religious experiences, his standing in the church, nor his wealth, maturity, or education.

Sin kills wherever it is allowed to reign. Sin had Jesus crucified, it killed Adam, and it brought shame and disrepute to David. Because of David's sin he had to pray *"Restore unto me the joy of thy salvation"* (Ps. 51:12). Sin ate away at Judas until he hung himself. It brought Ananias and Sapphira into an early grave, and it caused Demas to forsake Paul, and King Saul to lose his kingdom.

"...the soul that sinneth, it shall die." Yes, indeed, sin is the only cause of death for the spiritual man. He will never die from anything else. Sin has many faces, such as selfishness, covetousness, lust, greed, murmuring, fornication, backbiting, stealing, robbery, strife, and witchcraft; but sin will always be sin.

May we never see sin just as a social evil or a theological principle, but as an enemy of our soul which continually tries to bring to death that which is born of God.

God Unites, but Man Divides

━━∘⫯⫯⫯⫲ᒊᒍᒌᒌᒌᒌᒌᒌ━━

One man esteemeth one day above another:
another esteemeth every day alike. Let every man
be fully persuaded in his own mind.

—Romans 14:5

In this passage, the apostle Paul chides Christians over their divisions concerning diet and the day of worship. There were meat eaters and there were vegetarians in the church at Rome. There were seventh day worshippers who worshipped on Saturday, and there were first day worshippers who worshipped on Sunday. No doubt, there were also sprinklers and immersers when it came to baptism. And there were likely both advocates and opponents for the gift of tongues.

As time developed, each group eventually needed its own scholars to defend its peculiar doctrines, its own church headquarters, printing presses and publishers, missionary boards, and Bible colleges and seminaries to perpetuate the "purity of the doctrine." May it be said that division started in the first century?

Isn't it amazing that Christians, born of God, are all born in oneness? Paul said, *"Even when we were dead in sins, hath [God] quickened us together with Christ...And hath raised us up together, and made us sit together in heavenly places in Christ Jesus"* (Eph. 2:5–6). Yet, where is all this togetherness today? Since we are born in togetherness, and we shall reign with Christ in togetherness, then why can't we work together?

Oh, what the church can do to believers. You take a thousand believers from all over the world, who are born again today, and they are together in Christ. You have them come together a year later, and they are divided. God have mercy on us! Let us take Paul's chiding to heart and come together for what we are born again for: to worship God, to love one another, and to make disciples of all nations.

One Thing

—⋙〰⋘—

*Jesus said unto him, If thou wilt be perfect, go and
sell that thou hast, and give to the poor, and thou shalt
have treasure in heaven: and come and follow me.*

—Matthew 19:21

One of the prerequisites for us to abide in Jesus is for us
to turn away from all desires of the Self-will toward God's
perfect will. Notice, I say, a turn away from all Self-will.
Anything less than one hundred percent commitment to
Jesus will keep us short of abiding in Him and of being filled
with the Holy Spirit. Anything less than a one hundred
percent all-for-God attitude prevents us from following
Jesus, from being a true disciple.

The rich young man disqualified himself because he held
on to one thing, just *one* thing. Because of that one attachment to the Self-life, Jesus refused to take him as a disciple.
As the story is recorded in Mark 10, Jesus said unto him,
"One thing thou lackest..." (v. 21).

Oh, how many people do you know who are one hundred
percent for God? They alone are true disciples and true
followers of the Lord Jesus, through whom God by the Holy
Spirit accomplishes His purposes in this world. A ninety-
nine percent grade may permit us to pass in any school of
man. But a ninety-nine percent grade falls short of connecting us with discipleship. Hence, Jesus said, *"So likewise,
whosoever he be of you that forsaketh not all that he hath, he
cannot be my disciple"* (Luke 14:33). To abide in Jesus
requires a full repentance from and abandonment of
the Self-life.

What we learn from the rich young man is that a man
who is ninety-nine percent for God, although he will make
a better citizen, is no closer to the abundant life than a
nineteen percent believer. Neither one connects.

If there is a *one thing* in your life, give it up, and you will
be taking your first step after Jesus.

Get Right with Man

For if ye forgive men their trespasses, your heavenly Father will also forgive you: But if ye forgive not men their trespasses, neither will your Father forgive your trespasses.

—Matthew 6:14–15

An essential element for bringing us into an abiding relationship with the Lord Jesus Christ is in the confession of our sins whenever we violate a spiritual law. That confession, as we learn today, must not only be toward God, but also toward man.

Many a sincere worshipper has left the altar of prayer short of experiencing that abiding in Christ, because resentment and criticism toward father, mother, brother, sister, pastor, or choir leader has not been confessed.

We are in just as desperate a need to hear "get right with man" as to hear "get right with God." Our Lord tells us in the Sermon on the Mount that unless we are right with man we will not be right with God. The prodigal son not only had to say that he had sinned against God, but also that he had sinned against his father.

I am convinced that most altar confessions never translate into new spiritual relationships simply because the pride of man prevents many from making things right on the horizontal level. Therefore, God's offer for the forgiveness of sins never reaches men's destitute hearts.

Get right with God? Correct! But also get right with man! If we do not forgive others, God will not forgive us.

December 13

Invite Him In

━━∈◀Ⅲ\ ∫\Ⅲ▶∋━━

Behold, I stand at the door, and knock: if any man
hear my voice, and open the door, I will come in to
him, and will sup with him, and he with me.

—Revelation 3:20

Jesus will not enter a human heart but by invitation. He does not force Himself upon anyone; yet, if He sees a broken, hungry, contrite heart, He will knock at that heart's door. He will come as far as your door on His own, but for Him to enter into your heart, you must open the door. In other words, He will ring the doorbell, but you must unlock and open the door.

When you open the door as a penitent and contrite sinner, He will come in. Yes, He will. Just say, "Lord, forgive me of all my sins. Come into my heart, Lord Jesus," and He will come in. Receive Him with gratitude, and thank Him with all your heart. He likes that. Aren't you glad that there are no ifs, ands, or buts about him coming in? Jesus, did not say, "I might come in," but *"I will come in."*

Now, once He is in your heart, that is when you begin to taste of the Great Supper referred to in Luke 14. That is when He will sup with you and you with Him. He will bring to you all that you need in food: the appetizer, the salad, the soup, the main course, and the dessert. He will bring the dishes and the silverware. He will bring the napkins and the tablecloth. He will bring the spices and the seasonings.

Jesus never comes empty-handed to anyone's door. He will come with the spiritual riches that are far beyond anything the finest of palaces could offer. Now, since He has come in, won't you keep feasting with Him forever?

Overcome

*To him that overcometh will I grant to sit with
me in my throne, even as I also overcame, and
am set down with my Father in his throne.*
—Revelation 3:21

Please observe that Revelation 3:20, the Scripture we covered yesterday, should never be read without the next verse as given above. Verse 20 tells us how to start our journey of abiding in Christ, but verse 21 tells us how to continue it. Notice, this is the last message of Jesus' seven messages that He gave to the churches, and the key word in all these messages is *overcome.*

So then, Revelation 3:20 tells us how to begin our journey with Christ: by invitation. Revelation 3:21, in the context of all seven messages to the churches, tells us how to complete our journey with Christ: by overcoming. Oh, the marvelous rewards that await this overcoming life. It is this beautiful sequence of overcoming that leads us straight up to the throne room of God Himself.

To eat of the tree of life: overcome. To be spared the second death: overcome. To eat of the hidden manna: overcome. To receive the morning star and power over the nations: overcome. To be clothed in white raiment: overcome. To become a pillar in the temple of God: overcome. To sit with Christ in the Father's throne: overcome. To not have our name blotted out of the Book of Life: overcome!

Overcome what? Overcome our Self-life which will never take one step after Jesus, which will never submit to the lordship of Jesus. Overcome the lust of the flesh, the lust of the eye, and the pride of life, and eternity with God will be yours.

December 15

Love and Live

━━◦◖◗◦━━

And, behold, a certain lawyer stood up, and tempted him,
saying, Master, what shall I do to inherit eternal life?

—Luke 10:25

I do not know of any greater question that could be asked
by any man, on this dark side of eternity, in all of history,
"...what shall I do to inherit eternal life?" Notice first, as
recorded in the Gospels, there are only two men who ever
asked this question, and it is this lawyer and the rich young
ruler (Matt. 19:16). Notice secondly, that these two men may
have been the only ones who professed not to be saved.

Consider what Jesus' astounding answer to the question
was not. It was not, "You must be born again." That was
Jesus' answer to Nicodemus because he already had a zeal
for God like the apostle Paul before he was saved. Paul
claimed even in the unsaved state, *"Concerning
zeal...touching the righteousness...in the law, blameless"*
(Phil. 3:6). To Nicodemus and Paul, God was already number one in the unconverted state. But to the lawyer,
something else was number one before God. Jesus told him
that in order to have eternal life, he had to love the Lord
God with all his heart, soul, strength, and mind (Luke 10:27–
28).

Can we have a wholesome conversion without intending
to put God first? Can we come to a sound rebirth while we
still have other gods in our life? Oh, how many have tried
to be converted, and claimed to be converted, while still
holding on to some beggarly element of the world, and we
wonder why they never become praying and witnessing
Christians.

My friend, check your conversion experience. Was it
really of God or something imagined? If it was only
imagined, try again, but this time, determine to let God be
everything and to let everything else be nothing as you come
to Him for new life.

The Cost of Counting

*And Satan stood up against Israel, and
provoked David to number Israel.*

—1 Chronicles 21:1

Here was a man after God's own heart. And just as Satan succeeded in deceiving and defiling Eve by getting her to "figure," so now, he went after David to use the same trick on him.

It is natural to figure, to analyze, to see what we can do and how much we have. It is natural to try to understand, but the point is, we are not called to live in the natural but in the supernatural. Supernatural living is not by figuring but by trusting the Lord with all of our heart in childlike humility.

Joab protested the numbering of the troops, but David insisted on proceeding with it. So, the number came to 1,100,000 soldiers in Israel and 470,000 soldiers in Judah. Oh, how we like numbers, how we like to publish them, how we like to play with them, and how we like to compare them.

Our whole concept of stewardship is too much in the numbers. God wanted David to trust in Him and not in numbers. God wanted David to know that his security and victory were in the God of Abraham, Isaac, and Jacob and not in the arms of the flesh. He wanted him to believe his own words, *"Some trust in chariots, and some in horses: but we will remember the name of the Lord our God"* (Ps. 20:7).

Because David numbered the troops, God smote Israel, and seventy thousand of his men died by pestilence. Oh, the price of analyzing and figuring. Satan provoked David to number the troops. Do not let him do that to you.

Who Is in Control?

━━◄══╬◙◙╬══►━━

If my people, which are called by my name,
shall humble themselves, and pray,...then
will I hear from heaven.

—2 Chronicles 7:14

God gave dominion over the earth to Adam and Eve, and the marvel of it is that He did not remove it once they rebelled against Him. So, from the Fall onward, the earth has been under the dominion of men whose *"heart is deceitful above all things, and desperately wicked"* (Jer. 17:9). This should cause us to question the popular perception that God controls everything.

Yes, God can be in control of everything if He wants to, but He has chosen from the beginning to let man be the custodian of the earth. God will only step in to take over when His people humble themselves and pray and forsake their wicked ways (or when He is otherwise inclined to do so for whatever reason). The key for change is in the hearts of the righteous. *"The effectual fervent prayer of a righteous man availeth much"* (James 5:16).

So, let us abandon the spiritual indifference of the doctrine that says, "God is in control." Let us abandon the fatalistic thinking that says there is nothing that we can do about it, therefore we will irresponsibly do nothing.

God gave the keys of control over the earth to Adam, and Jesus gave the keys of control over the church to Peter and to the rest of us when He said, *"Again I say unto you, That if two of you shall agree on earth as touching any thing that they shall ask, it shall be done for them of my Father which is in heaven"* (Matt. 18:19). Men who pray are men who take control and who change the destinies of souls, nations, and circumstances.

Take Charge

...That if two of you shall agree on earth as touching any thing that they shall ask, it shall be done for them of my Father which is in heaven.
—Matthew 18:19

If there is sickness, marital conflict, division, or lukewarmness in the church, if the devil goes about like a roaring lion, or if there is financial need, it is time for us to take positive control in prayer.

Jesus is ever living to make intercession for us, but the keys to victory or defeat are mercifully laid into our hands as they were laid into the hands of Moses, Aaron, and Hur in the battle against the Amalekites (Ex. 17:8–16).

God sends the power—if we ask Him. He sends the healing—if we ask Him. He sends the conviction—if we ask Him. He draws sinners—if we ask Him. He sends the anointing—if we ask Him. He protects us—if we ask Him. He heals broken hearts—if we ask Him. He forgives us and gives us our daily bread—if we ask Him. So, who is in control?

Dear one, if God had everything in control, this would be an entirely different world. The church would be spotless and without blemish. The devil would long have been banished from the earth. There would be no hospitals, no prisons, no crime, no armies, and no divorces. If God had everything under control, Jesus would not have asked us to pray, *"Thy kingdom come. Thy will be done in earth, as it is in heaven"* (Matt. 6:10). Nor would He have told the Parable of the Unjust Judge to let us know that men ought always to pray and not to faint, nor would He Himself have prayed hours each day.

Yes, ask and ye shall receive. Seek and ye shall find. Knock, and it shall be opened unto you. Take charge.

The People Are Too Many

---⊸⫘⫘⫘⊸---

*And the Lord said unto Gideon, The people are yet
too many; bring them down unto the water,
and I will try them for thee there.*

—Judges 7:4

Thirty-two thousand chose to rally around Gideon at the
sound of his trumpet, but of those, twenty-two thousand
went home when given the opportunity to get out of the
battle. God said to them, "If you want to, you may go home,"
and they did!

What spirit, what characteristics do we find in home-
goers like that? They are people who will participate in a
missions project if their contributions are absolutely
necessary. But such people will only do the minimum
required.

The ten thousand remaining troops were then tested at
the water to determine the depth of their commitment. They
represent the sanctified in Christ Jesus. Yet, amongst them,
we must distinguish those who were able to enter the
vision of the leader from those who could not come to one
accord with him. The ones who lapped the water from one
hand, thus staying alert, were separated from those who
bowed down to drink, ignoring potential danger on the left
or right. The ones who lapped were still ready to strike,
and they were chosen to fight with Gideon.

These men portrayed the spirit of Elisha who said to
Elijah, *"As the Lord liveth, and as thy soul liveth, I will not
leave thee"* (2 Kings 2:2). These were men who were willing
to live and die for their leader's vision. For them, there was
nothing else worth living or dying for.

So, Gideon had three types of men: those who served
him because they had to, those who served because they
wanted to, and those who were entirely in one accord with
his vision and mission. Where are you with your Gideon?
What type of commitment do you have?

Self-Confidence Versus God-Confidence

*And Moses was learned in all the wisdom
of the Egyptians, and was mighty
in words and in deeds.*

—Acts 7:22

Notice the word "was": *"Moses...was mighty in words and in deeds."* The Amplified Bible says that Moses was mighty in his speech. But that, my friend, was in Egypt. Forty years later, from the wilderness, we have another story which (in Moses' words) is, *"I am not eloquent or a man of words...for I am slow of speech and have a heavy and awkward tongue"* (Ex. 4:10 AMPLIFIED).

In forty years, Moses went from an orator to a stammerer, as some would put it. He went from a degree of high self-confidence to no confidence in his own abilities. Indeed, when God gets ready to do something with us, He has to make us utterly dependent on Him. So He often strips us of our human strengths and natural gifts so that it will be all of Him and none of us.

As God did with Moses, so He also did with Saul of Tarsus. The first gift of God to Saul, the new convert, was blindness. How helpful it would have been if God had told Saul that it was only going to be a three-day blindness. But such was not the case. As far as Saul was concerned, he was to follow Jesus with permanent blindness from now on. Utter dependence was the message to Saul, just as it was to Moses.

God tried to teach utter dependence to Israel as soon as she got out of Egypt. He placed her in a land where there was no chance for survival, except by His mercy. And such was the number one plan of Jesus in teaching His disciples that just as He could do nothing without the Father, neither could they. Hence, it is not self-confidence but God-confidence that is needed in order to labor in the precious vineyard of our dear Lord.

December 21

No One Is Born an Atheist

━━◖◗━━

*That was the true Light, which lighteth
every man that cometh into the world.*

—John 1:9

One of the points brought out by many commentaries is that *"every man"* here means just that—every man. Since the Incarnation, each man coming into the world has received divine illumination unknown to persons who came into the world prior to Christ. Since the birth of Christ, the Holy Spirit has been here to *"reprove the world of sin, and of righteousness, and of judgment"* (John 16:8).

Indeed, Christ has brought an end to the "moral Dark Ages" which reigned from Adam to Pentecost. In those days, wickedness could reach such boiling points that God actually, at one time, had to destroy almost all of mankind, and at other times, entire nations and cities.

This light, brought by Jesus and the Holy Spirit, has put a moral restraint on humankind, but with it has also put a greater moral responsibility on every soul in the world. *"For unto whomsoever much is given, of him shall be much required"* (Luke 12:48).

So then, man is without excuse, his enlightened conscience either excusing him or condemning him for his thoughts and actions, as we learn from Romans 2. Yes, Jesus is the *"Light, which lighteth every man that cometh into the world."* What a comfort that is, as we witness to the roughest of sinners, the most fanatical Muslim, or the most devout atheist. We know that, as we witness for Jesus, there is something in each of these hearts that says, "Yes, yes, yes!," something that bears witness to the truth as we speak, even though suppressed at the moment.

My friend, this verse tells us that no one is born an atheist, and that witnessing can do so very much to brighten the dim light in the heart of the sinner.

Lights Off, Lights On

—◌▥▥◌

*And I will put enmity between thee and the woman,
and between thy seed and her seed; it shall bruise
thy head, and thou shalt bruise his heel.*

—Genesis 3:15

Genesis 3 is the darkest chapter in the Bible. All sin, suffering, war, divorce, fornication, drug addiction, family squabbles, jealousies, lying, anger, pride, murder, theft, criticism, resentment, adultery, homosexuality, and selfishness originate with this chapter. The chapter begins with *"Now the serpent..."* and it ends with *"so [God] drove out the man."* Then God placed a cherubim with a flaming sword at the east end of the garden, turning every way to keep man away from the tree of life.

Genesis 3 depicts one of the greatest tragedies of humankind. It shows God's first moral experience with man turning into disaster. Man failed and succumbed to evil, and then evil entered into the bloodstream of the human race.

Yet, how wonderful is our God, for as soon as the devil turned off the lights, God turned them back on. He placed a little candle, ever so tiny, yet with an unquenchable flame into that garden through a promise. This candle tells us that a woman would conceive and that her seed would bruise Satan's head. So, with the Incarnation and Pentecost, that little candle became a bright light, ever increasing in its brilliance. And so the prophecy was fulfilled, *"The people which sat in darkness saw great light; and to them which sat in the region and shadow of death light is sprung up"* (Matt. 4:16).

Friends, today is the day of salvation; now is the accepted time, for there is a light on for everyone in the world to come back home.

Keepers of the Candle

~~⊸⊸⊸⊸~~

*And I will bless them that bless thee, and
curse him that curseth thee: and in thee shall
all families of the earth be blessed.*

—Genesis 12:3

Advent, the coming of Christ into this world, begins in Genesis 3:15 with this prophecy, *"And I will put enmity between thee and the woman, and between thy seed and her seed; it shall bruise thy head, and thou shalt bruise his heel."* This is the first promise of a Savior to come who would put the heel of His foot on the devil's head. It is there in the garden that God lit the first candle pointing to the coming of Jesus. The promise made here is the candle of the hope of the coming Messiah.

Then, in Genesis 12:3, the promise is renewed and expanded and placed deeply into the heart of a specific man called Abram. Out of his seed would come blessings that would bless all the families of the earth.

But oh, what great event occurred between Genesis 3 and 12? Many say, "The Flood!" *"And God saw that the wickedness of man was great in the earth, and that every imagination of the thoughts of his heart was only evil continually"* (Gen. 6:5). Did this darkness put out the light? Can any darkness of any kind ever quench the flame of God's promise? No—never! As long as God has a keeper of the candle, even if He only has one man left, that is all He needs to pass the flame of hope from generation to generation.

Noah found grace in the eyes of the Lord, and so the candle of hope went from Eve to Noah, from Noah to Abraham, and on and on, until the fullness of time had come for the Savior to be born. And now my dear friends, it is we who are the lights of the world. Let us pass this light on to others also.

Go by Revelation

...behold, there came wise men from the east to Jerusalem, Saying, Where is he that is born King of the Jews? for we have seen his star in the east, and are come to worship him.

—Matthew 2:1–2

Here we have the first pilgrims ever to visit Jerusalem because of the Christ. Notice that these pilgrims did not go to Jerusalem out of a sense of curiosity, nor to study, nor to learn spiritual lessons. The first pilgrims went to Jerusalem by revelation. This, my friend, is the best way to travel anywhere: by revelation.

You can go to the Holy Land year after year, but unless you go by revelation, you find the stones cold, their voices silent, and you will return with your heart untouched and your pocket empty.

But, oh, my friend, if you go by revelation—if you can discern the voice of Jesus as the wise men could discern the stars, if you can go to the Holy Land at Christ's prompting and in His time—then you will be as wise as they were, and find exceeding great joy. You will find Christ in a richer way, and your heart will be enlarged to hold more of His love, peace, patience, kindness, and compassion than ever before.

You will return home wanting to give more gold, frankincense, and myrrh to His glorious kingdom. Yes, Herod sat in the middle of the Holy Land, but nothing touched him there. The wise men, however, came to that land by revelation, and everything there moved them closer to God.

If possible, wherever you go, go by revelation.

Unstoppable!

———————

*And she shall bring forth a son, and
thou shalt call his name JESUS: for he
shall save his people from their sins.*

—Matthew 1:21

This may very well be the most powerful proclamation in all of human history. The event was long in coming. God spoke of it to the Serpent when he told him that the seed of the woman would bruise his head (Gen. 3:15). Abram was told of it in veiled words, *"and in thee shall all families of the earth be blessed"* (Gen. 12:3). Balaam knew about it when he said, *"I shall see him, but not now: I shall behold him, but not nigh: there shall come a Star out of Jacob, and a Sceptre shall rise out of Israel"* (Num. 24:17). David's Psalms are full of messianic prophecies, and the prophets offered Messiah's coming as the only and ultimate hope for Israel and the world.

The four thousand years of biblical history before Christ's birth abound with messianic expectations. Oh, what a triumphant proclamation from that precious angel that memorable night, *"she shall bring forth a son, and thou shalt call his name JESUS."*

Nothing could stop it. It was an explosion of the goodness, mercy, love, and power of God in the making for millennia. And so shall be the second coming of our dear Lord. Nothing can stop it. He will surely come, and all eyes shall see Him and all men shall confess that Jesus Christ is Lord.

Be Not Troubled with Jesus

*When Herod the king had heard
these things, he was troubled, and
all Jerusalem with him.*

—Matthew 2:3

Yes, Herod was troubled and so were the people. But Herod was more troubled than anyone because he was jealous, and he felt threatened. Yet, the man who was about to come into the world had no desire to usurp Herod's kingdom at all.

The kingdom that Jesus was bringing was not of this world. His kingdom had nothing to do with earthly thrones, standing armies, political parties, geographical borders, or taxes. His kingdom was spiritual and universal. It was a kingdom of redemption, holiness, love, patience, and divine justice.

No, Jesus did not come to threaten Herod, but rather to deliver him from the misery of his sins, bondages, and destructive attitudes. Jesus came to offer His kingdom to Herod, as well as to any man, that by it and through it he would go to heaven and live forever with Him. But Herod could not and would not see that the One he wanted to destroy was the very One he needed to be saved.

How many millions of souls have unnecessarily been troubled with Jesus ever since Herod? Oh, friend, do not be troubled with Jesus. Don't feel threatened. Surrender to His will, and what He will give you is Himself, His kingdom, His righteousness, and an eternity of bliss and glory as well.

A New Neighborhood

*But he, willing to justify himself, said
unto Jesus, And who is my neighbor?*

—Luke 10:29

Indeed, this is seen to be an unnecessary question. Everyone knows that his neighbor is the person next door. But it is not so with Jesus, as His kingdom is not of this world. Therefore, Jesus' perspective of our brothers, sisters, and mothers is also different. *"For whosoever shall do the will of my Father which is in heaven, the same is my brother, and sister, and mother"* (Matt. 12:50). Jesus revolutionized our thoughts in reference to family, and He infinitely expanded our neighborhood.

In Luke 10, the Parable of the Good Samaritan teaches us that our neighbor could be anyone we meet anywhere on the face of the earth who has a need. Oh, now do we ever have neighbors. Yes, what a vast neighborhood the Lord has opened up to us all.

Now, another matter worth noting is that we most always, if not always, meet those neighbors of ours in need of something when we have other plans. So, whenever we meet a neighbor, we come to a point of conflict; shall we cancel our plans or break our commitments to help a neighbor as the Good Samaritan did? The question is, shall we save our life, our reputation with man or lose it for Christ's sake (Mark 10:39)? Shall we pass by on the other side in order to be faithful to our friends, our families, and our business partners at the expense of the neighbor's needs?

Obviously, the answer to the question is clear in the words of our Lord when He commended the Good Samaritan by saying, *"Go, and do thou likewise"* (Luke 10:37) to the lawyer who had asked, *"And who is my neighbor?"* And now we have the answer to the question of what it means to love our neighbor as ourselves.

Standing Tall in the Mud

And Moses besought the Lord his God, and said, Lord,
why doth thy wrath wax hot against thy people, which
thou has brought forth out of the land of Egypt
with great power, and with a mighty hand?

—Exodus 32:11

In this chapter, we have the great conflict between God and Moses over the destiny of God's people. God wanted to destroy His people for having made a golden calf. God spoke out of His holiness, but Moses spoke out of the moral mud of humankind: Lord, you promised; Lord, you can save us; Lord, what will the enemy say?; Lord, what will this do to your reputation? Israel was spared.

Aren't you glad that Moses did not desert the camp when the moral mud of God's people got knee deep? Aren't you glad that Samuel held steady for those twenty years when Israel was soaked in idolatry? Aren't you glad that the prophets did not escape to foreign lands while Israel was engaged in spiritual adultery? Aren't you glad that Jesus did not hesitate to enter the moral morass of humankind to walk before us in perfect love and holiness? Aren't you glad that He tolerated a lying thief amongst his apostles for three long years? Aren't you glad that he had the love to eat with publicans, tax collectors, and Pharisees, and to converse with harlots? Aren't you glad that Paul did not give up as Christians forsook him by the hundreds?

Ah, my friend, all these men stood up, and out, in the moral mud of their time. None of them became deserters. Now when the mud reaches your knees, will you go or stay?

Count the Levites

---

*Now the Levites were numbered from
the age of thirty years and upward: and
their number by their polls, man by man,
was thirty and eight thousand.*

—1 Chronicles 23:3

Soldiers in the Old Testament times were called upon occasionally, but only in times of emergency. Most of the time, these men were allowed to pursue their own plans. When needed, they showed up equipped. But on ordinary days, they took off their uniforms and hung their shields and spears in their closets.

Levites, on the other hand, were always on duty, busy for God, serving in His temple, and submissive to His will. Their life was regulated by the Word of the Lord. The Levites were holy and sanctified, seeking *"first the kingdom of God, and his righteousness"* (Matt. 6:33), to put this in New Testament language.

The parallel is that, even today, we have those who are part-timers, who worship when they want to and stay home when they choose to do so. And then we have those with the Levite spirit, yielding wholly unto God, full-timers for Jesus.

Dear ones, the strength of our church is built and measured by those who have the Levite spirit, who see the prayer meeting, and not the Sunday worship, as the most important service in the church. For here is where the battle is either won or lost.

Let us not deceive ourselves; the strength of our congregations is not in how many we have on Sunday mornings, but on how many we have on their knees during the week, wrestling *"against principalities, against powers, against the rulers of the darkness of this world"* (Eph. 6:12). Let us count the Levites and not the soldiers!

How to Win

--~◄**·◄⊸llll\ʄ⫶⫶ll⫶⫶m►**─

*And when Judah came toward the watch
tower in the wilderness, they looked unto the
multitude, and, behold, they were dead bodies
fallen to the earth, and none escaped.*
—2 Chronicles 20:24

Ponder the dilemma of King Jehoshaphat. He had three nations coming up against him. Did he number his troops? No! He trusted, he fasted, and he prayed.

A Levite by the name of Jahaziel had the revelation as to how the battle was to be won: by the Levites going ahead of the army, praising God! As they praised the Lord, the enemy nations fell upon one another, destroying each another.

Praise and prayer were also the significant force as Moses, Aaron, and Hur prayed for Israel's victory over Amalek, and as Joshua and the Israelites rejoiced to bring down Jericho's walls. Is it any wonder that the number one plan of the devil is to destroy the power that really determines the outcome of spiritual battles: prayer and praise?

Hence, one of the first things every new convert must know is the importance of prayer and praise. Without prayer, no battles will ever be won, and without praise, the negatives of life will soon bring lukewarmness to the newborn soul.

If there is no genuine church prayer meeting, let the new convert find a prayer partner, or two, to meet with regularly. *"And if one prevail against him, two shall withstand him; and a threefold cord is not quickly broken"* (Eccl. 4:12); *"For the weapons of our warfare are not carnal, but mighty through God to the pulling down of strong holds"* (2 Cor. 10:4). *"Rejoice evermore...In everything give thanks: for this is the will of God in Christ Jesus concerning you"* (1 Thess. 5:16–18).

Taking Pleasure

The Lord taketh pleasure
in them that fear him.

—Psalm 147:11

Observe that *"The Lord taketh pleasure in them that fear him."* To take pleasure is beyond being satisfied. It is beyond approval. It is to be delighted, thrilled, and impressed.

When a schoolteacher takes pleasure in a student's essay, it is more than putting an A or a B grade on it. Pleasure causes every load to be lighter and every day to be brighter.

"The Lord taketh pleasure in them that fear him." It is difficult to conceive that God takes pleasure in weak, mortal men. But, indeed, He does! Consider that God has so many things to take pleasure in: the heavens and their splendor, the seas and their secrets, the angels in their worship. But we read here that God takes pleasure in His obedient servants.

Solomon said that there were four things too wonderful for him to comprehend: the way of the eagle in the air, the way of the serpent upon the rock, the way of a ship in the sea, and the way of a man with a maid. But, the Almighty God takes more pleasure in those that fear Him and keep His commandments than any of these wonders.

Let Him take pleasure in you. Fear the Lord and keep His commandments, for this is the whole duty of man, and the Lord will smile upon you.

Bibliography

[1] **January 16**

Bounds, E. M. *The Complete Works of E. M. Bounds on Prayer.* Grand Rapids, MI: Baker Book House, 1990 (p. 447).

[2] **March 21**

Author unknown. *Standing in the Need of Prayer.* Lyrics reprinted with permission from *Alfred's Basic Adult Piano Course Lesson Book Level One.* Van Nuys, CA., Alfred Publishing Co., 1983 (p. 46).

[3] **May 7**

Helm, Loran W. *A Voice in the Wilderness.* Bourbon, IN: Evangel Voice Publications, 1973 (pp. 229-230, 244).

[4] **May 8**

Torrey, Bradford. *Not So in Haste, My Heart!* Public domain.

[5] **May 18**

Matheson, George. *Make Me a Captive, Lord.* From *Hymns of Faith & Life.* Winona Lake, IN: Light and Life Press, 1976 (hymn 305, stanza 1).

[6] **May 26**

Smith, Walter Chalmers. *Immortal, Invisible, God Only Wise.* From *Hymns of Faith & Life.* Winona Lake, IN: Light and Life Press, 1976 (hymn 3, stanza 2).

[7] **July 15**

Wesley, Susanna. Letter to John Wesley on her method of child-rearing. 24 July, 1732, Epworth, England. Public Domain.

[8] **October 11**

Wesley, Charles. *O for a Heart to Praise My God.* From *Hymns of Faith & Life.* Winona Lake, IN: Light and Life Press, 1976 (hymn 327, stanza 1).

Scripture Index

Genesis
2:16–17   November 6
2:18   December 5
2:22   May 25
2:24   March 23
3:6   October 23
3:9   January 8
3:15   December 22
3:16   June 2
3:19   February 9
6:9   January 6
9:22–23   October 28
9:24–27   October 29
12:3   December 23
12:10   January 27
14:23   January 14
16:2   April 22
31:34   July 11
37:3   May 17
37:24   June 7
37:24   November 15
37:28   November 17

Exodus
2:10   August 26
3:13–14   February 21
4:14   March 14
12:11   October 21
15:24   September 29
17:8   April 17
28:2–3   November 20
32:11   December 28
33:16   June 1
33:18   April 18

Numbers
11:31–32   July 18
12:2, 10   December 7
14:38   May 29
16:3   October 15
20:12   July 7
21:8   September 9

Deuteronomy
1:21   May 29
5:29   April 29
10:12   November 12

Joshua
1:3   April 15
1:6   September 14
6:20   May 6
7:6   May 2
24:15   April 24

Judges
7:4   December 19

Ruth
1:14   April 5

1 Samuel
8:5   July 19
8:7   July 20
15:22   June 12

2 Samuel
6:6–7   January 24
12:13–14   July 25
15:6   February 3

1 Kings
10:6–7   April 27
11:9–10   February 4
18:4   April 28
19:3   June 25
19:4   June 24
19:16   June 26
19:20   December 3
21:2–3,15   October 16

2 Kings
2:6   March 10
2:15   March 11

1 Chronicles
4:9–10   August 2
15:29   August 3
16:1   March 30
21:1   December 16
23:3   December 29
23:30   August 10

2 Chronicles
7:14   December 17
20:24   December 30

Job
1:20   April 16

Psalms
7:11   September 3
19:1   July 5
19:9   May 31
23:1   February 17
24:3–4   March 3
27:14   May 8
37:7   April 2
51:3   September 8
55:17   July 24
62:1   May 7
62:5   May 5
103:17–18   July 22
105:17–18   June 8

105:20–22	June 9	10:40	July 26
105:22	June 10	11:2-3	October 19
105:39	September 6	11:20	February 8
105:40	February 15	11:29	September 12
106:11–13	January 19	11:29–30	September 11
111:10	March 1	12:34	March 2
119:105	May 11	12:38–39	August 8
119:165	February 24	12:50	October 6
147:11	December 31	13:15	May 15
Proverbs		13:16	May 16
3:5	November 16	13:21	September 24
4:23	October 11	13:45–46	November 8
16:6	November 11	14:22	January 28
22:4	February 14	14:23	January 10
22:6	May 10	16:16–17	January 29
22:6	July 15	16:18	July 29
23:7	November 2	16:23	January 30
Isaiah		17:1	January 31
6:1	April 1	17:17–19	May 3
6:3	April 3	18:3	March 5
40:31	January 5	18:3	April 9
55:8	May 26	18:3	June 17
56:7	November 22	18:4	June 18
59:19	April 26	18:17	July 30
Jeremiah		18:19	December 18
17:9	October 31	18:20	May 24
Daniel		19:21	December 11
3:16–17	May 20	20:26–27	November 19
Ezekiel		21:22	July 1
18:4	August 31	22:37–38	August 13
18:4	December 9	24:12	February 16
22:30	May 19	24:13	January 20
Matthew		26:6–8	July 6
1:21	December 25	26:39	October 22
2:1–2	December 24	28:19	August 17
2:3	December 26	**Mark**	
3:1	September 4	1:35	October 4
4:1–2	May 1	3:33, 35	July 16
4:4	August 18	7:27	September 26
4:17	March 16	8:17	September 25
5:3	February 25	10:15	March 5
5:7	July 4	10:15	April 10
5:20	September 17	10:21	November 24
5:30	September 23	11:17	June 20
6:10	March 15	12:43–44	September 21
6:14-15	December 12	14:8	March 7
6:22	October 30	**Luke**	
7:12	February 10	1:13	November 5
7:21	March 6	2:36–37	November 28
9:9	April 30	3:14	February 11
9:37	January 15	4:3	October 18
10:38	September 13	4:4	March 27
		4:9	September 7

4:10–11	March 28	12:27	September 18
5:4–5	June 3	14:12	February 2
5:14	October 5	14:15	June 11
5:17	June 4	15:5	March 18
6:12	February 7	15:7	March 17
6:46–48	March 6	16:8	March 13
7:9	June 23	16:13	September 28
7:19	June 27	16:8–9	October 25
7:20	June 28	16:8, 10	October 26
9:23	January 12	16:8, 11	October 27
9:57	December 2	17:1	September 27
9:62	February 20	17:9	August 23
10:25	December 15	17:21	August 25
10:29	December 27	18:36	October 13
10:42	November 13	20:25	August 7
11:1	April 4	20:29	April 8
11:50	September 1	**Acts**	
13:23–24	November 4	2:42	August 15
14:18	April 14	2:42, 46	August 14
14:18, 21	March 14	4:13	June 29
14:25–27	May 30	4:35	March 12
14:26	August 16	5:1–2	October 1
14:27–28	December 1	5:12	August 20
14:33	April 13	5:14	August 21
15:18	March 21	6:1	October 2
16:19–21	June 16	7:22	December 20
17:12–13	June 14	8:29	August 22
19:7	May 21	9:11	May 13
19:7	July 9	9:11	May 14
19:14	February 22	12:5	June 30
21:8	July 23	13:52	April 7
24:49	September 10	14:19	July 10
John		15:1–2	October 3
1:6	January 16	20:35	July 5
1:9	December 21	**Romans**	
1:12	July 2	1:7	September 2
1:14	August 12	1:13	April 20
1:16	June 22	1:21	March 20
3:8	October 10	1:21	December 4
3:14–15	July 17	5:5	March 4
3:21	March 31	6:23	August 30
4:34	July 21	7:7	November 1
4:35	December 6	7:11	December 8
6:7	October 7	8:1	January 1
7:17	June 13	8:1	November 29
8:5–6	January 18	8:4	September 16
8:59–9:1	January 3	8:11	November 30
9:1–3	May 4	8:13–14	February 26
11:35	February 29	8:14	February 27
11:38–39	January 25	10:11	January 23
12:6	October 12	12:2	May 12
12:6	October 14	13:1	October 17
12:24	March 19	13:8	September 30

372

14:1–5   February 6
14:5   December 10
14:17   November 9
1 Corinthians
1:19   November 3
2:9   August 1
2:14–15   February 18
3:3   February 18
3:3   February 19
4:16   July 26
6:9–11   March 22
12:4–6   August 11
15:58   July 12
16:12   March 8
2 Corinthians
3:18   May 23
5:10   June 6
5:17   January 13
6:2   March 9
7:9   August 6
10:5   January 26
Galatians
2:20   January 11
3:24   September 15
5:15   March 29
Ephesians
1:22–23   June 5
2:20   July 27
3:14, 19   July 31
3:16   July 8
4:4–5   July 28
4:11–12   June 19
4:31   April 25
5:8–9   November 7
5:22   March 26
5:25   March 25
5:28   March 24
6:1   April 21
6:2–3   May 9
6:18   May 18
Philippians
1:3–5   November 27
1:9–10   April 11
2:7   January 22
2:14   April 6
2:21   November 25
3:8   November 23
3:10   July 14
3:14   January 21
4:15   November 26
Colossians
1:9   August 5
2:7   January 4

4:2   September 5
1 Thessalonians
2:18   April 19
1 Timothy
2:1–2   August 24
6:6   September 19
2 Timothy
1:15   January 2
2:3   July 13
3:1–4   August 29
3:5   August 27
3:5   August 28
3:16–17   August 19
4:10   October 20
Hebrews
3:19   February 28
4:9–10   February 23
4:12   February 1
4:15   May 27
7:17   November 18
10:25   November 14
11:1   August 9
11:8   June 21
11:25   April 23
11:31   May 22
12:2   April 12
13:5   September 20
13:7   January 17
13:15   October 24
13:17   July 26
James
2:13   February 5
4:6   February 12
1 Peter
1:16   April 3
2:5, 9   November 21
2:23   November 10
4:12   May 28
5:5   February 13
2 Peter
1:5–7   January 9
1 John
1:5   September 22
3:9   January 7
4:20   June 15
Jude
24   August 4
Revelation
2:4   July 3
3:20   December 13
3:21   December 14
22:8   October 8
22:20   October 9

To Order
Abiding in Christ
Contact:

BookMasters, Inc.
Mansfield, Ohio 44905
USA Toll Free: 1-800-247-6553
or
Your Local Bookstore